Architecture on the Edge of Postmodernism

Architecture on the Edge of Postmodernism

Collected Essays
1964–1988

Robert A. M. Stern

Edited by Cynthia Davidson

Yale University Press
New Haven and London

Designed by Pentagram Design
Set in ITC Galliard Pro by Yve Ludwig
Printed in China by Regent Publishing Services Limited

Stern, Robert A. M.
Architecture on the edge of postmodernism : collected essays, 1964–1988
/ Robert A. M. Stern ; edited by Cynthia Davidson.
     p. cm.
Includes bibliographical references and index.
ISBN 978-0-300-15397-2 (cloth : alk. paper)
 1. Modern movement (Architecture) 2. Architecture, Postmodern.
I. Davidson, Cynthia C. II. Title.
NA682.M63S74 2009
724'.6—dc22   2009002873
A catalogue record for this book is available from the British Library.

This paper meets the requirements of NSI/NISO Z 39.48–1992
(Permanence of Paper).

10 9 8 7 6 5 4 3 2 1

Contents

Editor's Preface

In 1965, Robert A. M. Stern left Yale University's School of Architecture, master's degree in hand, and returned to his native New York City for gainful employment. That April, New York Mayor Robert F. Wagner, Jr., had signed into law the Landmark Preservation Act, spurred largely by the demolition of McKim, Mead & White's Pennsylvania Station two years earlier. Eero Saarinen & Associates completed the "Black Rock" CBS Building at Sixth Avenue and 52nd Street in 1965, Andy Warhol proliferated his *Campbell's Soup Can,* and Le Corbusier walked into the Mediterranean at Roquebrune–Cap Martin, France, never to return. In retrospect, one could argue that these events alone—preservation, pop, and the death of an icon of modernism—forebode the coming stylistic changes in architecture, changes that Stern's generation would both embrace and produce.

The young Stern began his architecture career at the office of the modernist Richard Meier, but not before serving for a year as the first J. Clawson Mills Fellow of the Architectural League of New York, where, with the mentoring of Philip Johnson, he organized the important "40 Under 40" exhibition in 1966, presenting the diverse work of a new generation of architects much like the "40 Under 40" show the League had mounted in 1941. Since his years as an undergraduate at Columbia, Stern had shown an uncanny ability to be in the right place at the right time. In 1962 he attended the first in a series of symposia on modern architecture at Columbia, organized by Henry-Russell Hitchcock; by the second conference, in 1964, he was assistant to Hitchcock; at the third, in 1966, he presented a paper with Philip Johnson, in which they listed their respective "top ten" buildings from 1907 to 1917. The latter was a clear indication of Stern's interest in history; in fact, at Yale he had taken a year off from pursuing a master's in architecture to study for a master's in art history. The research he conducted for an art history thesis that he decided not to write eventually led to his first book, *George Howe,* a history published in 1975. As the 1960s became the '70s, Stern, while developing his own practice with John Hagmann, organized a response to the "New York Five" ("Stompin' at the Savoye," 1973), became a "Gray" in the Whites versus Grays debates ("Gray Architecture as Post-Modernism, or, Up and Down from Orthodoxy," 1976), and then became a member of Paolo Portoghesi's advisory commission for the 1980 Architecture Biennale in Venice, remembered today for its seminal *Strada Novissima* and "presence of the past" theme. As Stern told Charles Gandee in an interview for *Architectural Record* (1981): "Portoghesi assembled a commission of mostly Italians, with two Americans, myself and Udo Kultermann....I, as the American member of the commission closest to the situation in architecture—and with Portoghesi's idea that this would be a post-modernist Biennale—proposed the theme 'The Presence of the Past.'" In 1980—and in retrospect today—Strada Novissima was a critical moment in postmodern architecture, having success-fully put forward what Portoghesi called an intent to recognize the "creative reinterpretation of [the] historical heredity" of architecture and to repudiate the "binding orthodoxy of the International Style."

It is almost too soon to write the history of postmodern architecture, in one sense because we are arguably still in a postmodern era, but also because one can hardly name a style or concept in architecture that has replaced it. Nevertheless, looking today at the vast number of articles and lectures Stern has written over the past forty-five years, one finds two distinct categories: one, pure history, and the other, firsthand accounts of the transformations in architectural thinking and design that, following the Brutalist period of modernism, changed the look and practice of twentieth-century architecture. It is a selection of the latter that makes up the collection of essays presented here. While bracketing postmodernism within the roughly twenty years covered in this volume is, historically speaking, an oversimplification, one can argue that conceptually postmodern architecture was essentially, if not launched, at least unleashed with Robert Venturi's *Complexity and Contradiction* in 1966; and that a second phase of postmodernism was ush-ered in with the "Deconstructivist Architecture" show at the Museum of Modern Art in 1988, one that represented a completely other stylistic sensibility from the "po-mo" of the 1970s and early 1980s, as developed by Venturi, Charles Moore, Michael Graves, and Stern himself, among others. There is no question that, dur-ing these particular decades, architecture in large part left the social idealism of European modernism for a new sensibility, one more informed by context and architectural history, and that moved toward an expression of shape and color and historical quotation that ranged from the banal to the sublime.

While he was writing, Stern was also developing a practice, and his bias for classical architecture, history, and ornament—always clear in his writing—becomes more pronounced as his own architectural production appears. It is interesting to speculate whether it was his penchant for history—very few architects participated in Hitchcock's modern architecture symposia in the 1960s—or his decision to become a practicing architect and not a historian that made Stern one of the cata-lysts in the movement that rejoined architecture with history. And in the essays here, the "history" of the present.

Stern was always interested in historiography and historicism as opposed to the pure facts of history. Initially it was historiography that informed the historicism. But as his practice grew into larger-scale commissions, it was the historicism that became dominant. In one sense, these essays are also a record of that evolution.

For the sake of history, and the spirit of these essays, every attempt has been made to retain the idiosyncratic use of the term *postmodern,* as the variations in its appearance also reflect the changes in the general cultural sensibility of the concept of the postmodern—both philosophical and stylistic. A few clarifying footnotes are the only changes to Stern's original texts, writings that not only reveal a changing of the architectural "garde" but also largely predate the sweeping architectural histories of New York that the historiographer Stern has produced since the mid-1980s. These are the more intimate views, providing a close reading of current architectural events, 1964–1988, through the eyes of Robert A. M. Stern, curator, critic, historian, architect, and educator.

Cynthia Davidson

I

Pepsi-Cola Building
1964

Last year amidst great publicity—thrusts and counterthrusts of rival architectural factions, critical claques, journalists, antiquarians, and other assorted types—the City Club of New York, unable to find a single distinguished example of municipal architecture completed in the previous five years, chose not to confer its Albert S. Bard Award for excellence in civic architecture on any building at all. This year, turning to the commercial architecture of the past five years, that organization and its jury, consisting of Peter Blake, I. M. Pei, Edward L. Barnes, and Sidney W. Dean, Jr., claim to have found better pickings. The Pepsi-Cola Building, located at the corner of Park Avenue and Fifty-ninth Street, and designed by the mammoth firm of Skidmore, Owings and Merrill, simply known as SOM, has been given the award (fig. 1). While there can be no question that Pepsi is one of the sparest, most meticulously executed glass-cube office buildings yet, it hardly seems, to this writer at least, an appropriate choice for an organization presumably dedicated to the perpetuity of the *polis* in its broadest sense. Like a good deal of the work of SOM, Pepsi is an irresponsible piece of city building; a manifestation of how little we value the few bits of urbanity left to our cities.

Pepsi's urbanistic difficulties grow out of three separate, though closely related, attitudes: SOM's passionate belief in the superiority of the technological solution; an apparent contempt for the pre-existing urban surroundings; and a willingness to make architecture that will serve as a symbolic projection of the corporate client's identity, imagined or real, even at the expense of the total landscape of the city.

Taken by itself, Pepsi represents the finest flowering of SOM's slick professionalism. It is a remarkable technological achievement, a probable swan song in the tendency toward the dematerialization of the building fabric that began fifty years ago when European architects sought to apply the two-dimensional

techniques of such new developments in painting as cubism and De Stijl to the three-dimensional problems of architectural design. This synthesis, which eventually emerged as the International Style, was the dominant form of creative architectural expression until the 1950s, particularly in America, where, as applied to high-quality commercial building programs, it has become the special province of SOM.

The Pepsi-Cola Building enjoys an international reputation, especially in such technologically starved countries as England, where architects and critics regard with respect the big, bare bays of its aluminum and glass façades, the absolutely even fluorescent lighting, and the perfect air-conditioning, which makes possible, in our fickle climate, façades glazed without concern for orientation. There is no doubt that SOM, in its desire to simplify and clarify, has achieved a measure of perfection. The broad, unornamented spandrels, the generous nine-by-thirteen-foot windowpanes, and the thinnest of thin mullions are combined to produce what is surely the curtain wall par excellence, a protective envelope of almost no weight and extraordinary transparency that brings Pepsi closer, as a colleague suggests, to the cellophane wrapper of a package of cigarettes or to the glass bottle enclosing the drink.

But Pepsi's perfection is skin deep and derives from the architects' concern for the expression of what machines *can* do rather than from any profound interest in the expression of how buildings *are* used or perceived. Pepsi is sealed off against both the elements and the assaults of mere, imperfect humans. Look at it from the distance at night; it is a giant beacon adrift in a turbulent sea of traffic. Even in the daylight, Pepsi's perfection, so devoid of any expression of use or of the action of the elements upon its surfaces, makes it seem terribly removed from human experience. Where are those scale-giving elements which would relate Pepsi to adjoining buildings and to such basic human experiences as entrance and exit? No one can deny that SOM responded with great sensitivity to the formal potential of modern techniques. But in its unwillingness to exploit elements of use, the firm produced a disquieting overall effect. For example, the sizes of the windows seem far more influenced by the limits of glass technology, problems of transportation to the site, and processes of erection than by any concern for basic human proportions. Thus Pepsi does not relate in any profound way to the scale-rich environment that surrounds it—to the pre-existing order of man-made things or to man himself. It is almost completely abstracted from everyday experience and, as it stands on Park Avenue, brittle and shimmering, seems like F. Scott Fitzgerald's Ritz-sized diamond or like one of those exquisite jewels that from time to time ride artfully grubby model railroad locomotives in the windows at Tiffany's (fig. 2).

The intensity of SOM's search for self-contained perfection spills over into attitudes toward the relationship between Pepsi and its restricted, and totally urban, setting. That is to say, Pepsi is a small building on a small 100-by-125-foot corner site. Seeking to use the property efficiently and at the same time to project a distinct public image, SOM tried to create the illusion of a tower while covering almost the entire site. Its methods were ingenious. Elevators, stairs, and mechanical services are packaged in a unit conceived as a link between the existing neighboring buildings and the office "box." As SOM's official biographer, Ernst Danz, puts it: "The transparent box of glass is set off distinctly from the existing structures adjoining it. The service core on the south side is set back fifteen feet from the building line. The resulting recess divides the building visually from its taller neighbor."[1] Thus, as much as possible, Pepsi is divorced from the city which crowds in at every side.

To reinforce this separateness, Pepsi's lobby is tucked under the office "tower." Unfortunately, it does not relate in height to the generously proportioned "bases" of the adjoining buildings. Nor is its twelve-foot-high ceiling particularly adequate on its own terms. (Compare it, for example, with the spacious twenty-four-foot-high lobby of Mies van der Rohe's Seagram Building, a few blocks to the south.) Even more disruptive, from the point of view of Pepsi's relationship to its site and to the buildings around, is the twenty-foot setback along Fifty-ninth Street, which weakens the definition of that street at the point where it is most needed—that is, at the corner where it intersects Park Avenue. Make no mistake, Pepsi is set back from Fifty-ninth Street so that its "tower" can be given some breathing space, so that the illusion of its "free-standing-ness" and its purity of shape can be more readily perceived—and not, as one might be tempted to think, to provide a usable open space for pedestrians.

It is interesting to note that, of all the buildings erected on Park Avenue since the war, only those bleak glass-and-steel blockbusters built speculatively come near to defining the street in the manner of their apartment-house predecessors—which were, incidentally, also speculatively financed. Purely money-making propositions, these hopelessly insubstantial curtain-wall constructions can never provide the kind of spatial definition that the intricate masonry walls of their predecessors did. Yet the economics of the real-estate market at least demand that they fill the zoning envelope. Allowing no precious street frontage to go empty, the blocks are filled to their corners and the wall of the street is maintained, however imperfectly.

Such should have been the case with Pepsi. A tower in a city must be taller than most of the buildings around it. Yet Pepsi's meager eleven floors barely reach the height of the first setback of the Hotel Delmonico across the street—not its tower. Similarly, its meager 20-by-125-foot plaza, indeed its entire site, could be comfortably pocketed in the broad sweep of Seagram's approach. Pepsi huddles nervously against the back of the buildings next door as if to protect itself, one surmises, against its own ambitious desire to project (or perhaps create?) a distinct corporate image, a desire that is much stronger than commonsense economics—not to mention questions of urbanistic responsibility. This is quite understandable in terms of the development of the International Style, which was based on a belief that, as J. J. P. Oud, a leading architect of the De Stijl group, stated in the early 1920s,

> an architecture rationally based on the circumstances of life today would be in every sense opposed to the sort of architecture that has existed up till now. Without falling into barren rationalism it would remain, above all, objective, but within this objectivity would experience higher things. In the sharpest contrast to the untechnically-formed and colourless products of momentary inspiration as we know them, its ordained task will be, in perfect devotion to an almost impersonal method of technical creation, to shape organisms of clear form and pure proportions. In place of the natural attractions of uncultivated materials, the broken hues in glass, the irregularity of finishes, the paleness of colour, the clouding of glazes, the weathering of walls, etc. it would unfold the stimulating qualities of sophisticated materials, the limpidity of glass, the shine and roundness of finishes, lustrous and shining colours, the glitter of steel and so forth.
>
> Thus the development of the art of building goes toward an architecture more bound to matter than ever before in essence, but in appearance rising clear of material considerations; free from all Impressionistic creation of atmosphere, in the fullness of light, brought to purity of proportion and colour, organic clarity of form; an architecture that, in its freedom from inessentialism could surpass even Classical purity.[2]

Never in the history of Western architecture has a style grown up with less relationship to its environment, man-made or otherwise, or with less concern, polemics to the contrary notwithstanding, for the processes of daily use.

But the battle has been won. A "modern" architecture is established. The polemical stance of the International Style is now mere posturing. And yet the relationship of buildings to each other and of men to buildings has never been less satisfactory, the achievements of the "materialistic" past have never looked so good. The point is, I think, that though technology varies and, we hope, develops, modes of perception change very little—similarly, our psychological demands change very little as well. Architects must not only learn to live with the past, they must reexamine it. It contains much that is of value in these matters, much that, in our fleeting love affair with the technological manifestations of the modern age, put us out of touch with the aspirations and needs, in many ways unchanging, of mankind.

How much better it would have been had SOM and the Pepsi-Cola Company decided to accept things as they were, to recognize the difficulties of a corner site, the limitations of their program and their budget, and, more importantly, their responsibilities to the long-established order of Park Avenue, recently discussed with great perception by Vincent Scully, their responsibilities to the ways men perceive buildings in relationship to each other.[3] Architecture cannot be practiced in a vacuum. Indeed, it is the most public of all the arts, as such companies as Pepsi only too readily recognize when they seek to use architecture to project a corporate image. But part of architecture's responsibilities—as we are once again beginning to realize—is the recognition of what has gone before and, wherever possible, the anticipation of what may come. Too bad more attention wasn't paid to that Pepsi advertising campaign of a little while ago, which admonished a thirsty America: "Be sociable …"

2

Secrets of Paul Rudolph
His First Twenty-Five Years
1965

Paul Rudolph has been practicing architecture for twenty-five years. At forty-six years of age, he stands just over the threshold of architectural maturity. With the completion of the Art and Architecture Building at Yale University, New Haven, his reputation, neither secure nor unchallenged, is nonetheless firmly established internationally.

Many critics have speculated on Rudolph's future, but he has moved too fast for these writers. His mind is too quick, his pragmatism too great to adhere to any simplistic vision of a neatly charted course of action. I should like to leave the question of Rudolph's future to his own devising and, on this, the occasion of the first major presentation of his work to the architects of Japan, take the opportunity to concentrate on his career to date and his position in American architecture at this time.

Rudolph's rise to prominence has been meteoric. He is the son of a Methodist minister. He was raised in the South—economically and culturally the most backward region of the country—and did not have the architectural advantages of his contemporaries: neither Philip Johnson's wealth and social connections nor Eero Saarinen's unique heritage nor even Louis Kahn's deep associations with a place rich in architectural traditions. He was graduated from the Alabama Polytechnic Institute (now Auburn University) in 1940. After twelve months in the office of E. B. van Keuren in Birmingham, Alabama, where he learned how to make working drawings, Rudolph, extremely ambitious yet feeling no strong sense of direction in his work, enrolled in Walter Gropius's master's class at Harvard University. Rudolph acknowledged his debt to Gropius in an autobiographical statement that he prepared for the editors of *Perspecta: The Yale Architectural Journal,* in 1952:

"In 1941 there was a certain sense of urgency at Harvard. Most had lost faith in the École des Beaux-Arts system, but what was to fill the vacuum? Geniuses probably should not be burdened with any kind of architectural school; but those of us who are less fortunate need some direction and a method of approaching a problem. Although I had studied architecture for five years, I had no sense of direction. I found in Gropius's teaching a base on which one could build, not merely a formula, as so many others have.... Gropius's strength lies in his ability to analyze and make precisely clear the broad problems of our day.... He was able to incorporate many diverse ideas and still give a sense of direction."[1]

More recently, Rudolph, along with others, notably Vincent Scully, the well-known critic and historian of modern architecture who is a member of the faculty at Yale, has come to realize the "academic" nature of Gropius's curriculum. Gropius's methods were based on a highly limited experience. He had built little; not at all, at first, in America. Upon his works and the more extensive works of Le Corbusier, Gropius developed an academy whose only real achievement was the precise codification of a series of pictorial experiences in terms that might be applicable to the practice of architecture. Seldom was an architectural revolution—and a concomitant revolution in architectural education—premised on so little.

The war interrupted Rudolph's program of study, and for four years he served in the United States Naval Reserve. Stationed at the Brooklyn Navy Yard, he supervised the repair of ships, a job which made clear to him the "necessity of seeing a design from the workman's point of view and in terms of the sequences of the various trades involved." Many of his later experiments with structure were to grow out of these experiences, as well as out of his contact with the engineer Konrad Wachsmann, who, Rudolph has written, "stimulated my own thinking in terms of the industrialization of structure and mechanical equipment."[2]

After the war Rudolph returned to Harvard, and in 1947 he received his degree. His second stint at Harvard, though productive, was less stimulating. Having tasted the excitement of actual construction, he was not really interested in school projects and was anxious to get to work. One project remains from his Harvard days—typically, a single-family house designed originally as a sketch problem and developed later for an actual client, though never built. In this, the Finney House project of 1947 (fig. 1), we see fully developed, and brilliantly drafted, the constituent elements of Rudolph's later and best work at Sarasota: big, precise bays of space (here compromised by the shed roof) framed in wood of the thinnest section and braced with steel cables in tension, an "open" plan derived from the work of Mies van der Rohe, a clear contrast between the carefully contrived landscape and the house itself, and a deft integration of automobiles (and, in this case, boats) into the overall design.

After being graduated from Harvard, Rudolph accepted Ralph Twitchell's invitation to join him as his partner in Sarasota, Florida. Twitchell, more than thirty years Rudolph's senior and trained in the traditions of the École des Beaux-Arts, had pursued his architectural career in a desultory fashion, practicing in New England in the summer and Florida in the winter. Rudolph had worked with him briefly in the summer of 1941 before going to Harvard. At that time he designed a house on Siesta Key in which his enthusiasm for Wright, as yet undisciplined and unpurged by Gropius's methods, is reflected in the triangulated structural system, in the bent plan formation, in the treatment of the masonry piers of the garage, and in the overall spirit of the detailing. Not for another fifteen years would Rudolph consciously turn again to Wright—and then not to the details but to his masterful handling of space.

Rudolph has been so long surrounded by the aura of success, his career so ablaze with his own talent, ambition, and daring, that the incredible insignificance of the early programs with which he struggled—single-family houses of no particular pretensions and even smaller guest houses—has been overlooked. Into these modest structures he poured his talents and his heart.

Fig. 1. Finney House, aerial perspective, Siesta Key, Florida, 1947

Any explanation of Twitchell & Rudolph's enormous influence must take into consideration not only Rudolph's talent but also the importance assigned to the single-family house in the years just after the war, when it was the only important building type being pursued in this country. Now, at the moment when our attention is directed toward other programs, usually of a monumental and civic nature, the work of this period, work which once seemed so terribly interesting, seems to fade in significance. The late forties now seems a time of limited goals and limited vision, a time, as Vincent Scully has written, when architects, alone with the "two-by-four," made the rediscovery of the skeletal organization of the wood frame seem heroic. It was not a time of great architectural achievement, to be sure; not an especially propitious time for the emergence of a talent eager to rival the masters of the past and to test its skill with monumental building. It was, however, a time when an architect could make a reputation with a succession of small houses and, on this basis, Rudolph, in only two or three years, catapulted to national prominence.

Looking over the entirety of Rudolph's work, one is impressed on the one hand by its incredible variety and on the other by its spottiness. Nonetheless, as Scully writes: "No one can look at [it] ... without recognizing a sustained effort, unmatched by any other architect of his generation, to come to grips with all the problems of architecture—to achieve, in the end, an unmitigated integrity of the whole. Nothing is left out: space, materials, structure, services, massing, the conception and the detail, are alike sought out, worked over, agonized on ...

"The record of such a struggle can never be an even one ...

"Let us not say that failures are unimportant; they matter profoundly. But the struggle matters too, and in this age of easy packages it probably matters most of all. The force and character of [Rudolph's] buildings themselves would seem to indicate that this is so."[3]

Rudolph is an architect of great ingenuity and inventiveness. The variety of shapes which have emerged from his drawing board has astounded critics and led the less discerning among them to assume that he is an architect without either philosophical or formal principles, and that he is therefore an irresponsible architect. Rudolph himself makes little effort to correct this image. The son of a minister, he rather enjoys the luxury of being architecture's bad boy. And, indeed, he is something of a maverick. But his integrity is unimpeachable; his dedication to his art, complete. And, though it may seem quite the opposite case at times, it is Rudolph's strong philosophical commitment to architecture as the *art* of building that has caused him to run so frequently against the tide. For architecture, at least in America, is in flux. "Change," Rudolph insists, "is the only constant." More importantly, there are those who, unable to cope with the conflicting demands of architectural practice today, would have us fall back on the pseudofunctionalism of Gropius or on the technological determinism that, rightly or wrongly, has come

Fig. 2. Miller Residence, Casey Key, Florida, 1947–1948

Fig. 3. Denman Residence, Siesta Key, Florida, 1946–1947

to be associated with Mies. But Rudolph, for whom architecture is the game of life, thrives on the confusion, adhering to those general principles that he enumerated in his well-known article "Six Determinants of Architectural Form," which is perhaps the clearest statement of his point of view.[4] He has no patience with the endless succession of causes and slogans which serve to ease the conscience of the less gifted. He devotes himself, instead, to the evolution of his own talent, to the conception and execution of architecture on the grand scale too often associated only with the past.

From Rudolph's six determinants—urbanism, functionalism, regionalism, techniques of construction, psychological demands, the spirit of the times— emerge the formal preoccupations: clear articulation and efficient use of structure; elaborate silhouettes; vertical as well as horizontal continuity of space; almost baroque effects of light; startling juxtapositions of opposites; open and closed spaces; rough and smooth surfaces; the man-made and the natural. These in turn give rise to a number of formal devices which Rudolph has used to great effect: the pinwheel plan, the colonnade screen supporting the bold cornice, the articulated service tower, sculpted floors, floating platforms, bridges through space, inglenooks, and so on. The origins of these devices are complex: some are of Rudolph's own invention but many more are borrowed from the works of the form-givers of the first generation of modern architects: Wright, Le Corbusier, and Mies. Rudolph's eclecticism is broad and he has been almost eager to acknowledge his sources in the work of these men—and in the general formal preoccupations of our time. Through these he hopes to insure in architecture "a civilized standard of genius"; through these he feels that even the least inspired architect, once provided "with a range of well-tried, culturally vital forms and motifs," will be able to "convert the passive act of plagiarism into the creative act of building up and systematically enriching an architectural language appropriate to our times."[5]

In Rudolph's earliest buildings, his sense of structure was more evident than his command of architectural space. That interest in structure, however, was visual rather than technological. No matter how enthusiastic his belief in the necessity of a clear and legible structural system in the design of houses may at times have been, he has always been willing to subordinate such systems to the needs of the space. Thus, in the design of his first important commission with Twitchell, the Miller Residence of 1947–1948 on Casey Key, though the intention was, according to Rudolph, "to make unmistakably clear how each member is joined to its neighbor," he could see no objection to the doubling of the columns in the living room in order to articulate the separateness of the space under the clerestory (fig. 2). In the Denman Residence (1946–1947), contrary to principles of structural efficiency, he organized a series of trusses lengthwise in the living room "to oppose the length of the sunroom and give emphasis to the view by leading one's eye in this direction" (fig. 3).[6] In the Deeds Residence of 1948–1949, Rudolph followed a vigorous structural determinism to its logical conclusion, devising a "skeleton" or "skyscraper frame" of wood of such economy that the cost of the house was held down to approximately ten dollars a square foot (fig. 4). Three rows of four-by-six-inch wooden posts permit a simple spanning system using rafters, with the walls used only to provide enclosure and lateral stability. Here, Rudolph, taking advantage of the balmy climate, incorporated the traditional screened porch, or "Florida room," as it is often called, into the volume of the house, giving it an integral relationship to the daily life of its inhabitants and successfully countering the then universal tendency of that region to keep the indoors and outdoors distinct.

Seven months spent traveling in Europe as the Wheelwright Fellow made Rudolph acutely aware of the limitations of his approach. Until this time, the references in his work had been almost entirely "modern," his historical vision limited to the pseudoscientific syntheses of Giedion's polemic, *Space, Time and Architecture*, which was the only work of architectural history acceptable for study at Harvard. Travel in Europe opened Rudolph's eyes to the splendors of the past: "One can talk of architectural space," he wrote in *Perspecta* in 1952, "but there is no substitute for actually experiencing a building or a city, or seeing architectural space at various times of day and under all types of weather, and of seeing forms in use. With notable exceptions I was impressed much more by the great architecture of the past than by the contemporary efforts. I returned to this country with the reinforced conviction of the necessity of regaining the 'form sense' which helped to shape Western man's building until the nineteenth century. Other periods have always developed means of tying their architecture to previous works without compromising their own designs. This is also our task."[7]

Before leaving for Europe, Rudolph designed a small house using the "Lamolith" process of concrete construction. One of eight regional prototypes sponsored by the Revere Copper and Brass Company, it employed concrete for floor and roof slabs and for nonbearing partitions—the actual loads being carried on thin lally columns (fig. 5). Rudolph, very much preoccupied with the formal predilections of the International Style—and especially with its preference for lightness—turned for inspiration to Mies's Barcelona Pavilion and not, ironically, to Mies's far more sculpturally active Concrete Country House project of 1923. Only much later, after the examples of Le Corbusier's work at Marseille and Chandigarh, would he seek more sculpturally active forms in concrete.

While in Europe, Rudolph was asked to suggest means by which a number of his Revere Houses might be grouped to form a cohesive suburban development. His proposal, based in large part on Mies's courtyard house schemes of the 1930s, was accompanied by a letter of such polemical importance that the editors of *Architectural Forum* chose to publish it as a kind of manifesto in their efforts to infuse a sense of urbanistic responsibility into the overly sociological climate of

Fig. 4. Deeds Residence, Siesta Key, Florida, 1948–1949

Fig. 5. Revere Quality House, Siesta Key, Florida, 1948

the planning movement as it was developing in this country under the influence of Gropius and Martin Wagner. One of the first serious criticisms of this tendency to be made by a former student of Gropius, Rudolph's position on the subject, though he has developed it since in extensive discussions of the particular problems of New York and Washington, has remained unchanged in its basic criticism of the planners' substitution of graphs, charts, and statistics for a real sense of urban design:

> There have been acres of plans devoted in recent years to town planning, some of which have been highly developed, allotting splendid colored areas for various functions. Much worthy effort has been spent in finding better relationships between residential areas of all varieties and the town as whole. However, it seems to us that the detached house, so popular in America and receiving so much attention as an individual unit, has for the most part simply been lined up on each side of the planners' or speculative builders' beautifully located cul-de-sac and that is the end of it. When the houses themselves are identical the results are particularly disastrous. Relationships between one house and its neighbor and devices to relieve the monotony of too much repetition and still keep within economic bounds is a real and urgent architectural problem and to us an exciting one. …
>
> The one tool which is the architect's special weapon, the handling of inner and outer space, has seldom been applied to this problem. Our proposals are fundamentally concerned here with the relationships between the house and its private outdoor living and work spaces. Finally and possibly most important it is a search for means to create a coordinated whole out of the repetition of basically similar elements without creating monotony.[8]

Rudolph returned to Sarasota in 1949. The Russell House of 1949 seems merely an extension of his earlier work and does not reflect his European experiences. But, with the indecisive spatial modeling of the Siegrist House, Rudolph began to show a greater sophistication of approach, claiming that "the contemporary interior is seldom eloquent in expressing the subtle differences between a living area and a sleeping area, a residence or a store; even differences in region." And, with the Leavengood Residence of 1950–1951 at St. Petersburg, Florida, Rudolph's work begins to take on greater scope (fig. 6). Turning for inspiration to the precise

volumes of Le Corbusier's work of the 1920s and 1930s and coming quite close to the "farmers' houses" envisaged in the Agricultural Reorganization project of 1934, Rudolph raised a simple box of glass and wood on thin lally-column pilotis painted gold. Unfortunately, the clear functional expressionism of Le Corbusier's *parti* (services below, living above) is sacrificed by Rudolph in favor of a spectacular, though unresolved, vertical integration of space. Dining and kitchen are on the ground floor, sleeping and living spaces above. These are connected and extended visually by a two-story-high screened patio incorporated within the volume of the house, creating what the *Architectural Forum* described as "one of the most interesting rooms built in the U.S. this year."[9]

Fig. 6. Leavengood Residence, St. Petersburg, Florida, 1950–1951

Fig. 7. Walker Guest House, Sanibel Island, Florida, 1952–1953

Rudolph sought to clarify the ambiguities of the Leavengood Residence in his project for the Walker House on Sanibel Island, Florida. Here a clear functional separation is more successfully achieved and the stair tower is incorporated within a two-story open court. Though this house was not constructed (nor was the subsequent and widely admired first Cohen House, in which this same *parti* was handled with an easiness, generosity, and wit that have since been too noticeably absent in Rudolph's work), a guest house was built; this splendid design, completed in 1953 but actually closely related to the spirit of Rudolph's earliest houses, can be seen as the climax of Rudolph's search for refinement in the articulation of the wood frame. Selected in 1957 by the *Architectural Record* as one of the outstanding American houses of the century, the Walker Guest House (fig. 7), according to that magazine's editor, the late John Knox Shear, "In a sense ... almost sums up the principal characteristics of Paul Rudolph's contribution to date: its fine, spare frame is carefully scaled; the total structure—in plan or profile—presents a simple, retainable image; its voids and solids produce a rich play of light and shadow and a great sense of volume; all its parts are expressed with clarity and with great simplicity; it possesses the gift of near weightlessness so appropriate for a structure of small wooden members; its moving flaps permit a flexibility in use and appearance; and withal one gets the sense that while it is manifestly a product of its place and time, it is nevertheless an architecture developed out of disciplines and concerns which transcend the local and the immediate."[10]

In the Walker Guest House, Rudolph achieved a true regionalism—a regionalism not of materials but of form. The nine bays of the structural cage which surround the impure structure of the house itself recall the colonnaded verandas of the "Greek Revival" plantation houses that were built in the South in the 1840s and 1850s and which, to this day, constitute the region's most potent architectural image. Rudolph, reinterpreting the venerable forms of these plantation houses, devised the counterbalanced wooden shutters to serve as "the infilling wall in inclement weather, …as the ventilation elements, …as the overhang and …as the hurricane shutter. Thus with all the panels lowered, the house is a snug cottage, but when the panels are raised it becomes a large screened pavilion. The ventilating unit does not have to be of glass. Moving elements of non-breakable materials are easier to make."

Inside, the plan is compact and quite uninteresting spatially. To relieve any effects of claustrophobia that might develop, Rudolph used only two solid panels on each side. When all the panels are shut the space extends itself through the fixed panes of glass—forming, for the first time in his work, the "pinwheel" or flat spiral configuration plan that Rudolph has used as an organizing device so frequently in the ensuing years.

Like Mies's perfect pavilions, the strength of the Walker Guest House is of a negative kind—its purity of structure is achieved at great expense. Much is thrown away: variations in space, procession, and light all give way to an obsessive reverence for the uncompromised structural solution. Rudolph was quick to realize the limited scope of the Walker Guest House but it was not until recently that he has begun to acknowledge the inadequacy of that kind of architectural composition which seeks to solve only a limited number of problems in a building. As recently as 1961, he rallied to the defense of Mies, who "makes wonderful buildings only because he ignores many aspects of a building. If he solved more problems his buildings would be far less potent."[11]

Rudolph adhered to the unity of the Miesian approach throughout the fifties. For the most part, his organizing idea was the "right" one, growing naturally out of the particular problem—the "umbrella" of the Hiss House, the cantilevered wings giving rise to the varied spaces of the Applebee House, the siting at the Jewett Arts Center, the spatial interplay of the Deering House—but often it was a notion about structure or shape or space which had little to do with the program at hand—the tension roof of the Healy Guest House, the elaborately articulated columns at Greeley Laboratory, or the plywood vaults of the Knott Residence.

In trying to extend the vocabulary of modern architecture beyond the primitive structural-functional determinism of Gropius's methods, Rudolph often indulged in extremes—structural and spatial exhibitionism of great brilliance but little meaning. His Cocoon House (Healy Guest House) of 1950 (fig. 8), a scaled-down version, as Peter Blake has pointed out, of Le Corbusier's Pavilion des Temps Nouveaux, is a well-known example of Rudolph's structural exhibitionism. Rudolph's own analysis, if somewhat biased, can surely stand as an accurate evaluation of his achievement in design in this house and of his ultimate failure:

> The form of this cottage … is the result of using steel in tension for the roof structure. Architects and engineers have long recognized the beautiful efficiency and expressiveness of steel in pure tension, but no one, to our [Twitchell and Rudolph's] knowledge, has solved the problem of making the resultant structure stable. But why should a roof structure be stable if a way could be found to keep it watertight? One of us had seen the moth-balling process used to protect warships when they were put in storage in 1946.

This process involves covering gun turrets, etc., with a wire frame, spraying the frame first with a mixture of…plastics, and then giving the resulting "cocoon" a final coat of clear vinyl.

In a sense this is an anti-social building, for it ignores the neighboring assortment of non-committal houses. It can even be said that it dominates the bayou because of its placement, form, colors and materials. The surrounding structures are already covered with a profusion of lush growth; in this cottage, however, we wanted to demonstrate that harmony between the work of nature and the work of man can be brought about by clearly differentiating between the two.

Of course, this cottage is a tour de force. Building types requiring larger spans are perhaps more suitable for such a form of construction. But, unfortunately, most architectural experiments have to be made in small structures.[12]

The Cocoon House is the most extreme example of Rudolph's structural exhibitionism. In the two cottages for Mrs. Kate Wheelan, built in the following year, he employed a similar system of construction, combining tentlike roofs hanging from a ridge beam of wood and walls of lime block built to the height of the eaves, and was able to evolve a far more appropriate composition for a domestic program, one which faithfully captures the spirit of the camp and the sense of permanence and enclosure needed in a house.

Beginning with the Hook Guest House, Rudolph turned his attention to the use of plywood in vault systems, gradually evolving more and more complex means for buttressing. These experiments culminated in the over-articulated redundancies of the Knott Residence project of 1952, in which the structural system was "so much in ascendancy," as the English architect James Gowan pointed out, "that it becomes a practical nuisance."[13] Only in the design of the Sanderling Beach Club did Rudolph succeed in using plywood vaults to advantage, defining the single spaces of the cabanas in a manner reminiscent of some of Le Corbusier's

projects of the thirties and forties, especially his "Roq" and "Rob" scheme for Cap Martin of 1949.

It is only a jump in scale, fundamentally, that distinguishes the Sanderling Beach Club (fig. 9) from the project for the United States Embassy at Amman, Jordan. Similarly, the Riverview High School of 1956–1958, one of the most consistently worked out of his buildings, makes little advance over the Walker Guest House toward a positive integration of structure and space.

In the late 1950s, Rudolph's realization of the inadequacies of the structurally determined solution and the Miesian pavilion did not result in anything more positive than a plea for "an enrichment of architecture at the brink of mannerism." This plea for fundamentally decorative form is nowhere more respectfully heeded than in his first building at Yale, the Greeley Memorial Laboratory of 1957–1959 (fig. 10). Faced with a program calling only for undifferentiated loft space, Rudolph sought to enrich the building through an elaborate system of columns and capitals in whose complicated shapes are to be read the record of the transfer of thrusts from supported to support. Similarly, the exposed beams of the roof, held down to a uniform depth, are varied in width according to the stresses involved. Each joint, each change from tension to compression, is lovingly articulated to the point that the entire mass of the building is shredded apart and almost all that is left is a collection of details. Greeley Lab is saved from total aesthetic collapse by its siting. Set below the level of the street, the pavilion is placed on a strongly battered base containing storage rooms and workshops to counter the downslope of the hill. As one approaches from above, the plane of the roof (whose black and white gravel, reflecting the pattern of the beam structure below, seems Brazilian in spirit) carries the eye out to the towers of a nearby factory and to the distant eminence of West Rock.

One last example of structural exhibitionism remains to be discussed: the highly ambivalent Temple Street Parking Garage in New Haven (fig. 11). Here the bold sculptural scale of a freeway is compressed and restudied in terms of the city street. Though the unbending geometry of stacks of identically proportioned structural elements seems quite arbitrary in comparison with the arcuated sequences of Roman aqueducts, a more complicated rhythm might have completely overpowered the already teetering shapes of the surrounding buildings. The Temple Street Garage surely brings up as many questions as it proposes to

answer. Structure and scale aside, it brings to the forefront a fundamental urban problem of our time—how much should we invest in accommodating the automobile to the urban environment? Surely we must do something with it; but is Rudolph's answer perhaps too expensive and too prominent as well?

In any case, the Greeley Lab and the Temple Street Garage come at the end of a sequence of development in Rudolph's work, and by 1960 he was prepared to repudiate many of his previous efforts and interests. One remembers his disappointments on first viewing Katsura Palace in 1960: "If I had come to Japan ten years ago or fifteen years ago, I would have been absolutely captivated by the post-and-lintel system and the sequence of spaces.... I'm still captivated, but my own interests are now in a very different direction. Now I'm more interested in space and light. We can't just be beauty-makers. It has to be meaningful.... Architects like Louis Kahn, who often makes ugly things, are much more profound. The great danger to American architecture, especially right now, is that everyone wants to make it prettier, prettier, prettier."[14]

In 1954, Rudolph, addressing the convention of the American Institute of Architects on the "changing philosophy of architecture," stated that a "layman never demands that...structure be clearly expressed, but he often describes in eloquent terms architectural space and particular psychological implications desired." In this criticism and in his objection to the "apparent lack of interest in the environment in which the building is placed and the particular role it plays in the city as a whole" that is shown by most architects, Rudolph outlined the direction his work would take toward the assumption of more complete urbanistic responsibility in the design of buildings.[15]

Rudolph's first experiments in the positive handling of space were timid. In the "Good Design" exhibitions in Chicago (1952) and New York (1953), he was confined by the inherent difficulties of the program and the loft spaces in which the objects were to be displayed. Nonetheless, by abandoning all the conventional paraphernalia of such exhibitions and concentrating on the organization of spatial sequences modeled primarily in light, he succeeded in making an environment with very definite qualities of its own and, at the same time, one which contributed considerably to the rather insignificant objects on display. In 1955, Rudolph arranged the "Family of Man" exhibit at the Museum of Modern Art. Here Lucite was extensively used to make Steichen's beautiful selection

Fig. 11. Temple Street Parking Garage, New Haven, Connecticut, 1959–1963

of pictures float and to give a sense of the total exhibition space at all times.
At the center of the exhibit, Rudolph placed a series of family group portraits
from all over the world; from this point a variety of spaces devoted to different
themes unfolds.

In the Applebee House, Rudolph took the same restrictions of floor and ceiling plane that had been so confining in the "Good Design" and "Family of Man"
exhibitions and, by means of fourteen-foot cantilevers accompanied by stressed
walls reinforced with steel, produced a simple composition that, in juxtaposing the
security of a snug fireplace cave overlooking a sweeping open living area, begins
to respond to the need for the open and closed spaces that Rudolph finds psycho-
logically imperative in the design of a house. Rudolph had already begun to think
in terms of "open" and "closed"—the "gold-fish bowl and the cave"—in the Hiss
House and in his exuberant project for the Sigma Alpha Epsilon fraternity at the
University of Miami, a pavilion with regular structure around an open court, into
which he placed a cylindrical building containing a dining room below and a room
for secret rituals above. In both these projects one finds another of Rudolph's
spatial themes: the two-story living space pierced by a bridge.

In the Deering Residence, the direction of Rudolph's subsequent spatial investigations becomes clearly established: a complex series of platforms on five levels
describes a splendid procession from the constricted entry court to the broad sweep
of the "Florida Room" and beyond to the successively more restricted spaces of the
living room and sleeping areas (fig. 12). Unfortunately, all of these spatial subtleties
are concealed behind a classicizing colonnade that is interrupted only at the entry
points. Because there is little modeling of the light, the spaces seem a little dull and
repetitious, especially as compared with those of the subsequent Milam House, in
which the highly sculptural *brise-soleil* responds to the light requirements of each
room. Continuing in this vein and even more promising as a resolution of the
requirements of the Florida climate with the desire for a sculptural statement is
the Bostwick House project, in which the planarity of the Milam House is abandoned and each *brise-soleil* does in fact become an extension of a particular room.

In all these houses, Rudolph, impatient with the limited scope of the domestic program, strained to produce statements of far greater monumentality than many would find appropriate. Rudolph justifies part of that monumentality as a compensation for the uneventful flatness of the Florida landscape and, in designing a house for New England, where the landscape is one of gently rolling hills, he registers a very different set of responses. In the Silvas House, a cross-axial plan in a manner reminiscent of Wright is anchored to a central core containing fireplace and stairs. Nine levels spin off this core, separated from each other by the two-foot depth of the beams. With comparatively few openings and a surface sprayed with plaster to emphasize its quality as a thin skin, the Silvas House begins to accommodate itself to the craggy New England countryside in a manner quite unprecedented in his work in Florida.

But Rudolph's major work in the 1950s involves programs of a civic nature. In the Floating Islands project of 1952–1953, Rudolph, forced to make use of the circular reflecting pool already dug according to the plans of the previous architect, Frank Lloyd Wright, devised a plan of baroque grandeur (fig. 13). But, as the airy pavilions of thin plywood vault construction show, Rudolph was by no means able to follow through with buildings of equal power. He was, however, sensitive to the differences of scale between the pedestrian and the moving auto, and his handling of the transition between the two is assured: a bold electric sign and a ninety-foot-high tower of plywood vaults (each lighted by a single bulb) announced the entrance, while a broad *allée* leads from the parking through the portico of the restaurant pavilion to the amusement area itself, where a freer, more intricate rhythm of serpentining walkways prevails. Throughout, Rudolph's command of the complex geometry, the sureness with which he juxtaposes straight line and curve, rivals that of Wright himself. In 1955, Rudolph, who had not yet seen through to completion any building larger than a three-bedroom house, was commissioned to design the Jewett Arts Center for Wellesley College near Boston (fig. 14). Rudolph's design has come to be, in recent years, the "whipping-boy" for critics bent on scourging architects for a vast number of sins, especially the sin of eclecticism. Though there is justice in much of this criticism, too little has been said in defense of the building, and its proper place in the evolution of modern architecture in this country has yet to be established.

Imperfect though the Wellesley commission may be, it surely is not the abomination that its architect now deems it to be. True, it is not an integrated composition and the interiors are chaotic, to say the least. True, it is guilty of a kind of superficial, though well-intended, eclecticism which many, brought up among the orthodoxies of the International Style, find totally unacceptable. To these critics, the use of clustered columns, pointed skylights, screens, and especially oriel windows seems only a step away from a return to neo-Gothic itself. And there is something in these objections, for as Rudolph has himself pointed out, the "good neighbor" policy that he pursued at Wellesley—"mood architecture," he calls it—is an "extremely difficult, patently dangerous" policy that "often leads to a picturesqueness and new kind of eclecticism [with] one kind of architecture for a pseudo Gothic environment, another for a Georgian environment and so on. This is, of course, a 19th-century version of eclecticism where one changes the approach according to the site rather than the type of building."[16]

But the harmony of scale achieved between the old and the new at Wellesley goes far beyond the simple projection of a "mood" and encompasses a far wider

Fig. 13. Floating Islands Project, Leesburg, Florida, 1952–1953

Fig. 14. Jewett Arts Center, Wellesley College, Wellesley, Massachusetts, 1955–1958

Fig. 15. Blue Cross/Blue Shield Building, Boston, 1957–1960

range of values. For Rudolph, in his first large-scale work, succeeded in capturing the spirit of the past; only later, with the Art and Architecture Building at Yale, would he succeed in sensing its direction, the rhythm of its forms, its pitch and beat and be able to build upon them all. At Wellesley, Rudolph discredited for a long time to come the smug hostility to the preexisting past that had stood for so long between modern architecture and its urbanistic responsibilities.

Sarasota High School (1958) and the Blue Cross/Blue Shield Building (1957–1960) mark the transition to Rudolph's mature work (fig. 15). With them begins that search for a complete integration of services, structure, and space finally achieved in the design of the Art and Architecture Building. The sources of the high school lie in Rudolph's own work and in Le Corbusier's High Court at Chandigarh. The office building, with its highly ornamental synthesis of ducts and columns, is, in the spirit of its forms, if not in their execution, quite like Louis Sullivan. Both the high school and the office building are conceived as freestanding buildings. In the case of the former, the site is comparatively isolated, while in the case of the latter there was considerable appeal in a tower solution, and the pedestrian plaza provides a welcome open space in a densely built-up quarter of town.

There is no need to go very deeply into the design of the Art and Architecture Building. In the comparatively short time since its completion in the autumn of 1963, it has been published in almost every important journal of architecture and has become the subject of a not inconsiderable critical literature. I should only like to point out at this time that, imperfect though it may be, the "A&A" is nonetheless a building that addresses itself to the widest architectural issues: space, structure, services, materials, the urban context are all scrutinized in terms of a vocabulary that goes well beyond its inspiration in Wright and Le Corbusier to become, finally, Rudolph's own. And, as Rudolph recently told the students of architecture at Columbia University, "Pretty buildings or buildings that work" are not enough, for "any fool can make buildings work." Architecture becomes significant only if it can work "*urbanistically*...with the past and with the future."[17]

The Art and Architecture Building is the culmination of a sequence of events in the development of Rudolph's talent, but it is by no means a conclusion. In the recently completed factory and office building for Endo Laboratories, he has demonstrated that the principles and techniques embodied in the A&A can be applied to great advantage in a completely different kind of program (fig. 16).

Endo is, in many ways, a very Wrightian building and, in its overall massing, in the disciplined handling of the curves as well as in the use of mushroom columns, the influence of the Johnson Wax Company Building is quite clear. Unlike Johnson Wax, which turns almost completely in upon itself, Endo appears quite open, though a considerable part of it is hidden behind solid walls. Courtyards and ramps make gestures of invitation and provide, amidst the emptiness of the suburban Long Island landscape, a genuine pedestrian place. At the same time the clear articulation of functional parts—lobby, cafeteria, dog run, light turrets, and so on—is of sufficiently bold scale to be read by speeding motorists on the Meadowbrook Parkway a quarter of a mile away. In this sense, Endo is a demonstration of Rudolph's conviction that architects must make buildings large enough in scale and memorable enough in total image to be read from a moving car—only the automobile is "large enough to organize the city on a large scale"—while intricate enough in detail so as not to be overpowering from close up.

Another project growing out of the Art and Architecture Building is the Boston Government Service Center (fig. 17), in which a number of architectural firms have agreed to work in concert under Rudolph's direction to produce a unified building out of what was originally intended to be three separate buildings occupying an irregular site very near the well-known City Hall, by Kallmann, McKinnell & Knowles, which is now under construction. The program calls for extensive, unencumbered loft space. The only fixed elements besides the structure are the mechanical services and the vertical circulation, which have been grouped in highly sculptural towers (this is not true of the Mental Health Building, in which a number of the important spaces are "fixed" as well). The office space of the Employment Security Building and the Mental Health Building is arranged in a series of set-back terraces whose ultimate prototype lies in the work of the Italian Futurist architect Sant'Elia, though a more immediate source would no doubt be Le Corbusier's various projects in North Africa in the 1930s, as well as Sir Leslie Martin's recently completed buildings for Caius College, Cambridge, England. The set-back section is used in Boston to break down the scale of the court and to extend its space as in an amphitheater while the resultant arcade along its periphery gives a strong definition and more monumental scale to the street. A twenty-six-story tower, housing the Department of Health, Education, and Welfare, rises at the end of a pedestrian passage leading from the new City

Fig. 16. Endo Pharmaceutical Laboratories, Garden City, New York, 1960–1964

Fig. 17. Model, Boston Government Service Center, 1962–1971

Secrets of Paul Rudolph

Hall and gives the Siennese space of the court a focus. The use of the pinwheel configuration for the office tower is intended not only to enhance its role as a pivot at the symbolic gateway to the Government Center as a whole, but also to provide, on a given floor, far greater modulation of space than would be possible in a more conventional plan shape. Combined with the "ritual circle" of columns near the center, the pinwheel begins to suggest a hierarchy of spaces with private offices along the perimeter, attached secretary spaces, circulation corridor, and, in the center, office pools.

The Government Center is still under design; if it is built—and the likelihood of that happening is considerable—it will be an impressive demonstration of Rudolph's determination to see architecture extend itself beyond the mere provision of functional accommodation toward a true urbanity of form. The Boston Government Center is a manifesto that, once again, as in times of great urban expansion in the past, civic design is the architect's responsibility. The planners are not to be relied upon: "They are not now and never will be, for their heart is elsewhere," Rudolph says. Nor are the majority of architects, especially those still under the spell of International Style polemics. They "have abdicated from the traditional role" architects have played in the past "in large-scale, three-dimensional design." Yet there is no time for despair or nostalgia. "It has been said that the golden age of modern architecture is over and now we merely elaborate and embellish. How could it be so when there are so many untouched, even undefined forces of society crying for order?"

There is much in Rudolph's work that I have not touched on. A whole series of projects for mass housing, in particular, shows his urbanistic capabilities in a lower key and shows, as well, his ability to go far beyond the empty sociology and strangulating "systems" favored by most so-called "housing experts" to make, within the highly restrictive demands of governmental and economic agencies, *places* for people to live in; architecture, not housing.

I have tried to outline Rudolph's career, to describe some of his buildings and, most importantly, to sift out the philosophic principles which give his work a complex unity that many, overwhelmed by the variety of his forms, have thought absent. I have, I believe, been true to my promise, leaving to Rudolph the question of his future, concentrating on the works of his first twenty-five years of practice. His work, without any words of mine, provides testament enough, I am sure, to the range of Rudolph's talent, the freshness of his imagination, and the breadth of his concern.

3

Stompin' at the Savoye

1973

The almost simultaneous publication of *Five Architects* and *Learning from Las Vegas* marks, one hopes, an opportunity to step back and consider what it is that our architecture stands for at this time; it gives us a chance to evaluate opposing points of view that have been described as European/idealist on the one hand, American/pragmatic on the other, exclusive and inclusive, conceptual and perceptual, invulnerable and vulnerable. Although the two books, and for that matter the positions they embody, are pretty much opposite to each other, they are not of equal importance.[1]

Learning from Las Vegas, by Robert Venturi, Denise Scott Brown, and Steve Izenour, builds upon the most important architectural text of the 1960s, Venturi's *Complexity and Contradiction in Architecture.*[2] Whereas *Five Architects: Eisenman, Graves, Gwathmey, Hejduk, Meier* is a perhaps premature effort at polemical assertion by architects who really have no claims as a group, *Las Vegas* is a cohesive record of six productive years of work by Venturi and his partners. Together with the writings of Herbert Gans, Jane Jacobs, and some others, *Las Vegas* is helping us at least to break from the hot-house aesthetics of the 1920s, to see familiar things in fresh contexts, and to assimilate diverse experiences into our work.

Five Architects, and particularly its introductory essay by Colin Rowe, the intellectual guru of the group whose work is presented therein, contains an implicit reply to Venturi's work and especially to Vincent Scully's introduction to *Complexity and Contradiction.* In that introduction, Scully made claims not only for the book in relationship to that of Le Corbusier's *Towards a New Architecture* but also, by implication, for Venturi's position as logical complement to that of

Le Corbusier as form-giver. Such a claim sticks in Rowe's craw. After all, for the last fifteen years or so, as design critic and theorist, he has initiated architectural students into a systematized version of 1920s Corbusian form. The irony of his faithfulness to the most questionable aspects of Le Corbusier's philosophy is nowhere clearer than in his 1967 Museum of Modern Art project for Harlem, where despite previous efforts to develop Le Corbusier's ideas about town planning on the part of Shad Woods and others, and in the face of major reassessments by other participants in the exhibition, he and his team projected the most sweeping and absolute "ville radieuse" scheme ever.[3]

Rowe states in *Five Architects* that "rather than constantly to endorse the revolutionary myth, it might be more reasonable and more modest to recognize that, in the opening years of this century, great revolutions in thought occurred and that then profound visual discoveries resulted, that these are still unexplained, and that rather than assume intrinsic changes to be the prerogative of every generation, it might be more useful to recognize that certain changes are so enormous as to impose a directive which cannot be resolved in any individual life span." Thus, as Rowe sees it, the revolution of the twenties is so fundamental to our architecture as to preclude its own evolution. I think it is not. Indeed, there seems to be a certain inconsistency of position on Rowe's part as manifest by his sudden affection for Aldo van Eyck, under whose slogan his essay is written, and even more clearly by his suggestion that we place the work of the "five architects" in a "context of choices" that include "Miesian neo-classicism …; the New Brutalism …; the Futurist Revival …; and the *neo-art nouveau*," which I guess means Yale/ Philadelphia architects with "Shingle Style and Italian ramifications."[4] This concept of choice (stylistic choice to boot) reveals more about Rowe's misgivings (not to mention his predilections) than I would have imagined possible and, finally, casts doubt on the firmness of his convictions in the five architects as logical successors to Le Corbusier, even on his own terms.

Against Rowe's highly colored polemics, Kenneth Frampton's critical essay on the work is cool and remarkably forthright.[5] Frampton is to be commended for trying to make connections (Italian mannerism, the Shingle Style, Frank Lloyd Wright) between the work of the Five and an architectural culture outside that of De Stijl and cubism. But though his intention is to be commended, his claims cannot be substantiated. The work of the Five is so hermetic in its conception as to be virtually incapable of connection outside the puritanical cultural attitudes of the 1920s avant-garde. What I will attempt to do is to fill in around the edges of Frampton's essay, following his order of discussion, concentrating on operational aspects of the buildings discussed, many of which were not complete when the article was first formulated as a talk in 1969, and on subsequent developments in some of the architects' work, which shed light on his remarks.

I find the projects of John Hejduk included in *Five Architects* less convincing than his Wall House previously published in *Artforum* because, as they attempt in varying degrees to become habitable, they vitiate the intensity of their polemic (fig. 1). Thus the One-Half House bogs down in a series of expedient gestures toward useful accommodation that make the geometry of the inside spaces unclear as well as barely usable (fig. 2). Hejduk, like Eisenman, is probably best at a paper architecture and, as such, possibly quite valuable to other architects as a stimulant to clear thinking. But it must be kept in mind that without the transparent

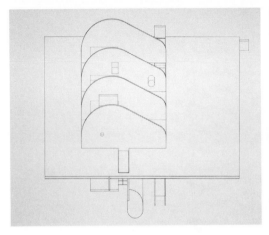

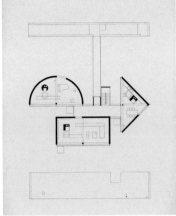

axonometric and isometric drawings which the Five favor, a large number of the conceptual and formalistic relationships developed become illegible.

Peter Eisenman has proved himself the unquestioned intellect among the Five, outgrowing the comfortable cubism of Meier and Graves. He has developed a philosophical position based on the belief, derived from the researches of Noam Chomsky, that architecture is a language which can be freed from cultural associations in an effort to get at the essential meanings of spaces and enclosures. To be candid, much that Eisenman writes gives me a headache; like his isometric drawings, it is too dense with information and in desperate need of editing. I disagree with Eisenman's philosophical stance most vehemently in regard to his belief that one can and presumably should divorce architectural experience from culture. Yet, my belief in the integrity of his search remains. How ironic that he, who, unlike Hejduk, has made no effort to accommodate program, has actually succeeded in building houses! What I do not believe is that so-called "deep structure" contributes at all to man's understanding of his place in relationship to the natural world and other man-made objects—the essential purpose of architecture. I do not believe that structure, no matter how "deep," is a particularly expressive tool in architecture. In fact, I think that the superfluity of walls, beams, and columns which characterizes his design contributes to his claustrophobia. Moreover, the increasing complexity of Eisenman's houses, as seen in Houses III and IV, indicates that the logic of the search notwithstanding, the results can be confusing from a perceptual point of view, as well as antihabitational on a strictly pragmatic basis (figs. 3 and 4).

Michael Graves takes cubism the most seriously of the Five. His buildings are like collage reveries inspired by prolonged examination of the early volumes of Le Corbusier's *Oeuvre complète*. At times, however, Graves's dependence on Le Corbusier can be unintentionally ironic. The Hanselmann House is an effort to pay homage to Le Corbusier's Curutchet House, but Graves fails to understand that the tension between the "façade" and the house behind it in Le Corbusier's prototype—a response to a complex urbanistic and programmatic situation—loses most of its meaning when cleaned up and straightened out, so to speak, and set in the Indiana countryside (figs. 5 and 6).

In the Benacerraf House Addition the dependent structure is so compulsive in its "modernity" that it deprives the original house of all meaning and calls

Fig. 1. John Hejduk, worm's-eye view of Wall House 1, 1968–1977. Reprographic copy, 89 x 92.5 cm.

Fig. 2. John Hejduk, floor plan for One-Half House, 1968–1974. Pen and black ink on panel, 101.5 x 76 cm.

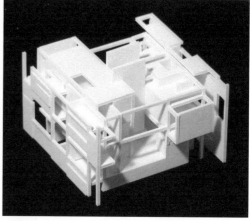

Fig. 3. Peter Eisenman, view from east, House III, Lakeville, Connecticut, 1969–1971

Fig. 4. Peter Eisenman, study model of House IV, Falls Village, Connecticut, 1971

Fig. 5. Michael Graves, Hanselmann House, Fort Wayne, Indiana, 1967

Fig. 6. Le Corbusier, Maison Curutchet, La Plata, Argentina, 1949

into question the validity of the neighboring buildings as well (fig. 7). The order of the new plan must compete with the order of the old one that it replaces but which continues its influence by means of the window placement and exterior wall configuration. (Compare the clumsiness of this stylistic confrontation with the skill of Venturi's Duke House conversion [fig. 8] in which a university program was accommodated within a preexisting dwelling.) Graves's new spatial order is to a remarkable extent contrary to the old; it includes a new and largely decorative grid of columns that appear to do little else than make furnishing difficult. As for the addition to the house at the rear, its excesses are obvious from an examination of the plan (all that roof deck resulting from a flat roof) and from the elevations where quantities of structure are employed to define literal and implied spaces, barely providing more than incidental sun protection for the spaces below.

Richard Meier is also a compulsive "modernist," though he takes chances by varying the rules of cubism in a way that Graves does not (but Erich Mendelsohn, Edward Durrell Stone, and William Lescaze did). His recent project for a house at Pound Ridge, New York, is better than either of his houses in the book, yet they all share a remarkable object quality, almost miniaturized in scale and slick in surface, that implies that they have been sheathed in vertical boarding painted white (fig. 9).

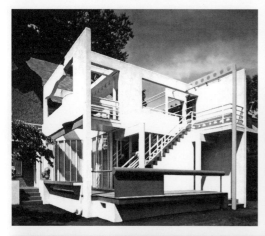

Meier's Smith House is very beautiful, but it is a façade that we admire. The overdesigned living spaces within, though spectacular in section, are narrow and seem trapped behind that expanse of largely fixed glass facing southeast (figs. 10 and 11). And a master bedroom right off the living room with one small window looking east across the roof of a tool shed seems not quite right. The Saltzman House has been completed since Frampton first prepared his criticism. As a result of Meier's insistence on an exterior expression fundamentally at odds with the materials used and, to be fair, the use of a contractor who built badly, the house has undergone the most serious vicissitudes in the face of a harsh climate marked by extremes of temperature and dampness.

Even as an object it disappoints and seems lumpish; perhaps because the plan, a square bisected along its diagonal by a path of circulation with open spaces along one side and closed along the other, is seriously violated at its ends (fig. 12). Also, the location of the upper stair is unresolved, while the inflected corner of the square produces an absolutely useless subspace at what should have been the climax of the design. I don't think I am carping to note that the bedrooms face west, with unshaded glass, a good deal of which is fixed; that the house, generally short on operable sash, is not adapted for air-conditioning; and that the three-story-high dining room, completely glazed along its southern end, is spectacular and intimidating in equal measure, and

Fig. 7. Michael Graves, Benacerraf House Addition, Princeton, New Jersey, 1969

Fig. 8. Robert Venturi, James B. Duke House Renovation, Institute of Fine Arts, New York, 1958

Fig. 9. Richard Meier, model of house in Pound Ridge, New York, 1969

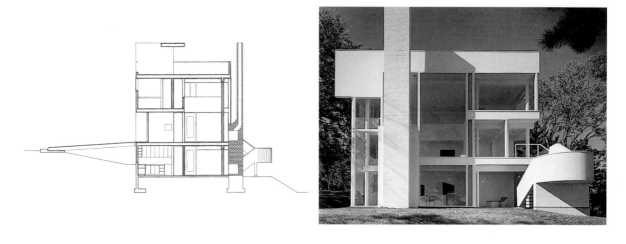

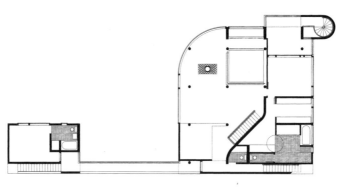

virtually uninhabitable during the daytime. The fundamental problem is with the conception of architecture as insistently new, abstract and divorced from the place in which it is built: from its landscape and from its architectural traditions which are, after all, the record of experience over a long period of time.

Of the five architects, Charles Gwathmey demonstrates the most consistent grasp of the technical and environmental aspects of architecture. He has not succumbed to the impossible dream—the dematerialized structure of wood painted white. He prefers, as in the design for his parents' house and studio, a vocabulary of natural stained cedar boarding, and in that house at least, as Frampton points out, he has "accommodated in very direct terms a local 'sub-culture' of weekend living, using and expressing local technique."

His larger houses, like those for the Steel families, suggest the limitations of his approach: the geometric relationships between the two houses, so clear in plan, simply are not legible in three dimensions (figs. 13 and 14). The desire to make the inside and the outside the same, so alien to the possibilities of architecture as enclosure, robs the house of much of its sculptural potential; as Gwathmey's buildings become bigger, and develop a more complex geometry, that geometry ceases to be capable of organizing the whole and, in fact, tends to fracture it. In a more recent house in East Hampton, Gwathmey recognizes this, and tries to organize the program within a single volume (fig. 15). Intended, no doubt (and for reasons beyond my comprehension), to relate to Le Corbusier's High Court at Chandigarh, it lacks the variety of scales and the structural thrust of the prototype.

Stompin' at the Savoye

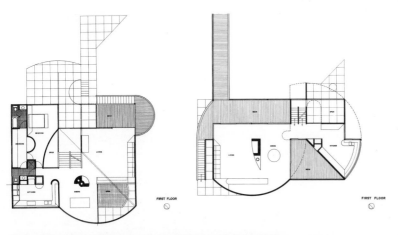

Gwathmey stands apart from the other four in his sympathy for the particulars of places; he alone seems concerned with the materiality of buildings. On the other hand, his new work at East Hampton and Princeton reveals a tendency to grossly oversimplify when dealing with problems of greater size or scale. He very badly needs to resolve the dilemma of his current work—to recapture the impromptu character of clashing geometries, active shapes reaching for light, articulating movement patterns within, gestures extended across time and space to older architectures.

Five Architects is a victim of bad timing. What was conceived in early 1969 as an informal report on works in progress has now become, more than three and one-half years later, a major publication with slick, thick paper and overworked graphics. Not only is it laden with an introduction (that makes claims for these architects as a "New York School") as well as a preface, not to mention the texts of the architects who chose to speak for themselves (Eisenman and Meier) and William La Riche's remarks on Graves; it is also burdened with so much technique, so much inflation of so little that seems really vital or important.

Despite its unfortunate slickness, size, and cost, *Las Vegas,* on the other hand, delivers important ideas, expressed in words as well as actual building designs. This book adds up to a consistent point of view, which, in drawing on so many aspects of our culture, does not (as is often implied) sacrifice design to life; nor, as in *Five Architects,* does it imply the substitution of one for the other.

Fig. 13. Charles Gwathmey, first-floor plans of Steel Houses, Bridgehampton, New York, 1968–1969

Fig. 14. Charles Gwathmey, Steel Houses, Bridgehampton, New York, 1968–1969

Fig. 15. Charles Gwathmey, Cogan House, East Hampton, New York, 1971–1972

4

Current Work/
Persistent Preoccupations

1974

I would like to discuss some of the work of our office in terms of the work of our contemporaries, in terms of the sources for the work in the history of architecture, and in terms of our concern for the larger issues of physical and cultural context, which I believe are inextricably bound up in the architectural act.[1] There are a number of reasons for my wanting to present our work in this manner. One of these is my conviction that, after fifty years of systematic polemicization, what has come to be called the *Modern Movement* (and I emphasize that phrase) and what is, and was never more than, a style, called the *International Style* (and I emphasize that phrase, as well) are not so much dead as still disconnected from the needs of the so-called public—the consumers of our architecture. The growing reaction among some architects to this style, with its presumed moral superiority, seems a very welcome thing. It took its first form among special groups in our society, and in non-Western cultural groups in general, in the 1960s. These groups formerly accepted modernist architecture because of a sense of cultural inferiority. Black people (in our country and in Africa), Asians, and Arabs all saw five or ten years before us that modernist form-making and modernist theory sacrificed traditional moral and social values on an altar of abstraction and purification, and that the nonrules of our architecture schools—which, of course, are rules—those homiletic honesties of function, structure, truth to materials, and so on, were destroying the crucial visual order of their worlds—and of ours as well.

Though the time to examine these rules should really be behind us, it is not. We must examine the rules, discover for ourselves their origins in certain cultural situations, and look about to see whether those same situations exist today, or see if, as I believe, they are no longer applicable.

We must understand how people really use buildings, what they really want from architects and from their architecture. Most importantly, we must rediscover without guilt that architecture is a visual medium, and in that discovery we may yet build upon the vocabularies of purist Parisian ateliers of the 1920s avant-garde as well as on a wide variety of other architectural moments in order to make a richer mix which is meaningful to a larger number of our constituencies. In opposition to the Esperanto of the International Style, we must recognize the polyglot vocabulary that is the reality of our situation; at the very least, we must tolerate—if not encourage—that freedom of architectural speech which Charles Moore so eloquently called for last week in his talk at the Architectural League. The time is at hand to go beyond the rigid limitations of the modernist movement, with its narrow aesthetic and intellectual limitations. We must find a new set of references and forge from them a new attitude toward form. I apologize for avoiding the word *style* but it has become such a dirty word. Yet I really believe, as Moore and the Venturis were the first to show us, that it is possible to have a high style of architecture which grows out of our real experience as architects and just plain people—if we would but let it.

To that end I wish to document the attempt of our office to enrich the mix. It is a collaborative attempt: the work of my partner John Hagmann, as well as of a number of others, mostly graduates of the architecture school at Columbia, all share this concern to extend the cultural connections of architecture. In presenting the work, I should like to indulge in some personal history, and—in so doing—to present it in terms of a wider range of issues and concerns than program, function, structure, materials: these wider issues and concerns I call our persistent preoccupations, our interests in the shape of the architecture around us—historical architecture, if you will—and our unabashed willingness to build upon those shapes. Our eclecticism, in short. By including some of the things that happened when John Hagmann and I were at the Yale Architecture School and by showing some of the work that our office has done since, I hope to describe our work in a larger context than simply that of the young, small office, or of housing typology, or even of issues of form and shapes—as fundamental as those issues are.

This wider framework of reference has come to be regarded, at least in the minds of some, as a kind of special bond between certain graduates of Yale and Penn in the 1960s and some of their teachers; a bond which, looking at it from the Olympian distance afforded by his situation high above Cayuga's waters at Cornell, Colin Rowe rather indelicately describes as a Yale/Philadelphia axis.

This so-called axis, students of cultural geography may be interested to note, connects New Haven and Essex, Connecticut, at one end with Philadelphia at the other. In so doing, it passes through certain areas of the West Side of Manhattan while it manages quite remarkably to bypass Princeton entirely. The axis does not, needless to say, extend to Cornell, though it has an implied diagonal emanating from Essex to certain areas of California and to DisneyWorlds on both coasts.

What, you may ask, does all this mean? It means, for one thing, that the culture of a place and the education of an architect are often decisive factors in the formulation of his work, and, by extension, that certain places at certain times where architecture is taught in a university as a humanistic discipline and not as mere technology, or, even worse, just design, are of fundamental importance to

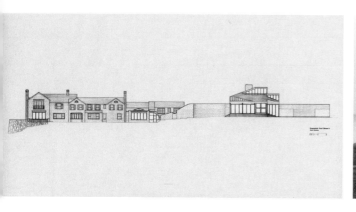

Fig. 1. Stern and Hagmann, south elevation, poolhouse, Greenwich, Connecticut, 1973–1974

Fig. 2. Stern and Hagmann, Lang Residence, Washington, Connecticut, 1973–1974

the development of architecture as something rather more important than simple problem-solving or mere professionalism. Harvard, under Walter Gropius and Sigfried Giedion, sought to be such a place but failed, I think because it too quickly became caught up in its own hermetic myth. Penn, in the 1960s, was more nearly such a place—with Louis Kahn, Venturi, Denise Scott Brown, and Aldo Giurgola as its leading teachers, but, sadly, with no architectural historians or graduate students in architectural history of comparable quality. It tended, therefore, to have a party line. Berkeley, when Moore and William W. Wurster and Joe Esherick dominated it, might have been such a place, but neither it nor Penn afforded the unique situation which, it seems to me (and I apologize for what may seem to some as the parochialism of much of this), made Yale so important. Because I believe that for an architectural education to flourish it must be undertaken in an atmosphere of humanistic investigation, I think Yale succeeded better in the 1950s and '60s than any other place. Its unique blend was distinguished by an enlightened university administration under Whitney Griswold and Kingman Brewster, which lent support not only to the program of the school but also embodied their spirit in a vigorous building program which gave enormous freedom to the talents of Eero Saarinen, Philip Johnson, Paul Rudolph, and, especially, Kahn, whose presence so many of us miss.

Those of us who have been privileged to hear and read and wise enough to listen to and learn from Kahn and from Vincent Scully have been able to go forward in architecture with a point of view of such generosity and complexity as to permit us to *include* varieties of experience in the architectural decision-making process. History, culture, the literal and the metaphoric functions of buildings—all of these are seen by them as a way toward the release of form; they are *not* seen as some constraining force in conflict with an idealized search for Platonic and Chomskian purity of expression.

What Scully and Kahn did for John Hagmann and me, as they had done for Tim Vreeland, Gio Pasanella, Jaque Robertson, Etel Kramer, M. J. Long, maybe even Charlie Gwathmey and others before, is to force us to see the fundamental limitations of the "modern architecture" MYTH. In so doing—and it was Scully in particular who did this for us—we were made to see architecture as a whole once again; to open us up to countless other aspects of architectural experience, notably the classic Greek, Frank Lloyd Wright, and, most meaningfully for our office at this stage in its development, the English "free architecture" of the 1890s and the American Shingle Style.

If Scully and Kahn can be seen as the pivots of this Yale/Philadelphia axis, then the issue of the Yale architectural journal *Perspecta,* which I edited in 1963–64 with the assistance of Hagmann, Norman Jackson, Alexander Purvis, and Craig Whitaker, among others, must be seen as its declaration of independence. This issue was ever so modestly intended to mark a major turning point in all our perceptions of what the parameters of architecture were. It was intended as a revolutionary document and it succeeded remarkably well as such, even to the point of marking Yale's transition from the vestiges of a Harvard/Bauhaus influence under Rudolph to Moore's unique blend of erudition and high-style Mickey Mouse.

In this issue of *Perspecta,* new relationships and linkages were implied by the juxtaposition of Aalto and Richardson, Kahn, Johnson, Rudolph, and Barnes. The writings and the buildings of Peter Millard, Charles Moore, Aldo Giurgola, and Bob Venturi were presented virtually for the first time.

The publication of this *Perspecta* and the search for a new department chairman to replace Rudolph heated things up at Yale quite a bit in 1964 and '65. So much so that they finally had to graduate me—in fact, Rudolph and I left New Haven on the same train, each for the last time, metaphorically speaking, in 1965. He to a career of spectacular proportions, all concrete and space and sculpture, and I to a little but ambitious shingled beach house which my one remaining friend in the world kindly let us design for his family on those fabled sandy strands of eastern Long Island.

Aside from these images—which you may or may not like—I'd like to leave with you a set of concerns that I hope you share. I say concerns and not theories; I leave the theories to my friend Peter Eisenman.

Fig. 3. Stern and Hagmann, elevations, Lang Residence, Washington, Connecticut, 1973–1974

Fig. 4. Stern and Hagmann, residence during construction, Montauk, New York, 1971–1974

Fig. 5. Robert A. M. Stern, residence, East Hampton, New York, 1968–1969

Concern for architecture as a humanistic discipline that neither ignores its past nor slavishly seeks to revive it, but rather seeks to learn from it. A concern that dares to see all architecture as one, a concern to make an architecture that is responsible to the context in which it is built—that is, to the people who use it, who simply see it as they pass by, to the process of its making and to the position it takes in the history of architecture itself.

In fullest respect to the memory of the finest architect I have ever known personally, I would like to cite the remarks Louis Kahn made at Yale in October 1964, and which are published in *Perspecta* 9/10. He said:

> Every architect's first act is that of either revitalizing a prevailing belief or finding a new belief which is just in the air somehow.
>
> It isn't a question of believing something yourself, because the reality you believe isn't your belief, it's the belief of everyone; you are simply the radar of this belief. You are the custodian of a belief that comes to you because, as an architect, you are in possession of those powers that sense the psychological entity of something. You're making something that belongs to all of us, otherwise you are producing very little or almost nothing—if not really nothing. Of course, that tells you that almost everybody fails, and it's quite true.

5

Post-Modern Architecture
1975

Paul Goldberger, the architecture critic of the *New York Times*, has written in an unpublished article that the *lack of single-minded ideological commitment* is the distinguishing factor separating the new crop of architects emerging in the mid-1970s from their predecessors. At last, it seems, the time is at hand for the architecture of "messy vitality rather than obvious unity," which Robert Venturi first called for in 1964. Diversity, heterogeneity, even eclecticism can now be spoken as the watchwords of post-modern architecture.

A confluence of events seems to mark this movement from the exclusionist neoclassicism of the late 1950s—still with us today in the work of such firms as Skidmore, Owings & Merrill—to the more inclusive, contextual, sometimes even ad-hoc work of the Venturis, Charles Moore, Aldo Giurgola, and their followers, among whom I number myself.

The so-called post-modern architecture of this group is now coming into its own as a style—or at least as an attitude, shedding its negative, anti-establishment tone and growing self-confident with its point of view. While not yet exactly a new establishment, it can be claimed to be, for the moment at least, a kind of institutionalized counterculture.

Before attempting to explain post-modern architecture I would like to make clear that the term *post-modern* is, in my mind at least, not a proper critical or art historical term at all but simply a convenient description for an attitude which I believe to be emerging and valid. This attitude can be described as cultural and historical inclusiveness; and as such it opens up for discussion the fundamental tenets of what for fifty years or more has been regarded as the Modern Movement in architecture.

More precisely, it suggests that the International Style of Mies, Le Corbusier, and Gropius was merely one aspect of modernism in architecture; that this International Style was iconoclastic, intent on breaking with the past—not only the architectural past, but also the political past; that it was idealistic in its belief in the power of architecture to mold society, puristic in its reliance on unadorned surfaces, simplistic in its pseudo-functionalism and pseudo-scientism. As such, to this day it has never received popular support in our culture, and—even in the twenty years before Venturi burst on the scene—it was being assaulted by the more creative talents within the profession, from Le Corbusier's Ronchamp in the 1950s through Alvar Aalto, Eero Saarinen, and Louis Kahn, and from outside the profession by such writers and literary critics as Norman Mailer and Jane Jacobs.

It is only recently that this twenty-year-long assault on orthodox modern architecture has come into its own and formed a proposition of its own that goes beyond negativism. Stuart Cohen, a young architect practicing in Chicago, which is probably the last bastion of orthodox modern architecture left in the United States, has, in a recent article about the work of Hardy, Holzman & Pfeiffer, described as "collage" the new attitude or methodological approach which informs post-modernism.[1] I tend to support Cohen's use of the term *collage* in this context, though I believe he ties it rather too nationalistically to a heightened sense of American tradition and the new American landscape.

I believe that Cohen's claim is correct to the extent that our architecture, if it is to succeed, must regain its basis in culture and in its own history. This is to say, architects must once again be prepared to call upon diverse elements in history and contemporary culture, and be prepared to respond knowledgeably and with enthusiasm to the particularities of place and lifestyle if our architecture is to go beyond the sterile neoclassicism of the late International Style, the architecture that has produced that "empty landscape of psychosis" which Norman Mailer so rightly claims many of our efforts at city building have become.[2]

I do not mean to call for a wholesale junking of modern architecture in favor of some naïve return to an earlier set of attitudes. Rather, I mean to suggest that we go back forty-five or fifty years to the critical juncture in the history of the architecture of this century in order that we examine the conditions which caused the International Style and not other progressive styles of the time to flourish.

Post-modernism seems to me to be the most positive direction available to direct architecture in its effort to go beyond the sterilities of the past twenty years. The mute, frozen, immobile qualities of so much of our best recent architecture clearly demonstrate that we must go beyond mere problem-solving, or overzealous concern for the problems of the building task itself, if we are to succeed in making architecture live again—for it is as symbol and metaphor, not as mere functional accommodation and technological innovation, that architecture speaks to people.

As a culture, as architects, we know so very much. What we must do is face this knowledge squarely—and in so doing squarely face the world around us, taking it for what it is, incrementally adapting the objects and ideas in it to our needs while we in turn adapt to its demands. Whereas the architects of the iconoclastic International Style rejected the world around them and sought to substitute a new one, we are at last learning to accept the context of our lives and our work.

In 1933, Talbot Hamlin, the architect and historian who was among the most articulate early critics of the International Style, in an article called "The International Style Lacks the Essence of Great Architecture,"[3] articulated the folly of the International Style's polemicists—Hamlin was critical not so much of Le Corbusier but of Henry-Russell Hitchcock, Max Taut, and others—who sought to build a castle of aesthetics on a foundation of functionalism. The layman, Hamlin wrote,

> is not an engineer, a philosopher or a sociologist, except in the most elementary manner. …He likes to have a feeling that things "work." But it's a qualitative, not a quantitative, interest.
>
> It is not quantitative functionalism [of the International Style] that is at the root of great architecture. It is not abstruse intellectual content of any kind, as analysis will show. …It is not conformity to any theory. It is never the result of labored and self-conscious puritanism. It is never a denial of joy in life.
>
> The root of great architecture is like the root of any created beauty, deep in the matrix of human consciousness. It is spontaneity, delight in form. It is superfluity—almost always a sense of "more than enough." It is the play of creative minds that makes living and building a delight as well as a task.

With this, I ask, where would you stay at DisneyWorld—the abstract Contemporary Hotel, with its round swimming pool in a wasteland of concrete, or the contextual, associative Polynesian Lodge, with waterfalls and intimate spaces set in lush greenery? I'm sure; are you?

Illustrations Shown with Lecture, Including Paired Comparisons

Pan Am Building, New York, Emery Roth & Sons with Walter Gropius and Pietro Belluschi, 1963

Chrysler Building, New York, William Van Alen, 1930

IDS Center, Minneapolis, Philip Johnson, 1973
Compared with Chrysler Building

Marin County Civic Center, San Rafael, California, Frank Lloyd Wright, 1958–69
Compared with Civic Center Competition, Thousand Oaks, California, Venturi and Rauch, 1969

Central Fire Station, New Haven, Earl P. Carlin with Paul E. Pozzi and Peter Millard Associates, 1959–62
Compared with Whitney Avenue Fire Station, New Haven, Carlin, Pozzi and Millard, 1962

Yale Mathematics Building Competition, New Haven, Venturi and Rauch, 1970

Library and Civic Plaza Competition, Biloxi, Stern and Hagmann, 1974

Whig & Clio Halls, Princeton, A. Page Brown, 1890–92, remodeled by Gwathmey/Siegel, 1970
Compared with University of Pennsylvania Museum, Philadelphia, Wilson Eyre,

Jr., Cope & Stewardson, and Frank Miles Day & Brother, 1896–99, remodeled by Mitchell/Giurgola, 1972

Guild House, Philadelphia, Venturi and Rauch in association with Cope & Lippincott, 1962–66

Contemporary City, Le Corbusier, 1922
Compared with Urbanization of Algiers Project A, Le Corbusier, 1932

Roehampton Estates, Surrey, London County Council, 1950–59
Compared with Park Hill Estate, Sheffield, Jack Lynn and Ivor Smith, 1957–61

Lower Manhattan Expressway project, Paul Rudolph, 1967–72

Mill Creek I and II, Philadelphia, Louis Kahn, 1953–63
Compared with Society Hill Towers, Philadelphia, I. M. Pei, 1965

Harlem River Park, Bronx, New York, Davis Brody & Associates, 1970–74

Waterside Plaza, New York, Davis Brody & Associates, 1966–74

Guild House
Compared with Crawford Manor, New Haven, Paul Rudolph, 1962–66

Brighton Beach Competition, Venturi and Rauch, 1968

West Plaza Condominiums, Coronado, California, Moore, Lyndon, Turnbull & Whitaker, 1962

Eigen Haard Flats, Amsterdam, Michael de Klerk, 1921
Compared with De Dageraad Houses, Amsterdam, Piet Kramer, 1923

Hillside Homes, Bronx, New York, Clarence Stein, 1932–35

Westminster City Council Houses, London, Sir Edwin Lutyens, 1928

Riverbend, New York, Davis Brody & Associates, 1964–67
Compared with Park Hill Estate

Twin Parks East, Bronx, New York, James Stewart Polshek, 1970–72

Twin Parks East, Bronx, New York, Gio Pasanella, 1970–73

Church Street South Housing, New Haven, Moore Grover Harper, 1969
Compared with Public Housing, Preston, Lancashire, James Stirling, 1957–60

Kresge College, Santa Cruz, California, Charles Moore, 1973

DisneyWorld, Orlando, Florida, ca. 1970–77

New England barn
Compared with Ingersoll Residence, Cornwall Bridge, Connecticut, Hardy & Prentice, 1966

Lang House, Washington, Connecticut, Stern and Hagmann, 1973–74

Eton College Schoolyard, Berkshire, England, ca. 1960

Governor Gore House, Waltham, Massachusetts, Jacques-Guillaume LeGrand and Rebecca Gore, 1805–6

Samuel Foreman House, Syracuse, New York, ca. 1830

Retirement House, Captiva Island, Florida, Charles Moore, 1971

Retirement House project, Southern Florida, Rem Koolhaas and Laurinda Spear, 1974

Zimmermann House, Fairfax, Virginia, William Turnbull, Jr., 1975

Housing development project, Williamsburg, Virginia, Charles Moore, 1973–74

Alexander House addition, Princeton, New Jersey, Michael Graves, 1973
Compared with Peter Eisenman, Falk House (House II), Hardwick, Vermont, 1969

DisneyWorld—juxtaposed reality
Compared with Leib House, Long Beach Island, New Jersey, Venturi and Rauch, 1969

Spaeth House II, East Hampton, New York, Hardy Holzman Pfeiffer, 1970
Compared with Porsche Monument House project, Daniel V. Scully, 1970

Twin Parks Northeast, Bronx, New York, Richard Meier, 1970–72
Compared with Church Street South Housing

Two swimming pools at DisneyWorld

6

Gray Architecture as Post-Modernism, or, Up and Down from Orthodoxy

1976

At the outset of this brief essay, I would like to suggest that the "White and Gray" debate is not (as has been suggested in the press) an encounter between polarities such as might have occurred in 1927 between advocates of the Beaux-Arts and apostles of International Style modernism. Rather, this debate, beginning at the University of California at Los Angeles in May 1974, has grown into an ongoing dialogue between two groups of architects who, in their built work and theoretical investigations, chart out and clarify a direction which architecture can take now that the orthodox Modernist Movement has drawn to a close.

Peter Eisenman, to my mind the principal theorist among the "White" architects, sees this new direction in a particular way, which he labels "Post-Functionalism." Eisenman seeks to free architecture from explicit cultural associations of any kind. My view of this new direction differs from Eisenman's: I call it "Post-Modernism," and I see it as a kind of philosophical pragmatism or pluralism which builds upon messages from "orthodox modernism" as well as from other defined historical trends.

For "Post-Modernism," and probably for "Post-Functionalism" as well, it is safe to say that the orthodox Modernist Movement is a closed issue, an historical fact of no greater contemporaneity than that of nineteenth-century academicism; and though messages can be received from both these historical periods, as from the past in general, nostalgia for either cannot be substituted for a fresh, realistic assessment of the issues as they are now. The struggle for both groups, then, is to return to our architecture that vitality of intention and form which seems so absent from the work of the late Modernists.

"Post-Modernism" and "Post-Functionalism" can both be seen as attempts to get out of the trap of orthodox Modernism now devoid of philosophic meaning and formal energy, and both are similar in their emphasis on the development of a strong formal basis for design. Beyond this, however, they are widely divergent, in that "Post-Functionalism" seeks to develop formal compositional themes as independent entities freed from cultural connotations, whereas "Post-Modernism" embodies a search for strategies that will make architecture more responsive to and visually cognizant of its own history, the physical context in which a given work of architecture is set, and the social, cultural, and political milieu which calls it into being. Contrary to what was said at the end of the 1960s, "Post-Modernism" is neither a sociology of the constructed nor the techno-socio-professional determinism of the orthodox Modern Movement; it affirms that architecture is made for the eye as well as for the mind, and that it includes both a conceptualized formation of space and the circumstantial modifications that a program can make this space undergo.

Implicit in this emergent Post-Modernist position is a recognition that the more than fifty-year history of the Modernist movement has been accompanied by no notable increase in affection on the part of the public for the design vocabulary that has been evolved. This is partially so because that movement has been obsessively concerned with abstraction and has eschewed explicit connections with familiar ideas and things. (Even the pipe railings of the 1920s are by now, for most of us, cut off from everyday reference; who among us has been on an ocean liner in the last twenty-five years?) For a Post-Modernist attitude to take root in a meaningful way, an effort must be made toward recapturing the affection of architecture's very disaffected constituency, the public.

The exhibition of drawings of the École des Beaux-Arts which was presented in 1975 at the Museum of Modern Art in New York, and the discussion of the significance of that exhibition in the press, at the Institute for Architecture and Urban Studies, at the Architectural League of New York, and within the frame of seminars at the School of Architecture at Columbia University, made it possible for architects of New York—many of the "Whites" and "Grays," in particular— to begin to reweave the fabric of the Modern period, which was so badly rent by the puritan revolution of the Modern Movement. It is not surprising that the tradition represented by the École des Beaux-Arts—the poetic tradition of design—should be examined with renewed sympathy, and that one of the hallmarks of the École's design methodology, the beautiful drawing, should be restored to a position of influence. A large part of the work of the "Grays" tends to establish connections with the formal, spatial, and decorative invention of the nineteenth century.

For the "Grays," at least, Venturi and Moore have laid the foundation for the philosophical structure of Post-Modernism. In the search for an architectural position able to draw on historic issues, including both Modernism and nineteenth-century eclecticism, they have reminded us of the power to achieve symbolic meaning through allusion—not only allusion to other movements in architectural history, but to historical and contemporary events of a social, political, and cultural nature as well. In organizing the Beaux-Arts exhibit, Arthur Drexler, long associated with the position of orthodox Modernism, has also made a contribution to the philosophical structure of Post-Modernism. The Beaux-Arts exhibit suggests that Modern architecture might find a way out of the dilemma of the late Modern Movement by entering a period where symbolism and allusion would take their place alongside issues of formal composition, functional fit, and constructional logic. In his introduction to the Beaux-Arts show's catalogue, Drexler admonished that "we could be well advised to examine our architectural pieties 'in the light of an increased awareness and appreciation of the nature of architecture' as it was understood in the nineteenth century."

The Beaux-Arts exhibition reminded us of the poverty of orthodox Modern architecture: trapped in the narcissism of its obsession with the process of its own making, sealed off from everyday experience and from high culture alike by its abstraction and the narrowing of its frame of reference within the Modern period to the canonical succession of events and images and personalities delimited by Giedion and Pevsner, and drained of energy as a result of a confusion between the values assigned to minimalism by a Mies van der Rohe with those assigned by an Emery Roth.

The work of the "Grays" presents certain strategies and attitudes that distinguish it from that of the "Whites." These strategies include (in no particular order):

The use of ornament. Though ornament is often the handmaiden of historical allusion, the decoration of the vertical plane need not be justified in historical or cultural terms; the decorated wall responds to an innate human need for elaboration and for the articulation of the building's elements in relation to human scale.

The manipulation of forms to introduce an explicit historical reference. This is not to be confused with the simplistic eclecticism that has too often in the past substituted pat, predigested typological imagery for more incisive analysis. The principle is rather that there are lessons to be learned from history as well as from technological innovation and behavioral science, that the history of buildings is the history of meaning in architecture. Moreover, for the Post-Modernist these lessons from history go beyond modes of spatial organization or structural expression to the heart of architecture itself: the relationship between form and shape and the meanings that particular shapes have assumed over the course of time. This Post-Modernist examination of historical precedent grows out of the conviction that appropriate references to historical architecture can enrich new work and thereby make it more familiar, accessible, and possibly even meaningful for the people who use buildings. It is, in short, a cue system that helps architects and users communicate better about their intentions.

The conscious and eclectic utilization of the formal strategies of orthodox Modernism, together with the strategies of the pre-Modern period. Borrowing from forms and strategies of both orthodox Modernism and the architecture that preceded it, Post-Modernism declares the past-ness of both; as such it makes a clear distinction between the architecture of the Modern period, which emerged in the middle of the eighteenth century in western Europe, and that puritanical phase of the Modern period which we call the Modern Movement.

The preference for incomplete or compromised geometries, voluntary distortion, and the recognition of growth of buildings over time. This is manifest in a marked preference for the Aalto of the fifties over the Corbusier of the twenties, for the plans of Lutyens over those of Voysey, and for the long love affair with the American

Shingle Style of the nineteenth century. These preferences are paired with an architecture that appeals to Platonic geometry, particularly in its general composition. Thus, geometrically pure rooms are linked together in an unaccustomed manner and create larger and frankly hybrid forms, tied together visually by the envelope of the exterior walls. These hybrid forms are rarely perceptible at first glance. For lack of a more appropriate term, I would call this an "episodic composition," which must be distinguished from the determinist composition of Modernist orthodoxy.

The use of rich colors and various materials that effect a materialization of architecture's imagery and perceptible qualities, as opposed to the materialization of technology and constructional systems that remain so overtly significant in brutalist architecture.

The emphasis on intermediate spaces, that is, the "pochés" of circulation, and on the borders, that is, on the thickness of the wall. From this comes an architecture made of spaces whose configuration is much more neutral and supple, from a functional point of view, than the so-called continuous spaces of the orthodox Modern Movement.

The configuration of spaces in terms of light and view as well as of use.

The adjustment of specific images charged with carrying the ideas of the building. It is thus possible for the architect to create simultaneously two premises or spatial units within one building or two buildings in a complex that do not resemble each other even if their compositional elements are the same. An attitude of this sort permits us to see the work of Eero Saarinen in a new light.

To return to the philosophical intentions of "Gray" architecture, the importance of the writings of Vincent Scully is evident: his vision of architecture as part of a larger whole, which is at the heart of the cultural formation of the "Grays" (many of whom were his students at Yale), often runs counter to arbitrary stylistic and cultural categories and puts a particular emphasis on the interrelationship of the building, the landscape, and culture. Scully has begun to influence not only architects but also historians like Neil Levine, who, in his account of the Beaux-Arts, assigns great importance to questions of communication and in particular to that of an *architecture parlante*. He has equally influenced George Hersey, whose studies on the associationism of mid-nineteenth-century English architecture make an important contribution to the philosophical foundation of the eclecticism emerging in the "Grays."

Not surprising, then, that Hersey should have been a client for whom Venturi achieved one of his most stunning houses. One finds at the root of the "gray" position a rejection of the anti-symbolic, anti-historical, hermetic, and highly abstract architecture of orthodox Modernism. Grayness seeks to move toward an acceptance of diversity; it prefers hybrids to pure forms; it encourages multiple and simultaneous readings in its effort to heighten expressive content. The layering of space characteristic of much "gray" architecture finds its complement in the overlay of cultural and art-historical references in the elevations. For "gray" architecture, "more is more."

"Gray" buildings have facades which tell stories. These facades are not the diaphanous veil of orthodox Modern architecture, nor are they the affirmation of deep structural secrets. They are mediators between the building as a "real" construct and those allusions and perceptions necessary to put the building in closer touch with the place in which it is made and with the beliefs and dreams of the architects who designed it, the clients who paid for it, and the civilization which permitted it to be built; to make buildings, in short, landmarks of a culture capable of transcending transitory usefulness as functional accommodation. "Gray" buildings are very much of a time and place; they are not intended as ideal constructs of perfected order; they select from the past in order to comment on the present.

7

New Directions in American Architecture
1976

In trying to define the present situation, at the edge of modernism, and also to suggest some of the directions that will take us beyond that edge into post-modernism, I would like to begin on a somewhat personal note by referring to a book I wrote in 1969 titled *New Directions in American Architecture,* to which I am currently providing a postscript to include even newer directions and ideas.[1] Those who have read the book remember that it opens by posing a confrontation between Venturi & Rauch's and Wells & Koetter's submissions to a competition for housing in Brooklyn held in 1968. This battle of Brighton Beach served me well, I believe, as a vehicle to explore the relationships between inclusionism and exclusionism, orthodox modernism and that as yet inchoate movement seeking to supplant the modernist orthodoxies of the 1950s and 1960s—not to mention those of the 1920s and 1930s—which then had no name, but which I and others have since come to describe as "post-modernism."

Much has happened in American architecture since 1969; we now have a climate such as has not existed since the 1930s, when traditionalists and modernists squared off in a battle of styles and ideologies that would determine the character of American architecture for a generation. While it can hardly be disputed that this battle of the styles was a real one, fought as it was over empty drafting boards in the years of the Great Depression and really resolved only by the events of the European diaspora caused by the Second World War, the struggle between ideas and ideologies now taking place, amidst a present-day, less-than-great Depression, seems to many to be rather small potatoes. Referring to today's battle of the styles, the architectural historian Rosemarie Bletter, speaking last June at the annual meeting of the Society of Architectural Historians, stated that the opposed White and

Gray groupings were merely "false polarization" and that all the new generation, from Robert Venturi and Charles Moore down to such younger Turks as Michael Graves and myself, were merely playing mannerist games and in retreat from the Holy Grail of modernism.[2] Yet the battles of Whites and Grays (not to mention the injection of other hues and tonalities such as the Silvers of Los Angeles), the clashing of axes, whether they connect Yale with Pennsylvania or Princeton with Cornell, are real and, I believe, important.

While I do not disagree with Bletter's claim that, given a wide view of things and set against the late orthodox modernism of the 1950s and 1960s, the Whites and Grays may well be far more alike and have far more in common than the debate would imply, I do not think that the myth of a monolithic view of the present situation can be effectively perpetuated anymore. Nor can one justifiably sustain that myth of monolithic modernism which Sigfried Giedion and others tried to project—and almost succeeded in projecting—during the 1920s and 1930s.

There is almost no one who would seriously dispute that modernist architecture was a far more complex scene than that, with Erich Mendelsohn, Hans Scharoun, Hugo Häring, Hannes Meyer, Bernard Bijvoet, Johannes Duiker, Pierre Chareau, and a host of other inventive talents entitled to play important roles in its history. Yet, virtually to a man, these architects were excluded from the councils of the CIAM just as they were from the canon of orthodox modernism as we were introduced to it in America in such books as Giedion's *Space, Time and Architecture,* Hitchcock and Johnson's *International Style,* Pevsner's *Pioneers of Modern Design,* and Hitchcock's *Modern Architecture: Romanticism and Reintegration,* although Hitchcock does discuss some of them.

In any case, I would submit that the new generation I wrote about in 1969, and key members of it whom I focused on in *Perspecta* 9/10 of 1965—I might add, inspired by an article of Donlyn Lyndon's published in *Casabella* in 1963—do represent a new point of view and not merely more of the same old thing, not merely a third generation of modernists.[3] This new generation is overturning a vast number of beliefs promulgated by modernism's first generation—the generation of Le Corbusier and Mies. The new generation is especially keen on putting as much distance as possible between itself and the second generation of modernists—the Anglo-American generation, if you will, the generation of Johnson, Rudolph, and Kevin Roche and, of course, Peter and Alison Smithson, who inherited as gospel the beliefs of their predecessors.

Before attempting to tackle the new and largely post-modernist generation, and to document some of its work, including some of my own, I should like to focus for a moment on the situation of late modernism in America, and in so doing set the scene for the emergence of the new revisions and attitudes. In the post–World War II building boom, the leaders of the second generation of modernists, then emerging out of Harvard for the most part, and out of the Midwest to a considerable number, shed the philosophical, political, and sociological idealism of the Modern Movement, holding on largely only to its forms, which, as they typically employed them, seemed particularly well suited to the needs of an expanding corporate and commercial bureaucracy anxious to build expeditiously, cheaply, and splashily. Though the economic pickings are slim these days for most of us, and though many of us feel that the cultural morsels that the second-generation modernists are able to throw at us are little more than crumbs, the leading practitioners of the postwar generation continue to build their dreams at a pretty good rate. And let us not forget that though the mock heroism of concrete piled to the sky and the technological bravura of the shiniest mirror-glass panel clipped to the minutest mullion may no longer hold for us the same religious power that it did for Le Corbusier or for Mies, it still seems to have a wide market in the so-called developing countries of the Near and Far East, where the concept of progress seems rooted in a vision of America that most of us rejected the night Lyndon Johnson told the nation it could have guns and butter, war in Vietnam and tranquility at home.

I would like, then, to begin this account of where we are at, or perhaps more accurately, where some of us younger architects think we are going, by looking at where the leaders of the profession, the second generation of modernists, are. I will do this by first looking at a building by Philip Johnson and then at one by Paul Rudolph, two architects whose work I discuss in some detail in my book. Then I shall touch on two transitional figures: Eero Saarinen and Louis Kahn.

Taking the work of Philip Johnson as represented by Pennzoil Place, now being completed in Houston, one can see that the real question about the minimalist strain in so much modernist architecture is whether or not it can sustain itself any longer and whether or not we, the public, the consumers of architecture, can support any longer its graph paper simplifications. In light of the enormous demands on our energy supplies and systems, and more importantly, in light of our own knowledge about the rich tradition and culture of architecture, many questions can be asked about the basic attitudes of this most dazzling abstract design. And if one considers the implications of such frozen minimalism for cities—and I could have taken some far more extreme examples by less sensitive designers— one begins to see why this style goes hand in hand with the development of the suburban office park.

Nature is needed to supply a foil; the richness of the city, which was part and parcel of the applied modernism of the Art Deco and Beaux-Arts–Baroque styles, has given way under the minimalist modernist banner to that urban landscape of the 1950s and 1960s, which Norman Mailer so aptly characterizes as "the empty landscape of the psychosis." And it has driven workers and executives alike from the center of our cities in droves.

The other side of the late modernist dilemma can be seen in the work of Paul Rudolph, whose search for expression without resort to applied decoration or sign has resulted in an obsession with the totally designed holistic object in which every part is manipulated again and again. One asks, as with minimalism, how long can overdesign sustain our interest and how many of us are willing to submit to the aesthetic will of the architect as we simply try to go about the ordinary tasks of daily life?

Two architects represent significant transitional positions in the discussion of the shift from modernism to post-modernism; both of these, Eero Saarinen and Louis Kahn, enjoyed relatively short careers and both, rather more significantly, by virtue of education and early practical experience, did not share the unbridled enthusiasm for and unquestioning acceptance of canonic, International Style modernism that characterizes representative figures among the second generation of modernists.

Kahn reintroduced the issue of the relationship of modern architecture to the architecture of the past; yet in the best of his work, as at the Salk Institute for Biological Studies at La Jolla, despite early experiments with a vocabulary that was explicitly referential to Roman prototypes, he expressed his ideas with rigorously abstract shapes inextricably bound to a specific building technology and a rigorous functionalism. And strangely, in the work in India and Pakistan, where Kahn seized on a locally available material—a crude red brick—he chose not to refer to the indigenous forms of the Indian subcontinent, or to those of ancient Rome, which he loved and which would have made some valuable connections for his Western-minded clients. Instead, Kahn proposed a set of forms that are disquieting in their abstractness and placelessness.

The other of the transitional figures I would like to discuss very briefly is Eero Saarinen. When I wrote *New Directions* in 1969, Saarinen had been dead for eight years, and there was no reason to include a discussion of his work in the book. More importantly, I did not then fully see the significance of Saarinen's achievement in design, and the liberating potential of his much-derided philosophy of the "style for the job." This philosophy was not an expedient pandering to the crass demands of the marketplace, as so many of his critics claimed it to be, but a genuine search for the appropriate solution to each building problem with which he was presented. Among Saarinen's last works, the two residential colleges at Yale—completed shortly after his death in 1961 at the age of fifty-one—flawed though they are, can be seen to represent a beginning resolution of his intention: two separate buildings whose deference to the forms of New Haven's neo-Gothic tradition is made manifest in both the plan and the image of the buildings, which surrender the "object fixation" of most second-generation modernist work to a strategy of building composition that can be described by some as environmental or urbanistic.

Now if one examines the period since I wrote *New Directions* or, more importantly, if one goes a bit further back in time to the years 1962–1963, when the pioneering figures of American post-modernism began to reach maturity, one can see that this new direction has had sufficient time to establish its goals and that the urgency of its message can be directly associated with major political and social events of the recent past, beginning with the assassination of an idealistic president in 1963, ending with the resignation of a cynical one, and focused on the war in Vietnam, the single most divisive event to have affected this country since the war between the states 100 years earlier.

Before focusing on some of the formal and social positions that constitute the post-modernist critique and program, I would like to comment briefly on two new positions that have emerged in American architecture, positions that do not seem to me at this point post-modernist but which in their blatant extremism contribute to our perceptions about the limitations of modernism and thereby serve to crystallize many post-modernist attitudes. The first of these, and certainly the more trivial, is the nihilist position embodied in the various fringe and splinter movements of the late 1960s: Drop City, Ant Farm, and various other less-well-known, build-your-own-yurt type movements, including Garbage Housing. All largely quiescent at the moment, these movements required an affluent, indulgent society to sustain their countercultural argument. Yet, in their antiestablishmentarianism, and more specifically in their antiprofessionalism, they did serve notice on the architectural profession that its relatively narrow goals were shockingly self-serving and that the boundaries of architecture extended well beyond the corridors of corporate and governmental bureaucracy.

A second position I would like to focus on is that of the so-called White architects, who seem to me to represent the playing out of modernism to its ultimate extreme; form is developed to a fever pitch at the expense of function or a sense of place, and buildings are pretty much self-sufficient not only in a technological sense but in terms of a hermetic view of landscape, physical context, and prevailing cultural milieu. Materials are denuded of their inherent characteristics in the search for abstraction and weightlessness. All these characterize the extreme, or rococo, phase, if you will permit me a Wölfflinian interpretation of the evolution of the modernist style.

But the most important tendency prevailing that I can detect outside postmodernism is that articulated by Peter Eisenman, who describes himself as a "post-functionalist." Unlike the architects of Ant Farm and Drop City, Eisenman is hardly what one might describe as a hero of the counterculturalists. His erudition in the history and theory of architecture is second to none; and in his capacity as head of the Institute for Architecture and Urban Studies in New York he has done more than any other figure in recent history to create a culture for architecture in the United States; yet his work in design is profoundly countercultural. His houses offer a critique of the pseudo-functionalism of orthodox modernism, claiming with considerable justification that in this respect he is the first true modernist. Recently, in an interview in *Newsweek* magazine, Eisenman proclaimed that none of his houses were "shaped for clients' needs. They are designed to *shake* them out of those needs."[4] Eisenman believes that architecture can change culture; he tells his clients for House VI that he would like to build them another house that they can live in!

Eisenman's post-functionalism, which I would argue is perhaps one of the most splendid sets of clothes that any emperor ever had woven for the delectation of an avant-garde panting for new thrills, takes as its formalist jumping-off point Colin Rowe's idea of phenomenological transparency. As Richard Pommer has recently written in *Artforum,* for Eisenman, modernism "is a function of the mind, which comprehends planes as transparent though they aren't. Architecture can thus be understood as a conception of layered planes, as in a Cubist painting. Structure, materials, walls, doors, etc., might mark the planes for the eye but need not be otherwise significant. The functional and technological (and by simple extension, the social) dogmas which had oppressed modern architecture could be forgotten."[5] But though Eisenman critiques the direction that modernism took as its early abstractions were compromised by the realities and practicalities implicit in professionalism, his position cannot be confused with a post-modernist one, and, more importantly, by virtue of its rigorous iconoclasm seems doomed to trivialities as it trivializes all human meaning. The action of life in its day-to-day unraveling renders Eisenman's abstractions, however high-minded, trivial because of his unwillingness to grapple with the particularities of life and places. How ironic that in his rejection of culture and function Eisenman lays bare the real implications of modernism. Though we have been told many conflicting things about architecture's external direction—for example, that it is the will of its epoch, that there are constituent facts upon which its ideas are based, and so on—it seems clear that much of the work of the postwar period rallied not around technology or function but around the abstractions of Le Corbusier's "play of forms under the light" and, regrettably, around a materialistic interpretation of Mies's purported diction that less is more, which, when you think about it, is one of the dumbest ideas imaginable. *Less is less,* and that is all there is to it, or so it seems to me. Conversely, I would submit, *more is more.* Eisenman rejects culture, but as Pommer points out, he cannot escape the trap of culture—for is not the vigorous cubism of early Le Corbusier via Colin Rowe and Robert Slutzky as culturally hidebound as any other physical scaffolding for organizing physical elements for the purpose of making buildings?

While I reject the argument that has been put forward in defense of Eisenman's position that he belongs together with John Hejduk and the Italian architect Aldo Rossi under the rubric "neo-rationalist"—that term is the opposite of what could be called the "neo-realist" position of the post-modernist group that includes Venturi, Moore, Hugh Hardy, and myself—I would prefer to leave that issue open for discussion, and simply conclude my discussion of post-functionalism with a question: Can an architecture that sees itself as "autonomous," transcending history and culture, speaking in its own language "almost itself," and eschewing communication of ideas "other than its own," sustain its argument over time at any scale other than the most private?

Nonetheless, "post-modernism" and "post-functionalism" have one important thing in common: they can both be seen as attempts to get out of the trap of orthodox modernism now devoid of philosophic meaning and formal energy. Yet, beyond this key point of commonality, they are widely divergent. Post-functionalism seeks to develop formal compositional themes as independent entities freed from cultural connotations, whereas post-modernism embodies a search for strategies that will reify the early ideology of functionalism and embody notions of realism and rationalism while making architecture more responsive to and visually cognizant of a) its history, b) the physical context in which a given work of architecture is set, and c) the social, cultural, and political milieu which it calls into being. Unlike the posturings of the late 1960s, post-modernism is not a kind of built sociology nor does it subscribe to the techno-socio-functional determinist line of the orthodox Modern Movement. A post-modernist attitude brings with it an affirmation of belief that architecture is for the eye as well as for the mind; it is inclusive of systematic concepts of space-making, as well as circumstantial modifications of form, in response to particular physical or programmatic situations.

Implicit in this emergent post-modernist position is a recognition that the more than fifty-year-long history of the Modern Movement has been accompanied by no notable increase in affection on the part of the public for the design vocabulary that has evolved. This is partially because that movement has been obsessively concerned with self-referential abstraction and has eschewed explicit connections with familiar ideas and things. (Even the pipe railings of the 1920s are, by now, for most of us, cut off from everyday reference; who among us has been on an ocean liner in the last twenty-five years?) For a post-modernist attitude to take root in a meaningful way, an effort must be made toward recapturing the affection of architecture's very disaffected constituency: the public.

The Museum of Modern Art's recent exhibition of drawings from the École des Beaux-Arts and the subsequent discussion of the meaning of that exhibition in the press, at the Institute for Architecture and Urban Studies, at the Architectural League, and in the architecture program of Columbia's architecture school, have brought architects—particularly many Whites and Grays—together. The Beaux-Arts show has been greeted with a sense of urgency and focus beyond the immediate concerns of career. And it is not surprising that, just as much of the discussion touches on the relationship between nineteenth-century pluralism, early twentieth-century utopianism, and the current situation, so too does much of the work of post-modernists seek to connect with nineteenth-century formal, spatial, and decorative invention. One can see the Beaux-Arts show as a kind of self-fulfilling prophecy from the Museum of Modern Art and in particular from Arthur Drexler, the mercurial director of its architecture department. It was Drexler who enabled the major opening chord of post-modernism to be sounded when he published the full manuscript of Venturi's *Complexity and Contradiction in Architecture* in 1966—brief selections having previously been published early in 1965 in *Perspecta*.[6] Venturi, at first alone and then in partnership with Denise Scott Brown, dominates the revisionism of the last ten or so years.

Drexler's decision to hold an exhibition of student work from the École des Beaux-Arts can be seen, if not exactly as a logical step beyond the publication of Venturi's book, then certainly as an important and eminently comprehensible one. Initially, the exhibition was viewed as a cautionary tale about draftsmanship, about educational process, about what architects can do when they have no real work in the office; such, of course, was a trivial response to the show. Soon, as William Ellis points out in the current *Oppositions*, the critics began to realize that such an exhibition, held within the sacred hall of modernism's great temple, was "probably as significant as a symptom of our condition as it may have been as a catalyst for imminent change." Ellis continues:

> The very least the show has done is to have made a public signal that modern architecture for some time has not occupied a very significant point in its own history; that, therefore, it may be ripe for new energies, new development, and that the revision of its early assumptions will inevitably be a part of that process of development—perhaps a more significant part than the mere repetition, dilution or expansion of those early assumptions.[7]

Venturi and to a considerable extent Charles Moore have laid the foundations for the philosophical structure of post-modernism. In the search for an architectural position able to draw on history, including both modernism and nineteenth-century eclecticism, they have reminded us of the power to achieve symbolic meaning through allusion—not only allusion to other movements in architectural history but also to historical and contemporary events of a social, political, and cultural nature. And Drexler, for so long associated with an orthodox modernist position, has added to the philosophical structure of post-modernism. In his talk "Alternatives to Modernism," recently delivered at Columbia University, Drexler not only called attention to the techniques of the Beaux-Arts but also asked that we "appreciate the superfluous as an act of free will in an architecture whose values are predicated on necessity." In so doing, he defined the realm of architecture as one that must go beyond the functional and technological determinism of the orthodox modernist period into a perception of the multiplicity of situations which cause architecture to convey meaning.

American suburbanism most pointedly calls into focus the inherent and as yet unresolved conflicts between the abstract idealism of the continental European-based philosophical systems that have largely dominated our American scene in the past forty years of American modernism, and the newer, more pragmatic Anglo-American strategies which are to a considerable extent at the heart of post-modernism.

The message that commercialized American suburbia responds to so effectively can be read loud and clear in the semantic dysfunction of the archetypal European modernist suburb, Le Corbusier's Pessac development (1922–1926). Always derided as a Casbah by its residents, who were from the first aware of its exotic, and to them inappropriate, building form and urban design, Pessac was unsuitable from metaphoric, political, and sociological points of view. The housing was good but, to make a pointed distinction, the "meaning" was wrong.

The American suburb as a distinct physical environment based on distinct social and cultural ideals, though it has its origins in Regency England, really got going in the 1850s at Llewellyn Park, New Jersey. American suburbanism evolved in an effort to help cope with the pressures brought on by rapid economic expansion, which were changing the character of urban life. It did not take hold until the time of the nation's centennial, from which time forward it became not merely a phenomenon of geography but one of character, inextricably interlocking nostalgia for the life and architecture of small-town pre-industrial America, especially and understandably the towns of New England and the coastal South, with the presumably beneficial realities of technology and economic growth.

Any rapid survey of the architecture of the American suburb perforce elicits a number of ironies, not the least of which involves the internationally revered "Prairie House" of Frank Lloyd Wright, which, as has often been pointed out, not only defers to New England prototypes in its emphasis on the fireplace mass and hearth as the literal focus of plan and mass and the symbolic focus of family life, but also relies on the urbanism of the New England small town for its own siting strategies. The distinctly comprehensible image of the Prairie House as a house in a town on a small lot has no precedent in the farm or ranch groupings of the American Midwest or West (nor, of course, does it relate to a European urban precedent). It can be understood only in terms of the small pre-industrial towns of the East Coast.

A number of specific conclusions can be drawn in regard to the contributions of architects to the sociological and functional successes, and more especially to the enduring symbolic power and relevance, of the American suburb as we know it. Our most innovative architects, beginning with H. H. Richardson and Wright, have focused great energies on suburban issues, especially that of the suburban house. To the extent that these issues have been understood and accurately reflected in their design, especially as they affect the typical American's hold on the isolated single-family house as an icon of cultural connection with the early republic and its colonial antecedents, and as an icon of the individual in a mass society, these architects have been able to make their ideas felt in the marketplace. So it is, for example, that Wright's designs for the Usonian and Cloverleaf houses have had no real impact while his site planning ideas have virtually dominated all suburban land planning in the last thirty years; and, conversely, Wright's Prairie Houses of 1900–1910, most of which were conceived for modest sites in Oak Park,

Illinois, one of the earliest communities developed along the subway-suburb-as-small-town model, now embody and in fact continue to define the acceptable image of a contemporary suburban house. Whole aspects of Prairie House planning and specific images of its design have been incorporated in all kinds of house types today, even the ubiquitous "split-level-raised-ranch-garrison-colonial." And, parenthetically, if the suburb is accepted as a legitimate urban form, then Wright must be acknowledged as a twentieth-century urbanist equal to if not greater than Le Corbusier, not only in terms of theoretical insight, but also in terms of actual impact on built form. And Wright's impact, so characteristically American in its pragmatism, goes with the grain of American life, while Le Corbusier's, so characteristically European in its idealism, seeks to counter prevailing attitudes.

Although the impact of Europe's nascent modernism of the 1890s and 1900s on the American suburban house was considerable (Voysey, Baillie-Scott, Muthesius, the Viennese Secession), European modernism since the 1920s has had little impact except in isolated cases of high-style innovation and in providing the impetus for debate, such as Wright's Broadacre City, which was conceived in response to Le Corbusier's Ville Radieuse.

The continuously evolving attitude toward the issue of the modest house on the modest suburban lot on the part of excellent though not necessarily innovative architects since Richardson's period can be easily established and should be studied by all who really care about the future of the American townscape. There have been a significant number of successful and occasionally innovative suburban town planning schemes that adapt the image of the small town to prevailing issues of marketplace and transportation. Yet the coherent pattern of development that might have been evolved from the appreciation and understanding of such a project as the brilliantly complex urban/suburban paradise of Forest Hills Gardens in New York has failed to emerge, in part because of the unwillingness or inability of high-style architects and planners to adjust their own ideas about building form to popular tastes.

Considerable comprehension of the messages of suburbia is beginning to find its way into the work of post-modernist architects. Though Venturi and Scott Brown have studied the suburbs, they have not yet made a direct transfer of their research into design. Charles Moore has, however, in his Owen Brown Village for Columbia, Maryland, and in his housing at Williamsburg, Virginia, which suggest a fresh look at the suburban house retaining traditional imagery. The preferred images work out with especial irony at Williamsburg, while upping the density of the development.

In a project prepared for the Venice Biennale, I have made an attempt to define a new kind of suburb to be built within the legal confines of the city, relatively close to its center, using urban land that has been abandoned and has no apparent higher value. This project, called Subway Suburb, is purely speculative. Yet it suggests uncharacteristic ways to develop the land in burned-out, marginal areas of the city that will connect with existing rapid transit services while also accommodating the automobile within the new development. To provide housing in the city at the densities of new, moderate-priced suburban development in outlying areas, the Subway Suburb accepts known functional paradigms and confines its invention to the realm of shape and symbol, reintroducing historical and cultural allusion into the design process: Regency Crescents, the University of Virginia, the small-town American porch, Forest Hills Gardens, are all consciously evoked. The basic housing type devised for Subway Suburb is based on the freestanding cottage of the American small town, circa 1900. Incentives to individual proprietorship of open space are provided through the reintroduction of identifiable front yards of substantial size, places which by their very nature will mark out a clearly definable turf maintained by the private citizen for the benefit of the community. Careful development of existing, workable, plan-and-volume types permits the establishment of a sense of hierarchy at the scale of town planning through the introduction of the following strategies: a) treating the corners as gateways to the individual blocks, and b) assigning a hierarchical posture to each street through the introduction of big-scale crescents and appropriate house types, the larger one- and two-family "villas" grouped about a common green that also acts as a neighborhood park for the community, while the "smaller" cottages on the other streets recall the highly regarded suburban images of the Elm streets and Maple avenues of small-town America.

Our proposal for elderly family housing intended for a site set in a scrub-oak forest at Brookhaven, Long Island, not only has within it an explicit critique of prevailing formal and organizational paradigms but also can be seen as a specific evocation of earlier American traditions of space-making and of building form. Car and house, wild and controlled natural landscape are all considered in this scheme in an attempt to provide a variety of useful places for people to meet in relationship to established precedents. The academical village of Jefferson is reinterpreted to foster a sense of community amidst the ennui of an old age isolated from the world of work and from our society's inability to provide for a more natural interaction in one place for people of all ages.

The rapid development of Singer Island, a middle-class resort just north of Palm Beach, has tended to inhibit the evolution of local character and a sense of place. Its growth has shown an obsessive concern for the requirements of vehicular traffic, and yet it has failed to adapt to, or exploit, the possibilities inherent in the particular form of suburbanism that the automobile creates. Our proposal outlines methods and strategies for the evolution of a sense of place unique to the island. In establishing a physical image for Singer Island that is easily identifiable, familiar in form, unified and coherent, the most compelling frame of reference seemed to be the instant "Florida/Spanish" of the late 1920s. At the same time, strategies were developed to mark out particular places and sequences of spaces that could be "read" from the moving automobile and experienced by the pedestrian (thus, they function not only as "billboards" but as useful objects as well). Rather than attempting to "beautify" all the buildings along the strip and make them "presentable," energies are concentrated on the entrance to the island from the mainland, on the shopping strip, and on a plaza focused on the town's symbol, the sailfish, and situated at the principal public access to the beach.

To conclude these few words about suburbs and suburbanism: Americans are uncomfortable in large, densely built cities. Our urbanism is shaped by the prejudices and preferences of our English cultural heritage and our geography, which is vast in scale. This is not to say that Americans are anti-urban; only that our urbanism is of a different kind, a subspecies suited to the nature of our cultural heritage and our geography. To a considerable extent, the actual density of so urban a city as New York, once one goes beyond the two dense cores on the island of Manhattan, is far lower than the city's image in literature and films would suggest. It can be argued that New York—outside of Manhattan—and most American cities, for that matter, are, like London, really a collection of small towns united not by a street grid or by a superhighway system but by a system of roads that largely preceded urbanization and by subways and elevated rail systems that made large-scale urbanization feasible.

This pattern of low-density residential "towns" focused on transportation hubs, usually grown up at the intersection of the old roads and the newer subway station stops, persisted until the end of the Second World War, forming a suburban species of urbanism. Only with the development of the vast parkway and interstate highway system of the post–World War II era has it become possible for the new sprawling suburbanism to develop, suburbanism without a sense of town, without rapid transit, and, by the nature of the new arterial highway system, free of direct connection to the city core from which it presumably draws at least some of its strength. Such an arrangement manifests the deep-rooted Anglo-American prosuburban prejudice which with the development of the automobile has now found the technological and economic basis for almost infinite expansion.

In this brief attempt to discuss new directions in American architecture, I am focusing on the suburb not only because I am interested in its history and its potential, but also because I believe that of all planning types the American suburb remains the most firmly rooted in the national value system. It does so because it continues to have meaning to a large majority of Americans: the image holds so much power that it is able to transcend the very severe deficiencies of the reality of suburban houses and suburbia in general; deficiencies that cooler heads, usually those of planners and architects, continuously remind us of, even as new suburbs spring up around them virtually overnight.

In developing our suburbs we have given architecture a notable lineage of suburban houses. For a long time the single-family house of modest size on a modest site was regarded by our best architects as a viable typological problem. Beginning with Downing and Davis and continuing almost until the present, our best architects have supplied us with inventive responses to the issues of privacy and communality, landscape and townscape, and, most fundamentally, symbolic imagery at the residential urban scale. Regrettably, this tradition of serious investigation of suburban typologies has recently been overwhelmed in the critical and historical literature of our period by the particular urbanistic biases of the theorists of the orthodox Modern Movement in architecture. Yet even in the new suburbanism of the 1950s and 1960s, it is the partial reading of examples such as Wright's Robie House that has characterized the commercial product. Though modernist architects have chosen to ignore the suburb even as they build many suburban houses, the suburbs have not gone away, and the particularly rootless character of our typical suburban houses can be seen as a cheapening and exaggeration of the situation Wright defined fifty years ago: the conflict between an image of the prairie and the realities of the small suburban lot is still with us. And though some of our leading architects and sociologists keep telling us to learn to love the large-scale land subdivisions such as Levittown, which is at best a dim reflection of the inventive prototypes it emulates, no real alternative propositions for suburban development have been offered. We are confronted by a failure of critical judgment accompanied by a far more serious "failure of nerve," which manifests itself in the refusal of architects at this point in time to deal straightforwardly with the phenomena of suburbs, and more importantly to accommodate a theory of architecture to the concept of suburbia.

Suburbs will not go away, nor should they: and there will be no new ideas about suburbs until our thinking frees itself from the orthodox modernist biases, the pervasive and especially peculiar anti-urbanistic ideas about cities that underlie virtually all of its form-making. Nor will we be able to deal confidently with the suburb until we free ourselves from the belief that the new suburban ideas (or, in fact, new suburbs) can grow only on virgin land beyond the edges of existing development.

I should like to close with a survey of individual house designs, because I believe them to be the most accurate barometer now available by which to evaluate the directions in which the winds of post-modernism blow. Because George Baird has addressed Venturi's work, I have eliminated it from my discussion, though, of course, Venturi's ideas and forms are never far from my mind.[8] In reviewing some of the work of the post-modernist architects, whom I regard as beginning to push toward a new American architecture, it seems appropriate for me to try to isolate a number of strategies which distinguish it from that of the orthodox modernists. As I see it, some of these strategies are as follows (in no particular order of importance):

1. The use of applied ornament, often intended to be historically allusive, and always used decoratively, that is, freed from issues of structural articulation.

2. The manipulation of form to achieve explicit historical reference.

3. The use of orthodox modernist formal strategies in a self-conscious (eclectic) manner, just as one borrows from or bases work upon strategies developed before the inception of orthodox modernism.

4. The emphasis on compromised geometry; this is sometimes described as a process of "willful deformation." It is manifested in a decided preference for Aalto of the 1950s rather than Corbu of the 1920s, for the plan strategies of Lutyens rather than Voysey, and a continuing love affair with the nineteenth-century American Shingle Style. These preferences go hand in hand with an increasing reluctance to create architecture that calls upon Platonic geometry, particularly in its governing parti. Thus, rooms that are uncompromised geometrically will often be interconnected in unusual ways to form larger, distinctly hybrid shapes held together visually only by the wrappings of the outer walls; these hybrid shapes are seldom perceived in a single glance. For want of a better term, I call this "episodic" composition; it should be seen in contrast to the "determinist" composition that accompanies orthodox modernism's passion for geometric containment. Put another way, the general avoidance of uncompromised shapes in favor of inflected or partially completed shapes suggests possibilities of a high degree of contextual integration and a decisive break with the object fixation of orthodox modernism. Such an attitude, for example, enables architects to see key works of Frank Lloyd Wright, such as the Coonley House and both Taliesins, anew.

5. The concentration of design manipulation on a) the places between—that is, the "poché" of circulation, and b) the edge—that is, the "thickened" wall. This

results in an architecture of "rooms" that are usually far more neutral in their configuration (and, ironically, more universally adaptable from a functional point of view) than the so-called flowing "spaces" or the universal space of the orthodox modernist movement.

6. The layering of spaces in response to light and view as well as to function.

7. The pursuit of specific images to convey ideas about the building; this makes it possible for an architect to design two buildings simultaneously and have each look different from the other (even though the program and indeed elements of the composition may be the same). Such an attitude makes it possible to see Eero Saarinen's work in a new context.

Turning to the philosophical intentions of post-modernist architecture, the impact of Vincent Scully's writings is clear: his comprehensive view—which is central to the cultural background of the movement and its leading proponents—often cuts across arbitrary stylistic and cultural categories, bringing into sharp focus the relationship of buildings to landscape and to the events which caused them to be made. And now Scully has begun to influence not only architects—I am glad to learn that Nathaniel Owings is among them—but other historians, such as Neil Levine, whose account of the Beaux-Arts emphasizes the communicative aspects of its methodology as embodied in its concern for an *architecture parlante,* and George Hersey, whose studies on the "associationism" of mid-nineteenth-century English architecture constitute a notable contribution to the philosophical foundation of the emergent eclecticism. Parenthetically, it is not at all inappropriate that Hersey should be the client for one of Venturi's most provocative house designs.

One finds at the root of the post-modernist position a rejection of the anti-symbolic, antihistorical, hermetic, and highly abstract architecture of orthodox modernism. Post-modernism seeks to move toward an acceptance of diversity; it prefers hybrids to pure forms; it encourages multiple and simultaneous readings in its effort to heighten expressive content. The layering of space characteristic of so much post-modernist architecture finds its complement in the overlay of cultural and art historical references in the elevations. For post-modernist architecture, more is more.

Post-modernist buildings have facades which tell stories. Those facades are not the diaphanous veils of orthodox modernist architecture, nor are they the affirmation of deep structural secrets. They are mediators between the building as a "real" construct and those allusions and perceptions necessary to put the building in closer touch with the place in which it is made, and the beliefs and dreams of the architects who designed it, the clients who paid for it, and the civilization which permitted it to be built; in short, to make buildings landmarks of a culture capable of transcending transitory usefulness as functional accommodation. Post-modernist buildings are very much of a time and a place; they are not intended as ideal constructs of perfected order; they select from the past in order to comment on the present.

While I do not believe that post-modernism seeks to make a case for that simplistic eclecticism which has too often in the past substituted pat, predigested typological imagery for more incisive analysis, I do believe that a knowing integration of lessons learned from admired buildings—and I refer not only to abstract

organization or structural strategies but also to specific design elements—can enrich our work and thereby make it more familiar and possibly more meaningful to the people who use it. In the same way that many architects talk about functional and political processes, which cause work to emerge in a particular way, and the constraints of site, budget, and so on, which also serve to shape it, many post-modernist architects are willing to talk about the forms of earlier architecture which have spoken so directly to them that phases of their language—fragments, if you will—have found their way into their own work, just as fragments of the literature of the past have found their way into much of the poetry and prose of our time.

While I could show many house designs that would point out principles of post-modernism perhaps more vividly than the work I include here, I have chosen to restrict my choices to houses that are largely suburban in their programs and in the lifestyles of their inhabitants, if not always in the specific details of their sites.

The house in Dobbs Ferry, New York, by Hardy Holzman Pfeiffer (fig. 1) conveys important messages about the key urbanistic distinction between front and back, a distinction lost in so much modernist "pavilionizing." As well, it celebrates its materiality by simply using a common American material—shingles—in a way that any carpenter could have done fifty years ago: discovering in the act of laying up course after course in wonderfully various patterns that shingles can be cut and organized to enrich the facade, to just plain please the eye, and also to alter one's perception of the scale of the house.

William Turnbull's Zimmermann House in Fairfax, Virginia (fig. 2), celebrates the value of leftover space, the differences between enclosure and semi-enclosure, and very many other issues of house design that we seemed to have lost sight of with the arrival of air-conditioning and giant-sized plate-glass windows, which turned the house into a sealed environment. Here, beautifully reinvoked, is the living, breathing architecture of the Tidewater tradition. In unbuilt projects by James V. Righter, Gerald Allen, and Richard Oliver one sees a joyous play with traditional imagery, as well as a distortion of geometry in order to expand the reach of small buildings into the landscape. And in Charles Moore's Lee Burns House in California (fig. 3), which seeks, however tentatively, to evoke the great and regionally appropriate Spanish fantasies of the 1920s, one can see a clear statement of the new post-modernist approach.

From my own work, I offer a new porch added on to a Shingle Style house on Long Island (see Chapter 4, fig. 5). The project has some particular interest in that it replaced a porch designed by an orthodox modernist in the early 1950s, which not only had become in need of serious repair but also failed because it didn't look enough like the old house. Porches seem, if not a theme, then a reality of the new movement. Michael Graves has done some of the more remarkable of these: the Benacerraf and, now, the Claghorn. The first was rather a bit too much: it was described by someone as a machine in the garden. But the Claghorn porch (fig. 4) is really very different. In fact, when Michael showed it to me, he said that he had done it for me! I looked and looked and then I thought that I began to understand that he had indeed done it for me, and had done it to advocate what I would say is a post-modernist point of view. It is a modest addition to an unexceptional Victorian house. It is a rich, evocative vocabulary of lattice, of gables, of balusters and dados, all rendered fresh and personal yet all familiar and

Fig. 1. Hardy Holzman Pfeiffer Associates, Von Bernuth Residence, Dobbs Ferry, New York, 1975

Fig. 2. William Turnbull, Jr., Zimmermann House, Fairfax, Virginia, 1975

New Directions in American Architecture

contextually appropriate. It has a sense of place, a hierarchy of front door, side door; it has lattice work, a layering and richness, and a suggestion of cool summer breezes, all those things you can really believe an architect should know about. And I, for one, find it extremely satisfying and beautiful.

Fig. 3. Charles Moore, Burns House, Santa Monica, California, 1974

Fig. 4. Michael Graves, Claghorn House Addition, Princeton, New Jersey, 1974

The Mercer House (fig. 5) probably represents my office's fullest and most enthusiastic reading of the Shingle Style to date. It is, in reality, a very extensive transformation of a 1950s ranch house whose foundations and framing, to a considerable extent, controlled our parti. The Mercer House is a critique of the modernist position that imposes its own formal values on a landscape with identifiable values of its own. By contrast, Charles Gwathmey's Cogan House, seen from the same vantage point along the beach, is an evocation of Le Corbusier's mechanomorphological cubism (see Chapter 3, fig. 15). It seems strange to me, as does its dry dematerialization of the wooden sheathing skin.

In the Mercer House, references are made to the Shingle Style context of the neighborhood in which it is built. While it is based on such Shingle Style prototypes as "Shingleside," built at Swampscott, Massachusetts (fig. 6), in 1880–1881, the Mercer House is also intended to be read as a comment on a particularly lovely, if somewhat idiosyncratic, example of that style a block or so away, the Schuyler Quackenbush House of 1898–1899 (fig. 7). In both houses a strong roof form gives shade to the principal rooms and to sheltered porch or verandah spaces. Whereas in the Quackenbush house, the porch faced the road, then a simple suburban lane used by an occasional horse cart or carriage, our design turns its back on the street (now a busy road giving access to the ocean beach) and faces the view. In so doing we have made what no longer really functions as a porch verandah but is rather an allusion to that lovely and now functionally superannuated interstitial space. The dominant roof form, so symbolic of houses to Americans, combined with the vestigial porch, permits a play of big and little scale and an incidental composition of the volumes and windows, which can be located according to requirements of ventilation and view rather than to abstract compositional or constructional systems.

The Lang House is an attempt to make connections between an average house in New England and some of the more extraordinary monuments in the history of architecture (see Chapter 15, fig. 5). In order to achieve this within the tight economic framework of a basically simple volume, color and applied

New Directions in American Architecture

Fig. 5. Stern and Hagmann, Mercer House, East Hampton, New York, 1972–1975

decoration are substituted for the complex spatial joinery which has character-ized most high-style residential architecture, including many of our own houses. The clients' interest in discussing with us the historical sources of image and form involved in the design of the house, rather than focusing solely on the func-tional aspects of the plan, provides tangible proof of my conviction that the manipulation of iconographic references must be an integral part of establishing a direction for architecture at this time. The Westchester County estate enabled us to address a variety of problems at a residential scale, in part because they rep-resent an atypical program of unusually extensive scope, and also because various strategies were required to mediate between the elaborate nature of the project and the desire for a relatively modest and unpretentious residential grouping. The siting of the house and the landscaping restrict movement around the ends of the building and force one to move through it to experience it: this is not the sort of building that can be readily grasped by a quick tour around its perimeter. Episodic organization is the key: the house is conceived as a collection of formal interventions which are connected up by the observer as he moves through the spaces. And the spaces the bounding walls of the house make in the landscape are as important as those which they define in the interior. The stucco finish of the house is both abstract and palpable at the same time, further linking the house with nature. At once images of Tuscan villas and of Frank Lloyd Wright's work at both Taliesins are collaged together, with the gloss glamour of Hollywood in the 1930s.

I should like to conclude by returning to the philosophical premises with which I began. I believe that design is, in part, a process of cultural assimilation. Though design includes problem-solving, the functional and technological paradigms for the vast majority of situations with which we deal are established. Our task is to question the formal paradigms that dog us at what I regard as the close of the orthodox phase of the Modern Movement. And such questioning cannot come only from within the wellspring of an individual architect's "talent," but also from a knowledge of history, a concern for the state of the art of architecture at a given moment, and a serious respect for the aspirations of clients. It must be continu-ously reaffirmed that individual buildings, no matter how remotely situated from other works of architecture, form part of a cultural and physical context, and architects are obliged to acknowledge these connections not only in their words but also in their deeds—that is, in the combinations of forms they establish and perhaps too casually call "design."

As a culture, as architects, we know so very much. What must be done is to face this knowledge squarely—and in so doing face the world around us, taking it for what it is, incrementally adapting the objects and ideas in it to our needs while we in turn adapt to its demands. My attitude toward form, based on a love for a knowledge of history, is not concerned with accurate replication. It is eclectic and uses collage and juxtaposition as techniques to give new meaning to familiar forms and, in so doing, to cover new ground. Mine is a confidence in the power of memory (history) combined with the action of people (function) to infuse design with richness and meaning. If architecture is to succeed in its efforts to partici-pate creatively in the present, it must go beyond the iconoclasm of the Modern Movement of the last fifty years, as well as the limited formalism of so much recent

work, and recapture for itself a basis in culture and the fullest possible reading of its own past.

The post-modernist use of history is not based on a jaded nostalgia for a moment—the individual architect's search for what John Hejduk calls one's personal belle epoque. One cannot deny that each of us has a favorite building, style, or moment, but that is not really important. What is important is that one follows a path in architecture in full recognition that he or she is a participant in an ongoing culture, one that includes the anticulture of much of modernism as it excludes the surfeit of culture of nineteenth-century revivalism. And if as one keeps this culture in mind one does not lose sight of the wide range of human experience that our American civilization represents—younger and brasher than Europe's, yes, but in a way as parochial, it seems to me—then, I think, like the architects of our early republic who seem so sympathetic to many of us now, we may yet again be able to forge a new, and I am still naive enough to believe, better, and more human place than the one we inherited.

Fig. 6. Arthur Little, Shingleside, Swampscott, Massachusetts, 1880–1881

Fig. 7. C. L. W. Eidlitz, Mrs. Schuyler Quackenbush House, East Hampton, New York, 1898–1899

8

Over and Under Forty
A Propos the "Crise à Quarante Ans" Among Second Generation American Modernists

1976

In 1951 Henry-Russell Hitchcock published in the first volume of *Perspecta: The Yale Architectural Journal* an account of the progress of the careers of the pioneer, or first generation, modernists—Frank Lloyd Wright, Mies van der Rohe, and Le Corbusier—as related to the fortieth birthday of each architect.[1] This landmark article has continued to interest me since I first read it sometime in the late 1950s, when I was beginning to consider in a serious way the issue of "careers" in architecture. When I became editor of an issue of *Perspecta* in the early sixties, I remained interested in Hitchcock's claims and was able to encourage Adolf Placzek to test their validity in terms of the careers of architects outside the Modern Movement.[2] And, of course, my interest in reviving in 1966 the "40 Under 40" exhibition initiated by the Architectural League in 1941 was another manifestation of the hold that Hitchcock's article and the proposition it contained continued to have over me: grossly put, this proposition states that architecture is an old man's art, one in which serious artistic life seldom begins before forty (or thereabouts). And if the art-historical biases of Hitchcock and Placzek seem too partial and particular a frame of reference, one can look at "forty" as do the French, who describe the great changes that often overtake a man of that age as the "crise à quarante ans."

In any case, when I was quite far along with this newest reincarnation of "40 Under 40," [*A+U* editor] Toshio Nakamura asked whether I would undertake to explore its themes in relationship to the careers of members of the second generation of modernists in order to more fully develop a frame of reference for the new compilation. While I believe one can gain some insight into the situation of American architecture at this moment, and especially the difference between the second and third generation, through an investigation of the careers of some of the leading members of the second generation in relationship to Hitchcock's and Placzek's observations about youth and age in architecture, such an assessment takes on particular meaning when viewed against the background of the major social, political, and cultural events affecting the careers of the second generation of American modernist architects: 1) the limited opportunities for building caused by the economic depression of the 1930s and the Second World War (1939–1945), and 2) the postwar building boom, which, though it was slow to develop at the war's end, grew to mammoth proportions during the late 1950s and early 1960s, only to be virtually halted again in yet another serious economic recession following the traumatic events associated with the American intervention in Vietnam. So disruptive to the orderly development of their careers was the Second World War, so devastating on the practice of architecture was the impact of the economic depression that preceded it, and so intellectually baffling was the battle of the styles—"traditionalism" vs. "modernism"—which tore the schools of architecture apart in the 1930s and 1940s, when many of this group were students, that the second generation of modern architects in America was peculiarly marked even before the strange and extraordinary boom period that propelled it to the first rank of international influence in the fifteen years or so that followed the conclusion of the hostilities in Korea.

In this brief discussion, I propose to examine the careers of a handful of Americans in the second generation in terms of Hitchcock's claim that first mature works seldom, if ever, come to architects much before their fortieth birthday and often not for a few years after, and to demonstrate its validity even for a generation so seemingly star-crossed by highly destructive events outside its control. Of the second generation modernist architects that I propose to discuss, I will include those whose careers I dealt with in my book *New Directions in American Architecture:* Philip Johnson, Kevin Roche, Paul Rudolph, and Louis Kahn. I should also like to include Eero Saarinen, whose importance as an architect impresses me more and more as my own generation's search for contextual relevance establishes itself as a dominant theme.[3]

Kahn, the oldest of the group, was born in Russia in 1901 and came to the United States with his family in 1905.[4] Kahn was educated in architecture in the American Beaux-Arts manner, under Paul Cret at the University of Pennsylvania. If for no other reason, his Beaux-Arts education in architecture set Kahn apart from the group, which was otherwise united by age and common interests and by the fact that each of the others came to architecture as a full-fledged enthusiast for modernism. Kahn began to pursue a career along the lines expected of a talented but not socially well connected architect at a time when architecture was still very much a "gentleman's" profession and "old-boy" contacts often paved one's way through it. The winds of change that modernism brought to American professional practice in the late 1920s were probably particularly appealing to Kahn by virtue of his inability to trade on an "impeccable" social pedigree, if not necessarily for reasons of social, ethical, or aesthetic commitment.

With the coming of the Depression Kahn began to work extensively in the area of "housing" research while building almost nothing. In 1941, at the age of forty, he was invited by George Howe to join him in a partnership to design workers' housing at Middletown and Coatesville in Pennsylvania.[5] Howe's invitation was decisive in propelling Kahn to a career in professional practice rather than theoretical research. In 1943, after accepting a position with the federal government in Washington, Howe withdrew from the firm, which now included Oscar Stonorov. Carver Court, built in Coatesville, Pennsylvania, between 1941 and 1943, the principal product of the firm, can hardly be considered significant as a premonition of the work that would establish Kahn's reputation in the mid-1950s, but it can be seen as a major fulfillment of his aspirations for housing reform over the previous ten years, and it remains an important milestone in the evolution of modernist low-density housing design in the United States.

In 1951 Howe was instrumental in bringing about the selection of Kahn as the architect for the extension to the Yale Art Gallery, generally considered his first work of enduring significance (fig. 1). From the point of view of this discussion, it is obvious that Kahn's career as a practicing architect only really began at his fortieth birthday, and that only ten years later, after economic conditions had changed and Howe had given him a significant opportunity to prove his abilities, did his mature work begin to emerge. It seems likely that Kahn did not have a "crise à quarante ans," because at the age of forty, after ten very dry years, he was enormously grateful to be given any opportunity to build at all. Later, while teaching and building at Yale and then at Pennsylvania, Kahn's dissatisfaction with the course of his professional progress and with the state of architecture as he saw it practiced around him manifested itself in an iconoclastic view of professionalism and, more importantly, in works of breathtaking clarity and originality. Thus it seems possible to argue that this "delayed reaction" was not without its benefits. It allowed Kahn sufficient time to observe the European modernist scenario play out its themes on its adoptive American soil, a scenario whose rhythm and form Kahn never seemed able to embrace fully. And the lapse in time gave Kahn a chance to recharge his perceptions of the kind of architecture he had first loved: trips to Italy rekindled his imagination so that when he got down to the serious work that distinguished his last ten years, he was able and ready to express in his own work that love for the buildings of the past, which had caused him to become an architect in the first place.

Eero Saarinen's career, too, takes exception to the orderly progress of things as Hitchcock outlines them.[6] But in Saarinen's case it is his early death in 1961 rather than a late flowering that alters the flow of events. Born in Finland in 1910, Saarinen immigrated with his family to the United States in 1923. Nine years younger than Kahn, he had a totally different background in architecture. The son of an internationally known architect, Saarinen was brought up at Cranbrook, where his father headed the Academy. Steeped in an atmosphere in which architecture, crafts, and the fine arts were taught and practiced side by side, Saarinen established enduring friendships and professional associations with Charles Eames and Henry Bertoia, who were closely associated with the Academy. Saarinen continued his education at Yale, arriving in New Haven at that most interesting moment when the School of Fine Arts, then under the direction of Everett V. Meeks, was struggling to extend its Beaux-Arts methodology to include modernist formal strategies largely based on French stripped classicism as translated into American terms by Cret and others. Upon graduation in 1934 and travel in Europe between 1934 and 1936, Saarinen returned to Michigan, where he was able to join his father in partnership. Even though the nation was deep in economic depression, the Cranbrook situation provided economic and cultural support to the Saarinen family; his father

attracted some clients, not least of which was the Academy itself. By 1939 Eero's impact on the firm could be seen in their submission to the competition for the extension of the Smithsonian Institution in Washington. World War II killed any chance for construction of this project, but it did bring to the Saarinen and Saarinen office, as it did to Howe and Kahn, opportunities to construct housing for defense workers.

Fig. 1. Louis I. Kahn, Yale University Art Gallery, New Haven, Connecticut, 1951–1953

Fig. 2. Eero Saarinen, Massachusetts Institute of Technology Chapel and Kresge Auditorium, Cambridge, Massachusetts, 1955

While this is not the appropriate place to undertake a discussion of the younger Saarinen's influence on his father's work in the late 1930s and early '40s, it is important to note that the Tabernacle Church of Christ at Columbus, Indiana, completed in 1940 and credited to Eliel, brought the Saarinen family into close contact with J. Irwin Miller, thereby establishing a business and personal relationship that was to extend beyond Eliel's death in 1950 and even Eero's in 1961 to his successor, Kevin Roche; a relationship which in its professional aspect would directly result in commissions for a bank and a second church in Columbus, two houses for the Miller family, and, indirectly, commissions for two major works for Yale, which Miller served as a trustee.[7]

After the conclusion of hostilities in 1945, the pace of building gradually increased as the nation's economy adjusted to the needs of peacetime. Each Saarinen submitted a proposal to the competition for the Jefferson National Expansion Memorial in 1948, and Eero emerged the winner; his boldly expressionistic and somewhat over-simplified design was not constructed until after his death. Enormously controversial, it enjoyed international attention and put the architectural world on notice that the younger Saarinen was a major talent in his own right. In 1946 Saarinen and Saarinen was commissioned by the General Motors Corporation to produce designs for a research and development facility to be built at Warren, Michigan. Work proceeded on the designs in the late '40s but did not get going in earnest until shortly before Eliel's death in 1950; so it is that the G.M. Technical Center, as it was built over a six-year period completed in 1957, marks the emergence of Eero's talent in full flood. Between 1951 and 1955, the remarkable outpouring of buildings that came from the office at Bloomfield Hills established Saarinen not only as a first class talent but as a maverick one as well; the

Kresge Auditorium and Chapel at MIT (1955) (fig. 2) and Concordia College, Fort Wayne, Indiana (1953–1958), put the modern architectural establishment on notice, self-consciously seeking to "enlarge its alphabet beyond ABC."[8] But it was not until 1956, when Saarinen was forty-six, that the really important original work began to unfold: the U.S. Embassy in London, the Ingalls Hockey Rink at Yale, and the TWA Terminal at Kennedy Airport in New York. So incredibly fertile was Saarinen's inventiveness by his mid-forties, that one is tempted to speculate on whether or not he would have been able to sustain both the pace of his career and the strength of his argument had he been given more time, and whether, like Le Corbusier and Mies, he would have exhausted the ideas of his early maturity and turned the direction of his later work around in pursuit of other, equally remarkable, ideas.

Philip Johnson, together with Kahn and Saarinen, defines the older end of the chronological spread that encompasses the more representative figures of the second generation of modernists.[9] Unlike Kahn, whose training was in the American Beaux-Arts method at its most confident, or Saarinen, whose education combined European arts and craft techniques learned from his father at Cranbrook with those of the American Beaux-Arts in retreat, Johnson's architectural pedigree is that of full-fledged orthodox modernism. And, of course, it is precisely this sense of a group of fellow professionals united by a common bond—in this case, a belief in modernism as an attitude and a desire to expand its formal vocabulary without too seriously questioning the inherent meaning of that vocabulary—that sets the second generation of modernists apart from the first, and, in the final analysis, gives Kahn and Saarinen rights only to collateral membership in it.

A passionate commitment to modernism has characterized Johnson's career since the late 1920s when, as an undergraduate at Harvard, he first became involved in architecture under the influence of Hitchcock and Alfred Barr. Johnson's initial relationship to architecture was largely that of a museum curator, critic, and ardent polemicist for the International Style. Only later did he "begin again" and undertake a systematic study of architecture in a professional school. Although Johnson was involved in a few design projects in the 1930s—for example, an apartment interior designed for Edward M. M. Warburg in 1934, and a number of innovative exhibits that he not only organized but also designed, such as "Machine Art" of 1934—Johnson had built nothing.

Johnson's first executed work was the house he designed and built for himself in Cambridge, Massachusetts, just after he finished at Harvard in 1942. An atrium house based on Mies's courtyard schemes of the 1930s, its crisp integration of Miesian classicism and an Americanized modernism—it is largely a wooden structure—reveals a sure talent but not necessarily an original one. After service in the military, Johnson settled in New York and produced a few works of some interest, including a house on the dunes at Sagaponack, New York, and a utility shed in New London, Ohio, while he simultaneously directed the Department of Architecture at the Museum of Modern Art. But his career as a designer did not gain the momentum that propelled him into the position of artistic leadership in the profession that is now his until 1949, when he completed the Glass House and Brick Guest House for his own use at New Canaan, Connecticut (fig. 3).

Johnson was born in 1906; at his fortieth birthday he was barely established as an architect, though he was reasonably well known as an architectural tastemaker. In fact, in his fortieth year Johnson was more extensively involved in the curatorial

Fig. 3. Philip Johnson, Glass House, New Canaan, Connecticut, 1949

work that had occupied him ten years earlier than in the practice of architecture: after a twelve-year hiatus, he was once again the director of the Museum of Modern Art's Department of Architecture, and he was busily engaged in preparing a critical monograph about the work of Mies van der Rohe timed to an exhibition at MoMA. Mies was the architect among the first generation of modernists whom Johnson most admired and whose work he then set out consciously to emulate in his own.

Even after the extensive publication of the Glass House and the authority that it lent his career, Johnson continued to practice in the most modest way for years, his career largely occupied with lesser works at residential scale. It was not until the late 1950s when, partly due to his curatorial and architectural work at the Museum of Modern Art, and partly due to the aura of "professionalism" that fell to him by virtue of his association with Mies on the Seagram Building, that Johnson emerged as *the* architect of the American cultural establishment. So, rather like Kahn, who was very nearly Johnson's contemporary, he too was a "late bloomer." Like Kahn, he had to wait until his fifties before the major commissions would come to him: the synagogue at Port Chester (1956), the museums at Utica (1957–1960), Forth Worth (1961), and Lincoln, Nebraska (1960–1963), and the New York State Theater (1958–1964).

Paul Rudolph is twelve years younger than Johnson, but he was Johnson's contemporary at Harvard, arriving in Cambridge to study under Gropius and Breuer after initial training at the Alabama Polytechnical Institute at Auburn.[10] Like Kahn, Rudolph began as an outsider to the architectural establishment, and except for the period when he was chairman of architecture at Yale (1958–1965) he has always chosen to remain rather at the edge of the power structure of the profession. Like Johnson, Rudolph was completely imbued with modernism; he recalls an opportunity for viewing Wright's Rosenbaum House in Alabama as the decisive event in his decision to pursue a career in architecture—a talented pianist, he also considered a career on the concert stage. World War II interrupted Rudolph's stay at Harvard, and he served in the Navy before returning to Cambridge to complete his program and receive his degree in 1947. Among the second generation of modernists, Rudolph was the most thoroughly "American"—a son of a Methodist preacher, he was raised in the backwaters of the American South and had traveled very little outside that region before going to Harvard. Rudolph had never been to Europe—not even as part of his naval service during World War II, when he was

Fig. 4. Paul Rudolph, Yale Art and Architecture Building, New Haven, Connecticut, 1963

Fig. 5. Kevin Roche John Dinkeloo and Associates, Richard C. Lee High School, New Haven, Connecticut, 1967

stationed at the Brooklyn Navy Yard—until he received a Wheelwright traveling fellowship from Harvard after his graduation in 1947.

Gropius solidified Rudolph's commitments to architecture and modernism: in *Perspecta* 1 Rudolph writes: "In 1941 there was a certain sense of urgency at Harvard. Most had lost faith in the École des Beaux-Arts system, but what must fill the vacuum? Geniuses probably should not be burdened with any kind of architectural school; but those of us who are less fortunate need some direction and a method of approaching a problem. Although I had studied architecture for five years, I had no sense of direction. I found in Gropius' teaching a base on which one could build, not merely a formula, as so many others have…. Gropius' strength lies in his ability to analyze and make precisely clear the broad problems of our day…. He was able to incorporate many diverse ideas and still give a sense of direction."[11]

As much due to seeing Europe as anything else, Rudolph became the first important designer of the second generation of modern architects in America to reject the limited historical vision of the Harvard "Bauhaus," as codified by Sigfried Giedion in *Space, Time and Architecture,* and to question it openly. After traveling in Europe in 1948, Rudolph returned to the States "with the reinforced conviction of the necessity of regaining the 'form sense' which helped to shape Western man's building until the nineteenth century. Other periods have always developed means of tying their architecture to previous works without compromising their own designs. This is also our task."[12]

On the eve of his fortieth birthday in 1958, Rudolph had firmly established his reputation as a designer of enormous talent and was about to embark on his decisive seven-year career as chairman of Yale's Department of Architecture. He had produced a not inconsiderable body of work, largely for residential clients in Florida, and was working on that cluster of major works of a more public nature, including the Jewett Arts Center for Wellesley College (1955–1958), the Blue Cross/Blue Shield Office Building in Boston (1957–1960), and the Sarasota High School (1958–1959), which would solidify his reputation in the United States and give him that first major introduction to an international audience that has subsequently been so receptive to his work. His best-known early work, however, the miniature Walker Guest House built in 1952–1953 on Sanibel Island, Florida, in its Miesian precision did not accurately represent the direction the work of his mature phase would take. While the Jewett Arts Center suggested the contextual

Over and Under Forty

concerns that would be a hallmark of that maturity, the use of an overtly sceno-graphic formal vocabulary to adjust the appearance of the new building to the neo-Gothic forms of the Wellesley campus did not, though at this writing the very historicism and eclecticism of the scheme for which Rudolph castigated himself seems more pertinent than ever. The Sarasota High School, which was under con-struction as Rudolph turned forty, did represent the formal direction Rudolph's work would follow, though its simple plan and cross-section did no more than anticipate the spatial elaboration of the mature work.

But within five years, with the completion of the Art and Architecture Building at Yale (fig. 4), Rudolph did make the major first statement that Hitchcock estab-lishes as the principal manifestation of mature style; and the well-known series of drawings and model photographs he would publish illustrating the evolution of that design from 1958 to 1962, when it took its final form, provides a unique insight into Rudolph's method as he solidified his mature manner.

So, if one returns again to the main theme of this brief essay, the critical demarcation of career goals that, according to Hitchcock's claims and Placzek's reaffirmation of those claims, occurs around forty, it is clear that Rudolph, despite what he has regarded as time largely wasted in early studies at Alabama, and despite the interruption of his later education by military service during World War II—which he has always regarded as very valuable training—was right "on schedule" by 1958. Though Rudolph's career has often been described as "mete-oric" in terms of the Hitchcock criteria, it would seem to have been no more so than that of Wright, Mies, or Le Corbusier. It is only in context of the progress of some of his fellow architects of the second generation that Rudolph seems a bit the "enfant terrible"; it is not so much that he was ahead as it is that the others, for reasons I have already discussed, were rather a bit behind.

Kevin Roche is very much at the younger end of the second generation of modernists and, ironically, he is the successor in practice to one of its older members, Eero Saarinen.[13] Roche was born in Ireland in 1922 and immigrated to the United States in 1948, having already completed his initial training in architecture; he continued his studies in the United States at the Illinois Institute of Technology.

Roche, like Harry Cobb and Gordon Bunshaft, but unlike most of the other major figures of his generation, did not follow the usual path to professional suc-cess; in the generally accepted sense of the term, these important corporate design architects have never "gone out on their own." Roche's career has been a progres-sion within an established framework—he worked for Eero Saarinen beginning in 1950, emerging as chief of design and, upon Saarinen's death, together with John Dinkeloo was given the responsibility for finishing up key Saarinen works. By virtue of his own remarkable talents, Roche (together with Dinkeloo) estab-lished an independent practice and has been able not only to sustain the Saarinen operation but also to transform it to suit his own, rather more impersonal views of architecture. Viewed in terms of Saarinen's work, Roche's output, like that of Cesar Pelli, another "alumnus" of Bloomfield Hills, can be seen as representative of that technologically innovative and formalistically abstract side of Saarinen's talent, while Robert Venturi, who worked alongside Roche in Bloomfield Hills in the early 1950s, and who remains an admirer and friend, can be said to represent Saarinen's semantically expressive side.

At forty, Roche, together with his partner, John Dinkeloo, was established as a major force: he had won the competition for the Oakland Museum shortly after Saarinen's death in 1961, and in 1962 he had on his drawing boards such diverse designs as that for the IBM Pavilion at the New York World's Fair, for the Richard C. Lee High School in New Haven (fig. 5), and for a multi-use facility at the Rochester Institute of Technology. Though each of these is a unique design and owes no particular stylistic debt to Saarinen, taken as a group, in their formal diversity they seem to reflect not only Saarinen's "style for the job" attitude but also his almost "gentle" sense of scale—"gentle," that is, in relationship to the colossal abstraction of Roche's work since then, such as the New Haven Coliseum (1965–1972) and the Fine Arts Building of the University of Massachusetts (1964–1974).

Roche's situation is most interesting in relationship to Hitchcock's observations. Whereas the careers of Mies, Le Corbusier, and Wright—not to mention Kahn, Johnson, Rudolph, and Saarinen—were clearly focused on the ultimate goal of independent practice, Roche seemed to be tracking in a very different direction. As director of design for Saarinen, he was a powerful figure but a pretty anonymous one. Yet when suddenly, by a quirk of fate, he was propelled into a role demanding a public persona, he seemed as ready as any of the others; and certainly each of his buildings since has been characterized by the full assurance of a mature designer who not only knows full well what he wants and can manipulate the available technology to get it, but also can find—and keep—the clients with bold enough vision of their own to sustain the enormity of Roche's own ideas.

I have written this in an attempt to establish a claim that a coherent generation of architects exists in America (and, I would submit, in many other countries of the Western-European world but most particularly in England—Stirling, the Smithsons, among others—and Japan—Tange, Maekawa, among others) that is united by age and by its relationship toward the orthodox modernism of the first generation of the masters. These architects also shared certain experiences: the economic depression of the 1930s; the disruption of the Second World War; the incredible boom in construction that followed it in the 1950s and early 1960s. To a considerable extent the second generation in America remains active at this writing; but the disruption to our national values that the Vietnam War represents and the uncertain economic conditions which were in large part a by-product of that war have undermined its influences and in some cases eroded its confidence in its own values.

Beginning about 1966, this generation has been challenged by a younger generation of architects who are as skeptical of the values of the second generation as that generation was uncritically enthusiastic over those of the first. In order to begin to understand what happened to cause a whole new generation of architects to be so skeptical of their immediate predecessors, many of whom were their teachers and early employers, one must begin to deal with some of the larger issues that describe the plight of modernism in the 1960s and 1970s. Of these issues, perhaps the most vexing of all is the one caused by the orgy of consumerism that followed the twenty-year or so period of deprivation that extended from the economic crash of 1929. In the period of unbridled prosperity and consumerism that followed the close of World War II, certain modernist images lent themselves to the programs of corporations and institutions and to the expedient, minimalist standards of fast-buck marketing operations: the presumed "functionalism" and technological determinism of the Modern Movement; the flat slab, the free plan, and free façade of Le Corbusier; the minimalist technological and spatial strategies of Mies. All these were only too easily perverted into the typical spec-built high-rise schemes of New York, Miami, or Los Angeles; the wall of glass, combined with a mindless dependence on mechanical ventilation systems to reduce façade design to a kind of architecture slip-covering indiscriminately used for any and all programs in all orientations, all climates, and all contexts.

As Hitchcock rather ironically points out in his introduction to Yukio Futagawa's book on Roche-Dinkeloo, the "architects and critics active in the formative period of the 'International Style,' were they to be with us now, would be amazed not only by its wide acceptance and the 'giant scale' of many of the examples produced"; but they would also have been "annoyed and doubtless shocked that an architecture they had associated with a socially reformed world should be receiving the support of such clients as the Federal Reserve Bank and the Ford Foundation."

It seems appropriate to conclude this brief essay with these observations, written at the very end of the era of second-generation modernism, as we began with a thesis Hitchcock proposed at its very beginning. So many of the smashed hopes of an earlier idealism seem implied in his remarks. I, for one, share this great historian's respect for the solid achievements of the second modernist generation, which is, after all, Hitchcock's own. At the same time I can share in his tone of dismay and disappointment: as a young architect, I have grown up with the work of the second generation; I entered architecture as it entered a more prosperous and optimistic time; now, my generation, perhaps the first post-modernist one, looks at the ideals of its teachers and early mentors—the ideals of modernism—and everywhere sees them in disarray.

9

The Old "40 Under 40"
A Retrospective Glance
1976

Ten years ago, in the winter of 1965–66, I served as program director of the Architectural League of New York, a post that had been created for me at the behest of Philip Johnson, who had challenged the then somewhat moribund League to come to life or give up. Fresh out of Yale's architecture school, twenty-six years old, and filled with opinions and, more importantly, an unbounded confidence in those opinions, I set out to organize a series of exhibitions and public events that would stimulate and provoke the architectural profession, which was then quite contentedly enjoying a period of unbridled prosperity and the complaisance that usually accompanies such good feeling. I based most of my efforts on my Yale experience, falling back on what I had seen and learned in connection with the preparation of *Perspecta* 9/10, the double volume that I edited in 1963–64 and that appeared in the spring of 1965. Backed by a triumvirate of establishment types (Robert Alan Jacobs, Robert Cutler, Philip Johnson) who had volunteered to advise me (that is, to curb my excesses), I proceeded to arrange exhibitions of the work of MLTW (Moore, Lyndon, Turnbull, Whitaker), Venturi & Rauch, and Mitchell/Giurgola. For each firm, this was the first exhibition of their work in New York. I shall never forget the look of horror in the eyes of architects lunching at the League's clubhouse on 40th Street as the now famous Grand's Restaurant Teacup—having been removed by the restaurant's owner from the façade for which it had been intended—was hoisted into place in the not inappropriately banal "Pine Room" gallery.

In any case, recalling an exhibition of young architects called "40 Under 40," which the League had organized in 1941, I consulted my gurus, who agreed that a new edition of such an event would be a fitting climax to my year at the League.

The American Federation of Arts, then under the direction of Roy Moyer, most kindly agreed to circulate the show nationally and to assist with the publication of a catalog, thus ensuring that the new "40 Under 40" would have a wide exposure in the press and in schools and museums.

Johnson was of course more than helpful; he did the best thing possible by taking full responsibility for overseeing the selection process and then giving me a very free rein in selecting the architects and projects to be shown. More important to me, he encouraged me to include a house project I was then working on and very kindly agreed to write a few words about it for the catalog. Except for this, I wrote all the text, and Sheila de Bretteville, also very much under forty, designed the catalog and the exhibition panels, which I installed at the AFA's galleries in New York.

At twenty-six, I was the youngest architect in the exhibition: Charles Gwathmey, at twenty-seven, was just a little older. At the opposite end of the spectrum, Robert Venturi, Lewis Davis, and Charles Moore just squeaked in. Peter Millard, Ehrman Mitchell, and Romaldo Giurgola were too old and couldn't be included, though it was as clear to me then as it is now that their work was related in intention and in form to those of the under-forty group. But when you play an arbitrary numbers game, you win some and you lose some.

Though I proclaimed loudly in my introduction to the catalog that the selection was not intended as "a definitive statement on the younger generation," I really was just covering my bases. Immodestly, and not uncharacteristically, I believed that I was enjoying the first and the last word on the subject. And, ten years later, I still believe it, though not with the same intensity, and I now recognize some notable errors of omission (as well as those of commission, which I deem wiser not to mention). My most notable sin of omission was my failure to include John Hejduk, whom I had known as a teacher at Yale but whom I had come to regard as a paper architect trapped in some sideline issue involving the architectural implications of Mondrian's paintings. While I have never really warmed up to Hejduk's Diamond Houses, I cannot but regret they were not included, because his more recent work, such as the Bye House and the Venice project of 1975, has tremendous meaning for me and surely for countless other architects (fig. 1). One of those quicker to see Hejduk's achievement was Stanley Tigerman, who brought Hejduk to the opening of the "40 Under 40" show in 1966, causing me a memorably, and with hindsight I can say deservedly, awkward moment.

As I pointed out in 1966, the idea of a show of architectural talent under forty years of age had validity beyond the sentimental gesture of reviving an old Architectural League event. Henry-Russell Hitchcock's discussion of the issue of youth and age in the careers of key modernist architects in an early issue of *Perspecta* and Adolf Placzek's extension of that discussion in *Perspecta* 9/10 had established forty as a meaningful benchmark in the evolution of an architect's career.

How strange the continuous shifting of sensibilities over the last ten years, not to mention the thirty-five that have elapsed since the first "40 Under 40" show in 1941. In 1966, despite the presence of at least one overtly Wrightian project in the exhibition (Thomas Holzbog's house in Wisconsin) and a number of definitely Miesian projects (or at least Miesian by way of Pei in his Kips Bay [fig. 2] and Mile High Center phases), I proclaimed rather noisily, and I believe accurately, that it is "Le Corbusier, Aalto, and Kahn who emerge … as dominate figures." Stimulated

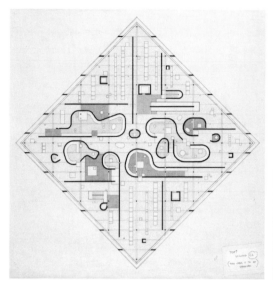

by the example of Richard Meier's tremendous breakthrough, from his Essex Fells
House of 1964 to the Smith House of 1965–67, both of which were included (the
latter in project form only), I proclaimed that "in the case of Le Corbusier, surprisingly, it is not his recent work, but his work of the late 1920s and early 1930s that
is most admired. 'Cardboard architecture' is for many the order of the day, with
an almost fanatical zeal being shown by some to re-create not only the spirit of an
earlier architecture but also its monuments." I can remember Johnson's reaction to
Meier's Smith House when he first saw it: "Gropius in front, Corbusier behind."

Aalto's influence was of a different order than Le Corbusier's. At the time it
seemed largely formal. Especially potent was the Saynatsalo grouping. Those who
studied with Venturi or who took the time to explore his plan ideas in detail were
of course led to Aalto's work of the late 1950s; not only the plans, but also the
details, especially the handling of the public interior space. And of course Kahn's
influence was seen then, as it still must be, in both conceptual and formalist terms,
though it should be noted that in the late sixties, as the more exaggerated of his
designs in India and Pakistan were built, questions grew in the minds of many of
us about those forms, and the direct influence of his work diminished notably.

Only two women were connected with the original compilation, Sheila de
Bretteville and Mary Otis Stevens. De Bretteville was the graphic designer responsible for the design of the exhibition panels and the catalog, and it is interesting
to note that soon after the exhibition opened she moved from New York to Los
Angeles with her husband, Peter (an architect included in the new "40 Under
40" group), and became a key participant in the feminist movement. A cofounder
of the Women's Building and the Feminist Studio Workshop, de Bretteville was
responsible for bringing the exhibition of the work of Eileen Gray to the United
States—to my knowledge, the first major exhibition on a woman architect to be
widely presented here.

In 1966 Mary Otis Stevens was the only woman architect whose work was
included in the show, and she was in partnership with her husband, Thomas
McNulty. Other women under forty were probably actively practicing at the time,
but I was unaware of their work. Certainly my failure to include women was not

based on any conscious sexist feelings; I had gone through Yale's architecture school in an era when there were a number of women students who were equal in their talents and energies to any man and who earned the esteem of their fellow students, male and female alike. Not least among these was Etel Kramer, whose work is included among the new "40 Under 40" but who was not an independent practitioner in 1966. Diana Agrest and Susana Torre were not yet on the scene in 1966, while I was not aware of any work produced by Judith Chaffee, another Yale graduate of great energy and talent. It remains unfortunate (though in part understandable, given the economic climate)—that among the many women now so actively involved in the profession, so few are able to establish their own professional practices. This is surely the case among men as well, but to a much lesser extent. Just as many architects dropped out of the profession to pursue other goals during the anti–Vietnam War period of the late sixties, it should be pointed out that a good number of women architects active in the feminist movement have chosen to abandon the role of traditional practice to work as activists. Thus, I think we are as yet unable to measure the potential impact women will make on the architectural profession until the achievements of the liberationist polemic have had more time to be felt in the schools as well as in the marketplace.

The feminist activism that encouraged women architects to pursue professional goals outside the bounds of conventional practice was preceded in the late 1960s by a proliferation of efforts to organize professional practice in more unconventional and more idealistic ways than the usual private office situation implies. The most serious of the new practice prototypes that I know is the Institute for Architecture and Urban Studies, which was established in 1967, one year after my "40 Under 40" exhibition.

It is my recollection that it was only with the publication in *Life* magazine of Peter Eisenman, Tony Eardley, and Michael Graves's linear city project that I was able to see the seriousness of Eisenman's approach to practice. Until then, I was so steeped in the pragmatism of the Yale/Rudolph situation that I was able to see very little validity in unbuilt architecture. We were told, and we believed, that the design and construction of "real" buildings was architectural research—and to some extent I still believe this to be so. But in 1966 I was able to accept work as serious only when it was produced in an office and "certified" by national publication. And certainly there is little in that dry, neo-Corbusian form of the linear city project to suggest the serious cubism of Graves's domestic work since, or the obsessive abstraction of Eisenman's houses.

For me, the focus of the show's content was the work of Robert Venturi. In the lobby space in front of the exhibition galleries I strategically placed models for the North Canton, Ohio, buildings. Especially poignant and provocative among these was that of the City Hall with its American flag, exaggerated in its size and ironic in its position on the façade, already challenging us to unpleasant thoughts about a nation at war in Vietnam. Surely, as I suggested in the catalog, the work and writings of Venturi, Moore, Lyndon, and Giurgola represented "new philosophical positions ... emerging among the older members of the 40 [while] their work ... offers new images, and their influence on the next generation seems secure."

Though I think I was fabricating something of a "white lie" when I wrote that the reputations of these so-called Philadelphia School architects were "so established . . . that their inclusion in this exhibition was seriously questioned by some," I was not too off the mark in calling attention to the fact that amidst a general prosperity in the profession, these acknowledged theorists and practitioners "had not yet been given commissions of sufficient size and scope and [were] therefore still unestablished." If I can recall accurately, I think that my hedging remarks about the establishmentarianism of the so-called "Philadelphia School" may well have been triggered by conflicts between the new vs. the newer young turks at various CASE meetings, and by a refusal of the Philadelphia group to play European-style, CIAM-style polemical games.

Much can be said of the progress of the "40 Under 40" architects since 1966. With the passage of time, what seemed an unkind trick of chronological gamesmanship when excluding Mitchell/Giurgola from the group while admitting Venturi & Rauch and MLTW has been prophetic in many ways. Surely the nature of the practice of the marginally older architectural firm has assumed a more characteristically establishment tone (fig. 3). Though Mitchell/Giurgola is, in my opinion, our most innovative corporate practice, it is quite different in its clientele and in its internal organization from the two younger firms, which do not seem to have "grown up" or evolved in quite the same way.

On the other hand, Mitchell/Giurgola's fortunes have been linked with Venturi & Rauch's in at least one critical instance: the rough justice meted out to each of them by the Fine Arts Commission in Washington. This connection also extends to the many critical points of philosophy that set serious architecture apart from what passes for quality in the marketplace, and the three firms, as I suggested at some length in my book *New Directions in American Architecture,* now constitute a newly established leadership in the profession.

Other older members of the 1966 "40 Under 40" group have gone on to spectacularly successful careers, enjoying the fruits of the late sixties architectural boom, a boom that affected in particularly felicitous ways those architects interested in working for and with government in the areas of housing and urban development, and those who were able to tap the "corporate" market.

Under the impact of government-sponsored programs a number of offices established themselves in the uniquely difficult area of multifamily housing design. Davis, Brody & Associates had a head start in this area, having established its interest in this kind of problem at Riverbend, included in project form in the 1966 show. In the late sixties the firm grew rapidly, emerging as an American corporate practice of high integrity, one whose capabilities for invention could be seen in the U.S. Pavilion at Osaka and whose skills in the rough and tumble of publicly assisted marketplace housing can be seen all over New York. Yet it is interesting, and for me more than a little disappointing, that their splendidly intelligent Riverbend project, having been built and declared a success by the profession and the users alike, was abandoned by the firm as a model for housing in favor of a prototype of flashier profile but one that is far less convincing in its implications for urbanism and dwelling-unit design.

The careers of Gio Pasanella and Hoberman and Wasserman took off as a result of the sudden boom in housing construction. And the practices of each have suffered mightily in the last two or three years as the governmental programs have dried up. Joe Wasserman observes, "For the past several years, the amount of new building in America, especially in the urban public sector, has dwindled

sharply, leaving many of us whose efforts were devoted to public clients without
any significant work. It is a disturbing time to be an architect, especially as we
(and our agency clients) have had a first chance to test ourselves and would now,
I believe, be able to tailor our work much more responsively to the needs of our
real clients, the users who usually remain 'unseen' in the design process."

Norman Hoberman has just withdrawn from the firm: David Beer, who was
a part of the firm in 1966, left shortly thereafter to join a large commercial firm,
Welton Beckett Associates, where he is now director of design of the New York
office. Der Scutt, like David Beer, has given up individual private practice for a
succession of similar situations in a number of established commercial offices.
Each man has succeeded in bringing some special increment of excellence to these
firms. Scutt made his decision because of his strong conviction "that the architect
has a responsibility to concern himself at an increasingly larger-scale of architectural practice with the public and private client," and that "one way to reach the
broadest command of large-scale commissions was to join a large commercial
firm. Few realize the difficulties associated with architectural practice in a large,
profit-motivated commercial firm."

Included in the compilation of course were a number of established architectural firms that were already engaged in large-scale commercial work, and
it is interesting to see that the progress of each of these firms has been steady
and predictable. In the case of the Cambridge Seven, where one of the design
partners is still under forty, as well as in the case of older firms such as Smith-
Entzeroth and Lundquist and Stonehill, that there has been a move away from the
relatively dry and technologically determined glazed-frame "sub-style" (as I called
it in 1966) to a freer, more circumstantially responsive model that is representative
of a wider reading of architectural issues.

James Stewart Polshek was unquestionably the *Wunderkind* of the 1966 compilation. Unlike many of his contemporaries, Polshek did not cut his "baby" teeth
on private luxury residences, finding them only "challenging technologically but
of little interest as plastic or formal problems, and programmatically inconsequen-
tial." As he writes: "My first two major buildings were both built in Japan and
completed before I was 34. Prior to that time, I had designed and built only two
small private residences. The result, for better or for worse, was that I skipped all
of the intermediate steps that an architect's career usually follows.

Fig. 3. Mitchell/Giurgola,
MDRT Foundation Hall,
American College, Bryn Mawr,
Pennsylvania, 1972

The Old "40 Under 40"

"Returning to the United States permanently in 1965, I commenced private practice. This was the middle of the building boom and after barely two years, I found my office inundated with moderate sized commissions. Over the next three to five years this involved me personally on the design of building types that I was totally inexperienced with—low-cost housing, historic preservation, and adaptive re-use (before this particular phrase was even known)."

Polshek accurately mirrors current concerns when he describes "the reutilization of existing buildings…as the most consuming of the generic problems now facing the profession, becoming a central preoccupation in American buildings in the '70s as inflation, skilled labor scarcities and energy and other resource depletions become facts we have to live with. All of this culminated (and the process is continuing) in a profound change in public attitudes regarding the built environment in the United States. It means that architects must have enormously diverse practices where the skills and knowledge required in such activities as building maintenance, operations research, industrial and interior design, industrialized building systems, design and procurement and health system planning will be absolutely necessary. The opportunities to build budget-free, unencumbered monuments to dying social and political institutions are of no interest to me and will in any event be few and far between."

For some of the 1966 "40 Under 40" groups, there have been some radical shifts of view point over the ten-year period. Tim Vreeland, for example, after spending the first ten years of his professional life "as an active member of the Philadelphia School," moved from Philadelphia to California after a year or two spent in New Mexico. In 1966 he was represented by a building and a town planning project. The former, designed in partnership with Frank Schlesinger, was a research laboratory built just behind Kahn's Richards Building at the University of Pennsylvania; their design was even more closely connected to their mentor's work, in that it was, in effect, a second-story addition to a building Kahn had designed in 1960. As I observed in the catalog in 1966, "The sympathy with which the new was added to the recently new [gave] rare but reassuring testimony that claims of a sense of the urbanistic on the part of younger talents are not entirely unfounded." Vreeland's second project was an urban design proposal for Cooper's Point and Pyne Point prepared in partnership with Oscar Newman, whose subsequent researches have resulted in a very remarkable book, *Defensible Space*.

Vreeland has found in Southern California a very congenial situation, discovering "an architecture unrestricted by an already strongly established tradition as existed in Philadelphia."

"I do not mean to imply that Southern California has no tradition of architecture. On the contrary, it has had a strong and important tradition beginning in the '20s that we are well aware of [and] which has been well chronicled in the writings of Esther McCoy and David Gebhard. In fact it is precisely their writing in books and in the pages of *Arts and Architecture*…that originally drew the attention of the Silvers—a loose affiliation of Los Angeles 'émigré' architects who came together in January 1974 to act as a host group for the visiting White and Gray architects from the East Coast, and who have continued to meet and exchange ideas ever since—to California and ultimately drew us here. It is that earlier tradition of case study houses, of light steel construction and the use of industrial components, which was part and parcel of the lack of cultural restraint, the freedom from a particular

The Old "40 Under 40"

architectural commitment that this place seems to promise, an escape from the orthodoxies such as cities like Chicago, New York or San Francisco demand of their architects. But by the time I arrived here I discovered, to my chagrin, that that was all over, had already passed into history. *Arts and Architecture* had folded; speculators' stud and stucco accounted for most of the building and the rest were imitation Sea Ranch. And I had to begin all over again."

"The absence of prevailing tradition" in Los Angeles ironically has given Vreeland the same sense of freedom to manipulate images in accord with site, program, users, and a sense of history that close contact with developed premodernist traditions has given other architects back East. He writes that the absence of a "prevailing tradition ... provides the searching architect with a blank screen upon which to project his inner-most images without interference. Los Angeles has always essentially played this role for the culture it has nurtured. It has encouraged fantasy—quick, easy fantasy—fantasy in a bean field like Beverly Hills—instant tradition. Make-believe is our chief product and export: the make-believe of the movies. Silver is the color of the movies: the silver nitrate of its films, the glitter of Hollywood, the silver screen.

"My recent work varies considerably in the style which each project adopts. Each is an exercise in a different style, a style appropriate to the job. I have come to believe over the past five years while practicing here in California that this is the task that faces the architect today: to find a style appropriate to each job—a task made simpler by virtue of practicing here in Los Angeles, where no previous images interfere with the Silver Screen upon which we project our imagery."

Charles Moore is another of the original group who has shifted the locale of his practice radically in the ten years, leaving Berkeley for New Haven, Connecticut, and ending up, ironically, in Los Angeles and on the faculty at UCLA with Vreeland. But Moore's search has led him to rather different conclusions about the same issues: "If, as I've come to believe, architecture is only worthwhile if it means something to the people who inhabit it, and if, in a dramatically pluralist society, the individual responses to any forms are wildly disparate, then the architect's chief hope (if he is to engage the inhabitant) is to develop a choreography of the familiar and the unfamiliar, to relax the user with forms well known, then awaken him with surprising shapes or colors or juxtapositions. In our work during the last decade, we've been especially concerned with the realm of the familiar, extending its range, and daring to get more and more specific.

"The fountain basin at August Perez's Piazza d'Italia in New Orleans, for instance, is to be shaped like the map of Italy (only very slightly abstracted), with the five architectural orders on walls surrounding it rendered, not exactly standardly, but certainly quite specifically in stainless steel and water. Ten years ago, in parallel circumstances at Lawrence Halprin's Lovejoy Fountain Plaza, in Portland, Oregon [fig. 4], we had *abstracted* a mountain waterfall into a set of concrete steps over which the water splashes, and would have found a more specific recall of the High Sierra unnecessary, and just a little tacky.

"But in the last ten years, people's expectations have changed a great deal: there is far less excitement about trying to plug in to a sleek, sterilized imaginary world of the future, and far more sympathy for making connections with the past, even with specific pieces of the past, in an urban-renewed world where so many connections have been wantonly destroyed. Ten years ago I thought Thomas

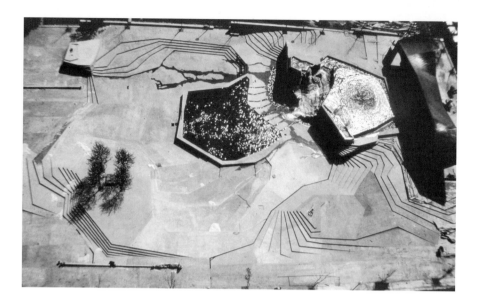

Jefferson's ten pavilions at the University of Virginia were beautiful, but perhaps a little quaint: the gesture of making ten architectural models for young scholars seemed so literal. Now, the gesture seems to me noble and necessary, and a worthy model for our own efforts.

"One change from Jefferson's concerns which interests me especially involves the chance to broaden the range of allowable sources, to find in very ordinary structures close at hand (so lately scorned) the familiar stuff of which people's memories are made, by way of which their engagement with their new buildings can begin. This was fairly easy in Northern California, where a lively carpenter's tradition has been continuous; it is much more confusing on the East Coast, where native traditions have been usurped by the A&P, or bludgeoned by European invaders, and it is confusing too in Southern California, where an endearing sleaze is a traditional environmental ingredient. In an increasingly well-traveled world, the imagery of far places and distant times has much more meaning than it used to for many people, but when the world traveler has simply been to a distant Holiday Inn, the need to find and to hang onto the special qualities of each place, whether Williamsburg or New Orleans or Los Angeles, becomes acute. My own pioneering during this decade has been in the realm of vernacular imagery. Special to places, ordinary, but not, I think, ugly, though it is often rejected as banal or tacky. If we can just get the familiar to work, the surprising seems to take care of itself."

In 1966 I concluded my introduction with the claim that "for the first time in fifty years there appears to be no revolution in architecture." I think I was right then, but I think the political events of 1967–69 triggered a period of questioning that is still very much with us and only now, as economic vicissitudes persist and, indeed, encourage the profession to reflect on the meaning of things, are we beginning to emerge from the negativism of the recent past and embark, with some confidence, on a new phase in our development, which has been described by some as "trans-industrial," by others as "post-functionalist," and by myself as "post-modernism." Surely, then, as Stanley Tigerman states, "the ten years of elapsed time since the original '40 Under 40' show has been incredibly important to the discipline of architecture, which is at least involved with the 'idea content' of not only its work, but of the society that work product purports to represent."

And Thomas Holzbog, mirroring the cautious optimism of this generation now in middle age, a generation that has watched the nation torn apart by war and a profession laid waste by economics and by self-doubt, states that "architects and planners have been preoccupied to such an extent with what is different in our time that they have lost touch with what is not different—with what is essentially the same—those norms which are taken for granted but contribute the bulk of our human condition. We cannot formulate a future on the dire insufficiencies of one generation's knowledge."

In the 1966 "40 Under 40" show, the catalogue and exhibition were arranged by building, not architect, and some buildings have different combinations of the same names associated with them, so there is no clear-cut list of forty architects or firms. The following is a list of every architect under the age of forty. (A few over-forty architects included in the catalogue because they worked on projects with under-forties are not listed here.) The architects/buildings were selected for the exhibition in autumn 1965.

1966 "40 Under 40"

James Baker

Hobart D. Betts

Gunnar Birkerts

Cambridge Seven, Inc.
  Louis J. Bakanowsky
  Ivan Chermayeff
  Peter Chermayeff
  Alden B. Christie
  Paul E. Dietrich
  Thomas Geismar
  Terry Rankine

Lewis Davis and Samuel Brody

Anthony Eardley, Peter Eisenman, and Michael Graves

Robert Entzeroth

John Fowler

Charles Gwathmey and Richard Henderson

Hugh Hardy and T. Merrill Prentice, Jr.

Norman Hoberman, Joseph Wasserman, and David Beer

Thomas J. Holzbog

Peter J. Hoppner

Hugh Newell Jacobsen

Donlyn Lyndon

Mary Otis Stevens McNulty

Richard Meier

Joseph Merz and Giovanni Pasanella

Robert Mittelstadt

Charles W. Moore

Oscar Newman

Rai Y. Okamoto

James Stewart Polshek

John Rauch

Jaquelin T. Robertson and Herman Lemaire

Frank Schlesinger

Der Scutt

Werner Seligmann

David Sellers, William Reinecke, and Edwin Owre (sculptor)

Robert A. M. Stern

John Jay Stonehill

Stanley Tigerman

William Turnbull, Jr.

Robert Venturi

Thomas R. Vreeland, Jr.

Ben Weese

Richard R. Whitaker

IO

Some Notes on the New "40 Under 40"
1976

Author's Note: In preparing this 1976 compilation of forty architects under forty years of age I used the same working method as the one I used in 1966 when I prepared a similar selection for the Architectural League of New York. This is a presentation of works of architecture made by men and women who were under forty years of age in September 1975, when the idea for the reincarnation of the "40 Under 40" exhibition was first discussed with Toshio Nakamura, the editor of *Architecture and Urbanism* in Japan. Each architect selected for the new compilation is engaged in independent practice. In the interest of providing the broadest selection of buildings and points of view in a compilation based on age, work by partnerships in which at least one member is under forty is included.

This compilation is not intended as a definitive statement on the younger generation, but rather as a presentation of the diversity of American architectural design as it can be seen in the work of younger members of the profession, who are at once the most flattering mirrors and the most severely caustic critics of their elders. The influence of the severe economic depression and the genuine promise of the Bicentennial spirit that is suffusing the country as I write, just ten days after the Fourth of July, make the decision to organize this new "40 Under 40" seem in some little measure poignant and appropriate.

In preparing the selection of the new "40 Under 40" group and the sections devoted to the "up-date" on the "40 Under 40" group organized ten years ago, I requested that the various architects submit statements about their work in relationship to their view of American issues. It was my intention to present these statements side by side with the individual presentations of the work, in lieu of the project-by-project editorial commentary I wrote for the catalog in 1966. But many of the architects felt uncomfortable in preparing such material, so in this fairly extensive essay I have included many ideas from the comments that were supplied.

One question might well be asked: "Why a new '40 Under 40' just ten years after the most recent one?" After all, the "40 Under 40" exhibition of 1966 followed its predecessor by twenty-five years; and that amount of time really does define a generation. There are a number of responses to this question that I feel are appropriate, the most obvious of which—aside from the facetious one that my time as a young architect is running out, and if the reincarnation of the event is postponed much longer I shall be too old to be included—is that, given both the Bicentennial and the disastrous economic state of the architectural profession, the year 1976 seems an appropriate one in which to examine the state of American architecture, particularly as it can be understood in the work and concerns of the younger practitioners. The Bicentennial has lifted the spirit of the nation, and especially of those of us in New York, which persists as the architectural center of the country. And the renewed sense of political purpose cannot but positively affect the profession's view of its own prospects.

Any discussion of professional prospects in 1976 has to be optimistic in contrast to the economic realities, which are very, very grim. In this respect, the "40 Under 40" group of today has much more in common with that of 1941 than that of 1966. Like the 1941 assemblage, and unlike that of 1966, there is both economic frustration and stylistic battle. In its catalog, the "40 Under 40" architects of 1941 described themselves as "the generation that did not build the New York skyline, the Gothic dormitories in the colleges, or the Triangle in Washington. We were just getting out of school or into practice when the stockbrokers were jumping out of windows. This was also the time of the big switch from Beaux-Arts to Bauhaus, from cornices to corner windows. We weren't sure what kind of architecture we wanted to do, but we were agreed on one thing; Roman baths were no place for railroad trains, nor medieval nunneries for undergraduates."[1] Today, the issues are similar, only, and rather provocatively, it is not the Beaux-Arts that is under fire, but modernism itself. And, among the very youngest of the architects under forty, as represented by the Arquitectonica group in Miami, or by Frank Israel, expatriated for two and a half years in London, or by Andrew MacNair in New York, there is not only great dissatisfaction with the current economic situation but also, in terms of formal and philosophical commitment, virtually complete separation from the orthodox modernism of the 1950s and '60s. From the unique perspective of the New York situation and its Janus-like interrelationship to American and European trends, MacNair, who organizes courses and lectures at the Institute for Architecture and Urban Studies, writes: "The current situation for young architects in America is difficult for me to assess except in terms of my view of the scene in New York. During a depression in building, a foggy economy, and a new conservatism in the schools, younger architects are either defining new groups, camps, and directions; faithfully following their historical masters and contemporary mentors; or they are trying to work quietly and privately on [their] own. I think that the entire movement of groups which formed in the late '60s and early '70s was an understandable response for young architects to take to the end of the era of rock bands with their groupies and to the beginning of an insecure building climate of the seventies. After the formation of European groups such as Archigram and Superstudio, there came ... teams for polemics such as the Five. As the sixties faded, the Five (the Whites) provoked worried repercussions from the Five on Five (the Grays) that the Five may be defining a rather narrow school exclusive of everybody, including the newest group, the Silvers from Los Angeles."

"Among other young architects," MacNair continues, "there are clearly two modes of thought, as seen in the 'Goodbye Five: Work Done by Five Architects' exhibition shown at the Institute for Architecture and Urban Studies last fall (1975). It is clear that there is the work which belongs to those who have been educated in schools and offices during a time when the practice of architecture was relatively stable. They were successful students who progressed continuously from undergraduate programs directly into graduate schools without the harassment of the Vietnam draft. They seemed to have quickly found not only historical mentors but also contemporary masters. These masters not only set the rules of the game in the few respectable schools in and around New York but also controlled the only desirable offices for practical training. This group of younger architects seems to continue to follow the paths of their mentors. They maintain an attitude towards client, building, and practice as synonymous with architecture and imperative for architects. Their projects reflect revisions and problems, vocabularies, and images more than adequately presented by Le Corbusier and Venturi."[2]

While MacNair sees the other body of work in "Goodbye Five" as belonging "to no group at all" and beyond categorization or classification, I would suggest that it is, as yet, unformed, largely because it is unbuilt and exists in a pictographic rather than tectonic way. MacNair's work belongs to that category, bearing heavy influences from Rem Koolhaas, who, like many young European architects, seems to be revitalizing that obsession with the American scene, which has not been so intense since the 1920s of Neutra, Mendelsohn, and Le Corbusier. So the circle has come full round again, or has it? Such is the question the answer to which is sought in this new "40 Under 40."

The new "40 Under 40" contains work by eight architects who were included in the 1966 compilation. Despite the fact that I am among these eight, I think it is possible to claim that, in many ways, the progress of these eight careers is the most revealing, if not necessarily the most significant, among the new forty. To substantiate this claim, let me present the eight "cases" on an individual basis.

Case 1: Peter Chermayeff is unique among the eight cases in that he has been continuously associated with a relatively large, corporate-type practice and one in which he was, at a very young age, a founding partner. In 1966 his firm, Cambridge Seven Associates, was represented in the catalog by the remarkable interior and exhibition design for Buckminster Fuller's dome, then under design for the United States Exhibition at Expo '67, surely our nation's most success-ful exposition pavilion to date (fig. 1). At the time, the firm was designing the New England Aquarium, a building as noted for its no-nonsense exterior form as for the innovative display techniques employed inside. Interestingly enough, the firm's attitudes have shifted away from one in which "external form remains

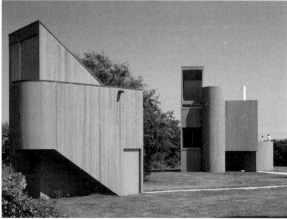

Fig. 1. Peter Chermayeff, United States Exhibition, Expo '67, Montreal, Canada, 1967

Fig. 2. Charles Gwathmey, Gwathmey Residence and Studio, Amagansett, New York, 1967

secondary…to the internal experience, to a 'freerer attitude'…not as constrained as it was in the early 60s when we started." Chermayeff notes that he now "feels more inclined to allow strong or idiosyncratic forms to emerge, but still not in a personal playful sense, still within the constraints of problem solving."

Chermayeff's belief in the primary role of "problem solving" in architecture is surely characteristic of the attitudes prevalent in the large-scale American office, though it is this aspect of modernism that seems to be most under fire from the younger members of the "Under 40" group.

Case 2: Charles Gwathmey's house for his parents at Amagansett, which was included in the first exhibition, remains a remarkably mature and resolved design, one that can be safely included in any list of important work in the decade (fig. 2). The additions that have been made to it over the last ten years—first the studio, which was shown in model form at the exhibition in New York (models were not circulated nationally), and later the house built on the adjacent lot for the actor Michael Tolan—elaborate with remarkable success the propositions advanced in the original house and suggest a kind of urbanistic interrelationship between free-standing object-buildings which, to my knowledge, no other such house grouping has so convincingly achieved since the main portion of Philip Johnson's Glass House complex was completed in the mid-1950s. Nonetheless, Gwathmey seemed unable to build upon the extraordinary success of the Amagansett grouping. Perhaps its completeness, its wonderful marriage of influences from Le Corbusier and from the American Shingle Style, and its superb sense of craftsmanship (which established a whole attitude toward buildings as craft, one that is reflected in the work of countless younger architects) made it too complete, too perfect, and therefore inhibiting. For the next few years, as Gwathmey's practice grew, his professional associations shifted, finally emerging as the firm Gwathmey Siegel. The direction of his work seems, to this observer at least, increasingly trapped in an over-elaborate geometry manipulated with skill but with too little reference to context. His inclusion in the New York "Five" continues to make little or no sense to me and, I think it can be safe to say, to many other observers of the scene as well.

Gwathmey Siegel is represented in this new compilation by a resort hotel proposed by the Playboy organization for Aruba. Obviously its design is the result of a move toward clarification and abstraction at the domestic scale, extending back in time to the work that followed the completion of the Steel Houses. Gwathmey

Siegel seems at the brink of entering the ranks of the world of corporate and institutional clients; it remains to be seen how much of the firm's formal panache can be brought along to serve its new patronage.

Case 3: Peter Hoppner's Mill House at Mad River Glen, Vermont, was the first building in the East that I know of to have shown direct influence from Charles Moore (fig. 3).

In its general form and in the use of bold super-graphics it anticipated much of the work that was to emerge under Moore's influence at Yale in the late 1960s. This is very surprising because Hoppner had no significant direct contact with Moore; he was, in fact, a student and later an employee of Paul Rudolph's. Hoppner has pursued a career in education and design over the last ten years "at the fringes" of the New York scene, struggling to establish for himself an appropriate attitude toward form-making, or, as he puts it, trying to "escape from an architecture of shape making, believing that kind of architecture to be overly willful and excessively obtrusive." Though with sardonic wit he calls attention to the "22 exterior corners" of the ski house, it seems to me that even that highly overwrought scheme, which I described in 1966 as "nervous and shack-like," is liberating in its attitude toward the relationship of form to use when viewed in contrast to much of the prevailing neoclassicism of the period, or the super-spatial articulations of those who aped and thereby exaggerated Paul Rudolph's call to architectural enrichment.

In the three "box" houses included (especially number three), Hoppner, like Tim Wood, who is one of the new "Under 40" architects, seems to be moving toward a positive attitude toward applied decoration, which can have significant implications for architecture at all scales. Hoppner is about to embark on a "mid-career" fellowship at the American Academy in Rome, and it will be instructive to observe the effect on his work of long exposure to that unique architectural hothouse.

Case 4: In 1966 Donlyn Lyndon, like William Turnbull (see Case 8), was a member of the MLTW affiliation, which at that time appeared to function as a fairly tight-knit professional partnership focused on work and teaching responsibilities in Berkeley, California (fig. 4). Charles Moore unquestionably seemed the wellspring for design invention within the group; and Lyndon was particularly known to me for his remarkably astute article assessing the American scene published

Fig. 3. Peter Hoppner, Mill House, Mad River Glen, Vermont, 1966

Fig. 4. Moore Lyndon Turnbull Whitaker MLTW, Condominium One, The Sea Ranch, California, 1965

Fig. 5. Robert Mittelstadt, Fremont Civic Center, Fremont, California, 1968

Fig. 6. David Sellers, Tack House, Prickly Mountain, Warren, Vermont, 1964

in *Casabella* in 1962. Since 1966, the partnership has evolved into a loose association, and Lyndon has shifted his academic affiliation to MIT and his practice to Cambridge, Massachusetts. He has built relatively little in the last ten years in comparison with the incredibly fertile Moore, but whatever Lyndon's oeuvre may lack in size, its importance is in large measure ensured by the intelligent relationship to significant issues established in his design for the dormitories for Pembroke College at Brown University, Providence, Rhode Island.

Case 5: Robert Mittelstadt was represented in 1966 by his extraordinary winning scheme for the Fremont, California, Civic Center competition of 1965, an incredibly ambitious project flush with the optimism of the pre-Vietnam 1960s (fig. 5). Mittelstadt now describes the competition and its professional aftermath as "the largest project I had ever been fully responsible for; ironically it remains the largest my firm has executed to date. The Fremont scheme was directly influenced by examples of urban design in Europe, by the work of Paul Rudolph, my mentor at Yale, and to some extent, by the work of James Stirling. The fact that the schematic design was done in Rome insured that the historic public spaces in Italy would provide the dominant influence on the master plan. While an employee of Paul Rudolph, I had been strongly influenced by the Boston Government Service Center, a scheme that seemed to invent a vocabulary of form and structure for public buildings that could adapt to almost any functional requirement, yet model dynamic urban space with disciplined plasticity. As an exercise in pure formalism, the Fremont project was ideal: a monument to a future metropolis, it was situated in a cabbage patch a half-mile from the nearest building.

"The abstract, theoretical beginnings of the Fremont project provided a strong contrast to the realities of architectural practice and of the work to come. . . . Predictably, work since Fremont manifests the gradual displacement of Rudolphian imagery by other formal influences.

Some Notes on the New "40 Under 40"

Fig. 7. Robert A. M. Stern, Wiseman House, Montauk, New York, 1965–1967

"For me, the shift away from the purely intuitive, formalist approach began in 1968 with two coincidental experiences: a teaching appointment at Berkeley and the climax of the Vietnam war resistance. Together these experiences served to dismantle my image of the burnished, high-tech world of early-sixties Camelot, to replace reflex and habit with a reassessment of all value systems."

Mittelstadt, rather like Hoppner, has continued to operate at the fringes of professional practice, devoting a good deal of energy and time to architectural education—trying unsuccessfully to return architectural education to a proper position in the academic hierarchies at Stanford University through the establishment of a nonprofessional undergraduate major—and building comparatively little.

Now embarked on a long search for connections with local form traditions, Mittelstadt has become increasingly concerned with the architectural implication of energy conservation issues and with a need to move in his own work beyond the "architectural styling" that he feels marked his early work. Clearly, this survey, as opposed to the one in 1966, finds his career and his ideas in a state of transition.

Case 6: Of the eight holdovers from 1966, David Sellers has been the most consistent in his outlook—doggedly persistent, one might even say. Very little appears to separate the intent, working method, and even the forms of Sellers' Tack House of 1965 (fig. 6) from his Rosen House of 1975. Sellers, who continues to find validity in the "hands-on experience in the process of construction" that caused him to seek an alternative to conventional urban practice in the hills of Vermont, has written that "if continuing education after architecture school involved one in actual construction, the inner city was eliminated as an appropriate area for pursuing professional goals."

Sellers' work at Goddard College has been remarkable in its combination of classroom and field techniques; and the buildings he has built there with the help of students clearly illustrate the limitations and strengths of his methodology, as it can be measured against projects of relatively large scope. Given its intellectual premises, the work at least shows a far more consistent relationship between the problem of the house and that of the large-scale building than one can observe in the work of many of the others among the eight cases under discussion. And though Sellers has wisely not chosen to go beyond the scale of work that can be realized with conventional wood-framing techniques, and though one cannot but be impressed by his consistent pursuit of a particular set of goals, one is also obliged to observe that those goals are perhaps more restricted in their ambitions and limited in their scope than those of any others of the "Under 40" groups.

Case 7: Robert A. M. Stern. It is very hard to write objectively about oneself. I make no claims, therefore, for doing so, and will simply remark on aspects of these ten years of my career as I now see them.

In 1966 I was represented in "40 Under 40" by my first house, the Wiseman House, then only a project (fig. 7). Philip Johnson accurately characterized it as "reflecting the Philadelphia School approach to architecture, especially that of [my] mentor Robert Venturi." Johnson went on to very kindly and encouragingly predict that the house would "be one of the most dramatic and 'far out' statements of the latest thinking in architecture." The house did get built, and when it was published in *Progressive Architecture* it caused a reader in Alaska to write a hate letter to the magazine—surely that marked it out for some distinction that even Johnson's praise could not compete with.

After a period at the Housing and Development Administration of the City of New York during the best of the Mayor Lindsay years, I set up shop in partnership with a colleague from Yale, John Hagmann, a partnership which, as I write this, is taking a new form because of Hagmann's withdrawal from it in June. Even as a student at Yale I was always mucking about in the netherworlds between design, architectural theory, criticism, and history. Such continues to be the case, as this very compilation attests. This concern for what might be called the "culture" of architecture is directly realized in the form our architecture has taken and, equally importantly, in the form my career has assumed. So, it is not odd that my work has become increasingly involved with issues of sign and symbol and the individual building as an overtly acknowledged participant in the continuum of history.

Our practice has been largely focused on the single-family house—a focus that has given us marvelous opportunities, not only to explore a host of bold, formal ideas, but also to learn a good deal about the craft of building, communing with the gods of Miesian detail rather more intimately than I would have ever admitted likely or possible in my Yale days. We have attempted to extend our scope and to address problems of larger scale and greater social use; none of these larger projects has yet been built (the great collapse of the Urban Development Corporation pretty much forestalling any hope to build our proposal for Roosevelt Island, financial stringencies cutting back on much of the proposal for Columbia). Nonetheless, it is not for want of trying that we have as yet been unable to realize the arguments established in the houses at a larger and more public scale.

Case 8: William Turnbull's contribution to the work of MLTW, like Lyndon's (Case 4) or Richard Whitaker's, was in 1966 vastly overshadowed by the then almost firmly established reputation of their partner Charles Moore. To this observer at least, it appears that over the years Turnbull has maintained a closer professional relationship to Moore than have the two other partners. Possibly this is because

Turnbull has not injected himself into professional and academic situations to the extent that Lyndon has at MIT and Whitaker has, first at the American Institute of Architects in Washington and now at the Circle Campus of the University of Illinois at Chicago. Possibly this is because Turnbull's practice has continued to parallel that of the MLTW group in its early days, comprising a good number of houses and an occasional commercial renovation. Now Turnbull is preparing drawings for an important public building, a library and museum for Biloxi, Mississippi, which was the subject of a unique limited competition held in 1974. Ironically, Moore was unable to accept an invitation to the competition, and Turnbull entered in his stead. Although Turnbull's work often refers to the work of the old MLTW partnership (this Biloxi project recalls the Faculty Club at Santa Barbara, for example), in the Zimmermann House he moves further toward his own realm.

While one is reluctant to make overall judgments about these eight "cases," or even to attempt to group the work in categories, one cannot fail to note that the ten-year period has been used by each architect either to reject early success (Mittelstadt and Hoppner) or to continue to pursue directions established at the outset, often, as in the case of Turnbull and myself, seeking to evolve new positions without overturning beliefs held now for ten or more years.

Many of the new "Under 40" group mirror ideas and forms of the work of members represented in the first compilation—surely a measure of the degree to which the talents of some of the older group have become established within the profession, if not necessarily within that body of public and private clients who must support an architect's practice in order to ensure continued productivity. For example, Michael Graves has built comparatively little; yet his work is widely admired and studied by other architects and by his students, one of whom, Peter Waldman, has built up a not insubstantial personal oeuvre that displays numerous influences from Graves. Waldman's frank acknowledgment of the "self-consciously superficial, decorated, and painterly" qualities of the facades of his Goodyear and Rubin House additions is perhaps unduly revealing, but it is not uncharacteristic of the new "Under 40" group in its willingness to admit that artistic developments are the product of a learning process and not born fully developed from the head of the architect. Waldman's architecture, with its intentional "polemical distinctions between appliqué, poché, and the assembled artifacts of remembered rituals," is perhaps overworked, but its serious concern for the relationship between form and the meaning form can establish in the mind of the viewer is not to be casually dismissed.

Charles Dagit and Peter Saylor find themselves followers of Aldo Giurgola "by style, if not by association." They liken their relationship to him to that between "weavers of oriental rugs, woven by different hands but of the same period and type." Their allegiance to Giurgola's example can be seen in the style of their drawing and the forms of the buildings themselves. Dagit and Saylor's buildings "evoke unsensational attitudes because [they] gladly accept unsensational problems. Alvar Aalto seems, to us, to represent this kind of ideal more than most. Fortunately, there is not enough money to build 'spectacular solutions.'"

Jerry Wells, Fred Koetter, and Mike Dennis, influenced by Colin Rowe's teaching at Cornell and by Werner Seligmann's teaching and design, find themselves in reaction against the "urban inadequacies" of the Modern Movement and what they describe as "the American Picturesque and Suburban traditions." Their work has been heavily influenced by Le Corbusier and by Swiss work of the 1950s, and the American qualities of their work are to be found largely in its "Yankee pragmatism and [in the] ad hoc ingenuity that manifests itself in modern manufacturing techniques and machines." By contrast, though Mark Ueland and J. Anthony Junker, literal contemporaries of Wells, Koetter, and Dennis, and products of that aspect of the so-called Philadelphia School that focuses around the work of Venturi, see American issues in terms of "its pragmatism, bluntness, persistent energy (right or wrong)," their formal focus is American not European. They are "in revolt against bareness," and their attitudes toward practice seem populist in style.

Dan Scully, Peter de Bretteville, and Thomas Beeby also claim influences from American know-how—so-called Yankee pragmatism. Each has turned that admiration or influence to specific use in his work: Beeby and de Bretteville have seen the existing technological hardware as a lost opportunity for formal stimulus, and pursue a direction of design best described as "high-tech." Beeby sees it as a means to connect with the Chicago tradition: "Our approach has been to utilize the lucid systematic qualities of construction long associated with the architecture of Chicago. We employ frame construction as a pragmatic necessity and an organizing aesthetic device." De Bretteville, it would appear, though he has not said so, seeks to connect with the California modernism of the late '40s and early '50s by using the lightweight steel technology that one associates with Eames, Koenig, Soriano, and the others who so influence Vreeland and his colleagues in the Los Angeles Silver group.

But it is Scully who has the most ironic and therefore most realistic view of American technology, seeing it in broad, consumer-oriented terms, combining a concern for energy conservation with a love for specific mechano-morphic images: "steam locomotives and Fearless Frank Furness; the Futurists; streamlined cars, trains and Norman Bel Geddes; a '51 Ford with '56 side trim; driving; Ant Farm, Baier, Venturi, and the Porsche 917–10."

"To our pleasure," Scully observes, "we have just been cruisin' on down the highway, constantly shifting up gear-popping hamburgers. Burn it out, man, throw it out the window. Farther on up the road I too am caught up in the automobile, in its social role, shapes, and mechanical aspects. Since I understand them, vehicles have often been the subject of my design imagery. If you can't put wheels on it, forget it." Though he, like most Americans, now realizes "the worldwide costs of energy and waste," making the auto the "bad-guy," in his work, as beneath the surface of most American psyches, protests to the contrary notwithstanding, "the appropriate/inappropriateness" of both the mechanicalness and imagery of vehicles "maintains its power."

No matter what particular direction in terms of style or professional attitude the younger members of the new forty are taking, they do seem to share a set of concerns about the future of the "modernism" they have inherited, and though this concern takes a variety of forms, it is usually triggered by a sense that the practical and philosophical issues of American architecture as this generation sees them are not adequately addressed in the prevailing modernist canon.

Tim Wood, for example, while accepting the continuing validity of modernism, or perhaps more precisely, the Modern Movement, argues that "modern architecture, in the commonly understood and much abused sense of the term, is being reviled today for what it has done and what it has failed to do historically."

"Everyone," Wood continues, "from highly cultivated architects, critics, and historians, to the man in the street, has vilified modern architecture unjustly because they have been goaded with increasing intensity for about thirty years, by most of the products of its idiot-twin, the International Style.

"We see attempts today in certain quarters to resurrect certain nineteenth-century architectural styles along with those drawing inspiration from reinterpretations of various types of American vernacular architecture, whether they be historically situated or excretions of our consumer/Pop culture. Fortunately for us," Wood rather ruefully continues, "most of the practitioners of these eclectic reformulations have absorbed the fundamentals of architecture via a solid academic grounding in modern architectural principles. In this they are not unlike the first generation of modern pathfinders, who were themselves thoroughly grounded in the principles of classical architecture when they went about upsetting what was still left of that system ...

"It is the majority of the remaining so-called modernists in America who are now in something of a quandary. They received their critical orientation more from the *images* of modernism that were prepackaged and imported as the International Style. That style served to revive the sagging energies [of] and give directions to more than one generation of American architects. The problem now is that most bought an empty package, an image without content, i.e., social content. Today [this] seems to be happening again. The search is on for a new package to sell. In fact, many are being offered to the disoriented and its dissatisfied public.

"The social content, to the extent that it exists, is derived from a perversely selective concept of aesthetic populism. This pseudo-pragmatism has as its central flaw the fact [that] it pretends to deliver what people want in a positive sense, but is instead exploiting a reaction to something else they will no longer tolerate. It is this year's model, superseding last year's in the best American tradition.

"The greatest danger in this situation for the future of architecture is that the coming generation of architects, like the third- and fourth-generation modernists, may be left with little fundamental understanding of either the underlying principles of all architecture (an historical basis) when the current model year is over."

There seems to be some argument among the group over Wood's claim that "architecture exists independent of particular cultural orientations [and] is therefore, in essence, a set of abstract, historically derived, formal principles." His indictment of the spurious populism that too often passes for a lack of rigor is surely justified, so long as one does not overlook the spurious aspects of much of the pseudo-cubism that is rather too glibly offered as an alternative.

Rodolfo Machado and Jorge Silvetti offer a more complex assessment of the pervasive modernist crisis, citing "two interrelated facts" as the basis of current debate: one, "the collapse of the anti-historical bias of the Modern Movement that [has] prevailed until recently," and two, "the failure of deterministic [functionalism] (with [its] corollaries of 'problem solving,' 'systems analysis,' etc.) as the generating force of design."

Machado and Silvetti, like Diana Agrest, Emilio Ambasz, and Mario Gandelsonas, see the dilemma of American architecture in relationship to the evolution and/or conclusion of the Modern Movement from a peculiarly privileged vantage point: they are Argentinian émigrés, each attracted to the States for political and economic reasons certainly, but most especially for the unique qualities of the American situation, its openness, its pragmatic acceptance of its own inherent contradictions.

Machado and Silvetti echo Wood's remarks in observing that "the American situation acquires special significance because of its own history; American architecture evolved as the product of a constant transformation and reinterpretation of European models, which, when removed from their original context acquired distinctly different meanings (this holds true not only for classical models but also for those of modern architecture).

"This process of constant re-semanticization (that to many critics appears either heretic or naïve) suddenly seems to be American architecture's main asset at a moment characterized by theoretical questioning and critical experimentations, because that 'heretic' tradition contains inherently liberating and de-mythifying possibilities if used consciously and systematically."

Machado and Silvetti feel that the "Modern Movement needs to be viewed in a broad cultural context." They see it as "an episode in the history of Western architecture," and though they do not so much as say so, they suggest that the episode is a closed one when they say that "the designer finds the whole past of architecture (Modern Movement included) as material to interpret, to reflect upon, to respond to and use." And they contradict the claims of Wood when they insist on design as "the *product* of a multiplicity of *factors rooted in culture.*"

Machado and Silvetti see a "theory of types" emerging, not based on function in the Corbusian sense, but based on issues of "space, icon, and symbol." It is as part of a process of "de-mythification, criticism, and liberation of the designer's potential," rather than a shriveling away from choice and context, that Machado and Silvetti wish to have their work viewed.

Coy Howard echoes Machado and Silvetti's concerns with the functional determinism of orthodox modernism, though he is more involved with behavioral issues than they. Howard observes that "all great innovations, which inaugurate a new era, consist in a sudden shift of attention and displacement of emphasis onto some previously neglected aspect of experience—some blacked-out range of the existential spectrum.

"Modern architecture, for too long, has maintained its functionalist focus in America, obscuring the more significant levels of its domain. We should recognize that architecture is not simply the inevitable consequence of needs, as the functionalists suggest; that both needs and the forms which respond to these needs demand high levels of social and psychological perceptiveness and formal skills, and that these skills are a scarcer and more precious commodity than the organizational talent we have for so long been praising."

A new "40 Under 40" is emerging confident that a new set of ideas are emerging, and they are excited to be present at the birth. Frank Israel, with one modest house under his belt, is representative of the generation raised in architecture since 1966. Though not the youngest to be included in the survey, he is the youngest to have built independently. Israel, writing about the late '60s, when he was an undergraduate at Penn and, later, a graduate student, first at Yale and then at Columbia, states, "The orderly mood in America and its universities has changed. External and internal pressures of war in Indochina and the university expansion into poor urban communities outraged many students and educators. I recall wandering [around] the Columbia campus in the spring of 1968 before I entered the School of Architecture there the following fall. The atmosphere was confused and uncertain. This mood prevailed during my 2½ years there."

Israel is very much the child of the late sixties. For him, Venturi's first book was a milestone, and he is "still struck by Vincent Scully's image of Venturi in his introduction to the book as 'this generation's answer to the grandiose pretensions of modern architecture...Venturi shrugs his shoulders ruefully and moves on.'" Israel's Snell House is, by his own admission, "directly influenced by the work of Romaldo Giurgola" and by Venturi's "formal attitudes"; and he is also the only one of the new forty to admit direct influence from the 1966 catalog; to wit, Gio Pasanella's Lemon House. After finishing at Columbia, Israel worked for Pasanella, whose "critical guidance during the design and implementation [of the Snell House was] crucial. Pasanella demonstrated how an architectural work may complete itself; it is not necessary to detail everything."

Israel is the only genuine expatriate of the new forty, spending two years as a Fellow of the American Academy in Rome, and now working in London for Llewellyn, Davies as part of the design team for Shahestan Pahlavi, the new center of Tehran. Perhaps his distance from the American scene gives his view of it greater clarity than those of us mired in it: "If American architects have always been involved in a reinterpretation of the European past, then that time seems to be over. The original intention of sending architects to the American Academy in Rome was to 'bring IT home.' Today this process is reversing itself. In Italy and France architects look to America to learn. The Great New York Debate of Gray vs. White goes on in the cafes of Rome, Venturi is discussed with enthusiasm in Barcelona, and though the New York Five were battered last fall in London, their words and work are still being discussed there."

I began this essay with a question, and it seems not inappropriate to end with a question: What then, if anything, connects the new "40 Under 40," and distinguishes it from the generation just older? It seems to me that the new "40 Under 40" regard themselves as distant from the canonical modernism of the '20s and early '30s as from the orthodox modernism of the '50s and '60s. As Machado suggests, they feel as willing to re-explore the styles of the former, if not the latter, in a revivalist or eclectic way as they are willing to explore images found in pre-modern architecture, the vernacular, or in the applied consumer modernism of industrial design or the roadside strip. It can be inferred from many of the new forty that this sense of distance is liberating; eclecticism, or what Machado and Silvetti describe as "polyphonism," has been taken out of the architectural closet. At last, or perhaps once again, as in the Edwardian era of the late nineteenth and early twentieth centuries, architects are able to sustain "architecture without guilt...reintroducing into architecture the notions of seduction, eroticism, and pleasure (the designer's through his creation and the beholder's through the perception of the forms)."

The "sense of distance" from modernism surely is not reason enough to justify the sudden philosophical shift from the functional and technological determinism that forms the basis of modernist theory. Implicit in the new eclecticism is a growing sense that modern architecture as it has developed to date has been pitifully short on "meaning." This is particularly obvious, as Allan Greenberg points out, in those kinds of projects where the things modern architecture has been successful with—the manipulation of shape, natural light, interior space—count for precious little: that is, in the design of large-scale public buildings and of monuments. "Public buildings," Greenberg notes, "embody civic values, and in order to fully express the complex role played by the institution in our lives, a deep grasp of its function is essential." But that is not enough, because "when one compares the rich vocabulary and sophisticated levels of meaning, symbolism, and association achieved by architects of the past, using classical and Gothic forms . . . with the forms and meanings generated by modern buildings, it is clear that the architect of today labors at a distinct disadvantage." While Greenberg believes that "our tools are limited to scale, color, texture, signs, inscriptions and, to a very limited extent, mouldings . . . [and] the visual and iconographic richness of the past cannot be generated," others are prepared to delve into and borrow from earlier architectures where these qualities did exist in an effort to infuse their work with a vitality and meaning so generally regarded as absent from modernism. This process of design research and recycling is, of course, eclecticism.

One can put this a bit cynically, a bit sardonically, and a bit ruefully, as do George Hartman and Warren Cox, who define their position in a very American way: as "basically pragmatic until [we] start to design [when] avowed concerns of site, program and appropriateness . . . [seem] constantly undermined by the latest influence," leading them to recall the "immortal words of that not so immortal architect, Leopold Eidlitz, who said that: 'American architecture is the art of covering one thing with another to imitate a third thing, which if genuine would not be desirable.'"

Somewhat cryptically, James Righter reiterates Hartman and Cox's claims: "American architecture is eclectic. Eclecticism is choice. Vulnerability acknowledges many choices."

So it is, then, the "40 Under 40" of 1976 finds young American architects economically and culturally vulnerable and embarked on a search for direction in a time of transition. At least for myself, and I think for very many of the others included in this compilation, the cherished orthodoxies of the Modern Movement are being supplanted by new concerns and beliefs; while these may not yet define a theory of architecture, they do go a considerable distance toward mapping out a methodology of design. The following is a nonhierarchical outline of the beliefs that inform my own work; beliefs that I believe are shared to not inconsiderable extent by the "40 Under 40" architects:

1) Applied ornament is no crime.

2) Buildings that refer to other buildings in the history of architecture are more meaningful than those that do not (this used to be called "eclecticism").

3) Buildings that refer and defer to the buildings around them gain strength over those that do not (this might be called "contextual integration").

4) Buildings that associate with ideas about specific events that caused them to be made are more meaningful than those which do not; the pursuit of specific images to convey ideas about buildings is relevant to design.

5) Architecture is a storytelling or communicative art. Our facades are not diaphanous veils; nor are they the affirmation of deep structural secrets. They are mediators between buildings as "real" constructs, and those illusions and perceptions necessary to put buildings in closer contact with their social, cultural, and historical milieu.

While we do not seek to make a case for that simplistic eclecticism which has too often in the past substituted pat, predigested typological imagery for more incisive analysis, we do believe that a knowing integration of lessons learned from buildings we admire—and I refer not only to abstract organizational or structural strategies, but also to specific design elements—can enrich our own work, and thereby make it more familiar and, possibly, more meaningful to the people who use it. In the same way that we talk about functional programs which cause our work to emerge in a particular way, and about the constraints of site, budget, and so on, which also serve to shape it, we are willing to talk about the forms of earlier architecture which have spoken so directly to us that phrases of their language— fragments, if you will—have found their way into our own work just as fragments of the literature of the past have found their way into much of the poetry and prose of our time.

1976 "40 Under 40"

1. Diana Agrest and Mario Gandelsonas
2. Emilio Ambasz
3. Architects in Cahoots and Associates
4. Arquitectonica
5. Backen, Arrigoni & Ross, Inc.
6. Booth & Nagle
7. Peter de Bretteville
8. Peter Chermayeff
9. Chimacoff/Peterson
10. Stuart Cohen
11. Dagit/Saylor
12. Peter Gluck
13. Allan Greenberg
14. Gwathmey/Siegel
15. Frances Halsband
16. Hammond Beeby and Associates
17. Hardy Holzman Pfeiffer Associates
18. Hartman/Cox
19. Craig Hodgetts and Robert Mangurian
20. Peter J. Hoppner
21. Coy Howard

22. Franklin David Israel

23. Etel Thea Kramer

24. Levinson, Lebowitz, Zaprauskis

25. Donlyn Lyndon

26. Machado/Silvetti

27. Andrew Pierce MacNair

28. Robert Mittelstadt

29. Potters/Williams

30. James Volney Righter

31. Jon Michael Schwarting

32. Daniel Scully

33. David Sellers

34. Robert A. M. Stern

35. Susana Torre

36. William Turnbull, Jr.

37. Ueland and Junker

38. Peter David Waldman

39. Wells/Koetter/Dennis

40. Timothy Daniel Wood

II

On the Beaux-Arts Exhibition

1977

Editor's Note: The "Beaux-Arts Exhibition" forum held at the Institute for Architecture and Urban Studies on January 22, 1976, was a response to the Museum of Modern Art's exhibition Architecture of the École des Beaux-Arts, held October 29, 1975–January 4, 1976. William Ellis, an assistant professor of architecture at City College of New York and a fellow of the institute, edited comments by the forum participants for publication in *Oppositions.* The participants were George Baird, William J. Conklin, Ulrich Franzen, James S. Rossant, Paul Rudolph, Denise Scott Brown, Vincent Scully, Peter Smithson, Robert Venturi, Anthony Vidler, Henry Cobb, Arthur Drexler, and Robert Stern. Stern's response is excerpted here.

There has been a notable absence of serious speculation about whether the Beaux-Arts exhibition and, in a larger sense, the nineteenth-century academic tradition of Western architecture offer useful messages with regard to *context* today; and more importantly, whether or not present-day sensibilities correspond more to the late nineteenth century than to the so-called heroic period of modernism.

Most of the commentary inspired by the exhibition has ignored the relationship between the museum's decision to organize the exhibit at this time rather than ten years ago, when the historical investigations of Reyner Banham, William Jordy, and even my own began to call attention to the influence of the École's program on the early history of the Modern Movement, and when, through the examples of Louis Kahn's work, its influence was being felt in contemporary practice. The interest of a decade or so ago focused on the ordering principles of Beaux-Arts design rather than on its semantic implications. It was largely concerned with classicizing ideas of space-making rather than those lessons of image and decoration which seem more important today. Thus the question of timing seems critical. Had the museum presented a Beaux-Arts exhibition in 1965, its intentions might have been directed toward further buttressing its long-established advocacy of orthodox modernism. But its appearance in 1975 suggests that MoMA is attempting to reestablish its credentials in the rapidly changing post-modernist architectural scene.

It seems to me that the museum's timing is right, because, as I hope to make clear, architects seem ready to receive a diversity of images and messages from the nineteenth century. We are entering a period once again when architecture will become involved with symbolism and allusion as well as with issues of abstract formal composition. And for the first time in many years, architects seem capable of holding more than one idea of architecture in their heads at once without feeling guilty or schizoid. They are able to develop different solutions for different situations. Universal order is no longer a goal or even much talked about. Cultural pluralism and post-modernism go hand in hand. And this, more than any other single factor, seems to me to explain why post-modernist architects, as they emerge as a group, and *not* orthodox modernists can learn from and allude to historical precedent, in particular to that of the nineteenth century. Arthur Drexler seems to recognize this when he states in his very cautious preface to the catalogue that we would be well advised to examine our architectural priorities in light of an increased awareness and appreciation of the nature of architecture as it was understood in the nineteenth century.

So we are confronted by a provocative exhibition presented with virtually no reference to the cultural situation that a) presumably called it into being, b) caused it to be regarded as important, and c) caused it to be received so enthusiastically, if so uncritically. How very different, one might observe, from the then newly founded MoMA's first and to date most effective intervention in architecture—the Modern Architecture exhibit of 1932. That exhibition catalogue and the separate but simultaneously published book, *The International Style,* gave the new architecture an instant pedigree and provided the would-be modernist with what amounted to a handbook of how to think and design.[1]

Thus far the only substantive criticism of the Beaux-Arts exhibition to be published has focused on the drawings rather than on the buildings the drawings represent. But even these comments have not gone very far; thus it seems appropriate to make some observations at this time. The drawings are a mixed blessing. Some are beautiful. Many more, at least for me, are lugubrious and lifeless, especially when one compares them to real buildings. Even the best of them are not really beautiful enough to be in the Museum of Modern Art unless they are viewed in the context of executed work. They do, however, seem to offer the following lessons. First, the lesson of size. Without great size, a) the development of ornamental detail is impossible; b) it is difficult to include in the initial architectural conception those elements of design which give architecture its semantic character—the size, the plaques, the painted sculpture, and the carved symbols that mediate between the grandeur and abstraction of the overall design and the particularities of programmatic, urbanistic, and cultural content.

The second lesson is that of graphic appropriateness. The drawings in the exhibition are renderings rather than sketches, and if *charrettes* in the French studio system of the nineteenth century were anything like what they were in the waning days of the Beaux-Arts in America, not to mention today, the drawings are probably by no means the exclusive work of the architects whose projects are depicted. Nonetheless, they are full-dress examples of the kinds of drawings which are inextricably involved with the design values that the students and teachers of the École held dear. They are large in size and they are also to a remarkable extent perceptual rather than conceptual in intention. Though the Beaux-Arts knew about axonometric projection, to my knowledge it was used by Auguste Choisy—from whose book Le Corbusier picked it up—only as an analytical tool. For the purpose of design, as opposed to analysis, the plan was the focus of energy and concern. Drawn large, and with much attention lavished on the floor surface, the typical Beaux-Arts plan drawing was as decorated and embellished as the elevations and sections—at least one of which was cut along the axis perpendicular to the principal façade. The elevations and sections show the character of the building on its exterior and reveal the extent to which that character infused the bounding walls of the principal interior spaces.

The third lesson is that of color. One of the most obvious charms of the Beaux-Arts drawings we see in the museum is the use of delicate washes of color. The use of color is not a device to tart up the drawing, as in so much current rendering, but rather an element in the design process; an element we have lost and that we should probably seek to recapture.

A number of myths about twentieth-century architecture have gained such unquestioned currency that the nineteenth century has all too easily been weighed in the balance and found wanting, a conclusion that is unfair and uninformed.

The first myth is that of typological primacy; I will remind you only of the pitfalls that this particular notion has led architecture through: for example, the fifty-year-old search of the Modern Movement for typological perfection in the area of housing. As a result, we have watched the extinction of a noble tradition of housing design in Paris, Amsterdam, London, and New York, whose built examples, now fifty to a hundred years old, continue to function and to be admired, despite the polemic of the Modern Movement and CIAM; from the Beaux-Arts Parisian apartment house to the low-rise Beaux-Arts solutions of Clarence Stein, rich and humanistically responsible housing design was produced for all classes while the Modern Movement's polemicists, who preached reform, mass-production, and the like, have succeeded in producing very little in the way of housing that is admired outside its own circle. Ironically, the myth of typological primacy has recently been confounded by the architectural passion of the 1970s—the recycling of old buildings. Everybody is doing it, and it is an amusing about-face in light of the modernist search for the typological grail.

The second modernist myth, that of constructional honesty and technological responsiveness, seems as obvious as the sins that have been committed in its name. For me, the exhibition put to rest the unsubstantiated conviction that raw concrete and exposed brick or cinder block are beautiful, carry special values, or even hold some special morality. Certainly the general public has always preferred expressive camouflage to the "let it all hang out bare bones aesthetic."

The final myth is the criminality of ornament. First of all, Adolf Loos never really believed in it in his work, and I would rather put my money on the Kärntner Bar and the Josephine Baker House than on his rather contrary, narrow-minded essay on ornament, which few architects in the Anglo-Saxon world ever read before Reyner Banham's translation in the late 1950s. But more importantly, orthodox modernism never really believed in architecture without embellishment; only it surrendered that search for a semantically charged ornamental system, which every prior architecture had undertaken, in favor of an obsession with "integral" ornament: the ⅝-inch shadow joint, the veneered plane, the ubiquitous abstract easel painting, and small-scale constructivist sculpture.

The Beaux-Arts exhibition reminds us of the poverty of our orthodox modernist architecture. Trapped in hermetic abstraction, the Modern Movement fails us because it seals us off from the very cultural and visual connections that were the stock-in-trade not only of the Beaux-Arts but of nineteenth-century architectural pluralism—or eclecticism, if you prefer the word.

The nineteenth century believed in an architecture that did not concern itself merely with a functional, constructional, spatial fit. It struggled toward semantic articulateness. To the Vitruvian triad it added a fourth goal—appropriateness—and it is the continuous struggle to make forms which are meaningful in a broad cultural context that the architecture of the nineteenth century offers great lessons for today. Robert Venturi and Charles Moore began to redefine for us a modern position in architecture that draws on historic issues—modernism and nineteenth-century eclecticism—to establish a new working strategy that I will call post-modernism for want of a better term. I believe that to succeed, the postmodernist attitude must be re-established or re-affirmed, in word and deed; the beliefs which were implicit in the vast amount of architecture of the nineteenth century, especially the belief in the power of architecture to achieve symbolic meaning through allusion not only to other moments in architectural history but to historical and contemporary events of the social, political, and cultural nature, are central to the emerging post-modern position. And a post-modernist attitude must also carry with it an affirmation of belief that architecture is for the eye as well as the mind. Such seems to be our best hope for capturing the affection of our very disaffected constituency: the public. After all, architecture is not built sociology or even built theory. It is art, and I thank the Museum of Modern Art for giving us cause for the first time in a very long time to think about architecture as art again.

12

Drawing Towards a More Modern Architecture

1977

Two exhibitions of contemporary American architectural drawings being held in New York—at the Cooper-Hewitt Museum and at The Drawing Center from September 20, 1977, to November 6, 1977—underline the recently revived interest in architectural draftsmanship. To understand this revival, one has only to look to the current reassessments of the positivist dogmatisms of the Modern Movement. The increasingly relaxed and inclusivist view of architectural production has opened up broad perspectives formerly denied to architectural investigation. This new freedom has unleashed considerable creative energy—particularly among younger designers.

To give expression to this freedom, and to explore its potentials, some architects have turned to literature (for example, Bernard Tschumi) and painting (for example, Rem Koolhaas) as more appropriately immediate media in which to work. The consequence of these activities is reflected in the work selected for this issue of *Architectural Design*.

The drawings in these exhibitions transcend the conventions for uniformity and minimalism—which are part of an ingrained and self-defeating Modern Movement sensibility that supposedly guarded against ambiguity with a fine line drafting style that tried to tell it the way it really was, but which, to the utter confusion of all but the initiated, appeared to say next to nothing. Instead, these drawings reveal a range of techniques, which are richly evocative not only to those who view them, but also to those engaged in their production.

It is to this twofold power of drawings—to be the medium of creation for both the viewer and the designer—that these two exhibitions are addressed. The organizers of the two exhibitions, Richard Oliver at the Cooper-Hewitt and Robert Stern at The Drawing Center, trace in their respective essays the growth of a new sensibility in contemporary architectural draftsmanship and what it may mean to both architects and those who come in contact with architectural drawings....

Guest editor Robert A. M. Stern outlines the threefold purpose behind the selection and presentation of the drawings included in his exhibition, "Drawing Towards a More Modern Architecture." He also seeks to explain the recent renewal of interest in architectural drawings as an important tool in the design process. The leaders of the Modern Movement relegated drawings to second-class status and relied on three-dimensional scale models to develop their ideas in keeping with their formal preoccupation with the building as a freestanding object in space. With the waning of the Modern Movement and the emergence of a new approach to architecture, which Mr. Stern labels post-modernism, drawing has been restored to an important role in the conceptualizing process.

My purpose in selecting these drawings for exhibition and for publication in this catalogue is threefold at the very least:

1. To present a diversified selection of architectural drawings which will themselves be beautiful to look at and which will be illustrative of the variety of ways individual architects choose to express their ideas in two dimensions at this time. The drawings represent both holographic examples by the architects selected for inclusion in the exhibition and drawings by members of the architects' design staffs. They have been selected because they are the product of a design process that not only is important in terms of the current state of the art, but also one which sets considerable store on the act of drawing as a part of the conceptual process.

2. To illustrate the current situation in American architecture by means of drawings. It can be argued that the predominant tradition of Western architecture in this century—the Modern Movement and its International Style—is in its final, waning phase, and that a new attitude and perhaps even a new style tentatively described as "post-modernism" has begun to manifest itself in a serious way.[1] This exhibition focuses on the debate between the late modernist group and the Post-Modernists, a debate which has taken earlier form as one between "exclusivists" and "inclusivists," "Whites" and "Grays."

3. To extend the generally accepted perception of what constitutes an architectural drawing to include any number of strategies for the two-dimensional depiction of architectural ideas that have come to supplement the classic techniques of chalk, paint, pencil, pen, and ink.

The seemingly sudden surge of interest in architectural drawings, particularly in New York, bears some explanation. In the preface to the book *Two Hundred Years of American Architectural Drawings,* David Gebhard and Deborah Nevins offer one explanation for the American architects' lack of interest in drawing. They write:

> Intellectual content has never been a consistent strong point in the practice of architecture in the United States. The use of drawings to solve theoretical problems has been

until recently almost nonexistent. Elsewhere the built building has been only one aspect of the art of architecture and not always the most seminal position in the design of a building—regardless of the profundity or lack of profundity of intent. But in the United States the illusion of architecture as business has meant that drawing has been played down. The result has been that initial sketches have not been saved, and most architects have purposely eschewed the use of more formal methods of drawings.[2]

But the anti-intellectualism of American architectural practice that David Gebhard and Deborah Nevins describe does not sufficiently explain the Modern Movement's distrust of drawings. It does not explain why, for example, drawings had fallen into equal disrepute in Western European practice during the past forty or fifty years.

Two other explanations can be offered to clarify the Modern Movement's attitude toward drawings. The first explanation lies in the educational theory and formal preferences of those among its leadership who devoted themselves to teaching; the second lies in considering the larger issues of the relationship of the Modern Movement to the history of Modern architecture itself.

It now seems clear that the leading educators of the Modern Movement, such as Walter Gropius and Marcel Breuer, in their puritanical attack on what many now regard as the richness and diversity of the nineteenth- and twentieth-century architecture that preceded the revolution of the 1920s—but which the authors of that revolution quite understandably regarded as its excesses—relegated drawings to second-class status as "renderings," that is, tarted-up drawings expediently conceived for presentation (that is, selling) purposes after the conceptual process of a building's design was complete. Three-dimensional study and presentation models were emphasized at the expense of architectural drawings not only because these leaders were in reaction against the virtuoso draftsmanship fostered by many of their academic predecessors, but also because cardboard models more accurately mirrored what they believed to be the appropriate form-expression for Modern architecture (though of course they eschewed almost any discussion of style as such). White cardboard models, isolated on a broom-clean datum plane, encased in a glass or plastic display box, and raised off the floor on a pedestal, idealized and miniaturized the new architecture; the "weightless" cubism of the canonical International Style and the kind of models that could be easily fabricated in a university drafting room or an architect's office formed a perfect marriage of form, intention, and production capabilities. The miniaturized object quality of models not only focussed virtually all design energies on the problems raised by conceiving of buildings-in-the-round, but also diminished the potential for expression that a single wall plane, a "façade," might have in its own right, and the elaboration of detail based on structure was, at least in the canonical International Style, jettisoned in favor of the smooth, rendered stucco surfaces that mirrored the model-makers' craft to perfection; not without reason did Reyner Banham describe Gropius as "the great grey visage of the white cardboard style."

The second explanation for the hostility of the Modern Movement toward drawings is inextricably intertwined with the attitude toward ornament. Joseph Rykwert has pointed out that the Modern period has been torn between fundamentally opposed kinds of architecture: "that of the poets and that of the Polytechnicians," with the latter dominating the so-called Modern Movement of the middle third of this century.[3] The poetic side of Modern architecture and the focus of the Modern Movement's revolutionary ire was the École des Beaux-Arts. As Rykwert notes, "The final triumph of the Polytechnicians [was] a destructive attack on all ornament." And with the destruction of ornament came the destruction of the *raison d'être* for the kind of drawings that the École fostered: the lavishly embellished depictions of compositional elements (the plan, the façade, the section), all of them writ large and brilliantly polychromed.

Much more than the art of drawing was sacrificed when the Modern Movement jettisoned its "poetic" heritage of the nineteenth century. Kenneth Clark, in the 1943 essay "Ornament in Modern Architecture," observes that the decay of ornament can be traced "not to machines, but to the state of mind ... scientific or materialistic (just as we can call its converse religious or superstitious) according to its manifestations and our prejudices. Let us agree to call it the *measuring* or *quantitative* frame of mind. Now the measuring frame of mind ... is fatal to art, because art cannot be measured: and it is particularly fatal to public art—and architectural ornament is a form of public art—because there the test of measurement is most naturally applied."[4]

That loss of nerve, of confidence in the "image-making" or emblematic power of architecture that accompanied the emergence of the late nineteenth and early twentieth centuries' "measuring or quantitative frame of mind" was given powerful, if perverse, theoretical justification in the writings and work of Adolf Loos, whose classic essay "Ornament and Crime" codifies the false split between the pleasures of the intellect and the pleasures of the eye, and goes on to "integrate" ornament and architecture. He thereby established at the very inception of the Modern Movement that holistic view of architecture characteristic of the polytechnical mind; and when this was combined with the mechanomorphology of the canonical International Style, buildings became reduced to the category of machine parts.

This view of buildings in turn fosters the emphasis on three-dimensional models, as we have seen; it also encourages the use of axonometric projection—an analytical drawing tool wrenched by Le Corbusier from the textbooks of Auguste Choisy. The axonometric is a drawing of the polytechnician and not of the poet, not just because it involves measure (all architectural drawings are "measured" to some extent), but because it provides the designer and the observer with a conceptual rather than a perceptual view of buildings. No buildings have ever been seen in axonometric, whereas one can imagine a point in space where perspective drawing accurately mirrors the "real thing." Though the vertical surfaces of an axonometric are measurable, they are distorted in a way that is conceptual rather than perceptual; and the very use of the drawings (at least until John Hejduk developed his variation, which "accurately" projects one vertical plane) represented a deliberate attempt to jettison frontality in architecture in favor of the holistic notion of a total-object-in-space.

Thus one can claim that the rebirth of interest in drawing should not be seen so much as a manifestation of a new respect for theory on the part of the American architect, but as a manifestation of the shift from Modern Movement polytechnicism to Post-Modern Movement poetry; and if poetry is too presumptuous a term at this moment, at least one can say that in its concern with semantic issues, Post-Modernism seeks to recapture that emblematic quality and that confidence in architecture as an act of cultural affirmation, about which Sir Kenneth Clark wrote so convincingly.

As architects try to reweave the fabric of the Modern period, which was so badly rent by the puritan revolution of the Modern Movement, it is not surprising that the tradition represented by the École des Beaux-Arts—the poetic tradition of design—should be examined with renewed sympathy, and that one of the hallmarks of the École's design methodology, the beautiful drawing, should be restored to a position of influence. In this context of looking backward to go forward, a key event to trigger the release of so much of the drawing we now see was the exhibition of nineteenth-century drawings culled from the archives of the École des Beaux-Arts by Arthur Drexler and presented in 1975 at the Museum of Modern Art. While it is true that the rebirth of interest in drawings owes much to the example of Kahn, Rudolph, and Hejduk, among American architects, and to the influence from abroad of Rossi, Koolhaas, Vriesendorp, and Zenghelis, I think it safe to say that it is the Museum of Modern Art that has played the decisive role. The Beaux-Arts exhibit was the culmination of what seems in retrospect a systematic build-up—beginning with the exhibition of the work of the students of The Cooper Union (where Hejduk and his colleagues forged a new academy with a curriculum based on drawing as an analytical and design tool) and followed by the exhibition organized by Emilio Ambasz and called "Architectural Studies and Projects."[5] Ambasz's show did not seem particularly committed to any idea about the role of drawing in the design process or about the state of architecture; it seemed to place value on the drawings per se ahead of any value they might have as cultural documents.

Such, very definitely, was not the case with the Beaux-Arts exhibition, which seems to me to have been conceived by Drexler as a polemic against the Modern Movement and as a re-affirmation of a nineteenth-century attitude toward the semantic and poetic role of architecture, an attitude in which ornament functions as the communicator of cultural ideas and aesthetic intentions. The Beaux-Arts exhibit combined with the previous MoMA show to suggest that Modern architecture might find a way out of the dilemma of the late Modern Movement by entering a period when symbolism and allusion would take their place alongside issues of formal composition, functional fit, and constructional logic. In his introduction to the Beaux-Arts show catalogue, Drexler admonished that "we would be well advised to reexamine our architectural pieties" in light of an increased awareness and appreciation of the nature of architecture as it was understood in the nineteenth century.

The Beaux-Arts exhibition reminded us of the poverty of orthodox modern architecture: trapped in the narcissism of its obsession with the process of its own making, sealed off from everyday experience and from high culture alike by its abstraction and the narrowing of its frame of reference within the modern period to the canonical succession of events and images and personalities delimited by Giedion and Pevsner, and drained of energy as a result of a confusion between the values assigned to minimalism by a Mies van der Rohe with those assigned by an Emery Roth.

I have called this exhibition "Drawing Towards a More Modern Architecture" with not a little irony. Given the alarming state of the economy, especially as it affects the younger architects, those who wish to make things happen must do so as they can: small commissions; unbuilt projects; drawings for buildings that often go no further than that. These are the realities that undercut the otherwise exhilarating adventure of discovering architecture and architectural drawing again.

Cooper-Hewitt Participants

Bohlin & Powell—Peter Q. Bohlin and James D. Brown

Chimacoff & Peterson—Alan Chimacoff, Steven K. Peterson, and Barbara Littenberg Chimacoff

James Coote

Roger C. Ferri

Kliment & Halsband—R. M. Kliment and Frances Halsband

Lauretta Vinciarelli & Leonardo Fodera

Charles Moore—Charles W. Moore, William Grover, Robert Harper, Glen Arbonies

Venturi & Rauch

Allan Greenberg

Meltzer Oliver Solomon

Needham/McCaffrey—Janet Needham McCaffrey and Robin McCaffrey

Sheer/Torre—Susana Torre, Clinton Sheer

John Hejduk

George Ranalli

Robert A. M. Stern

Drawing Center Participants

Michael Graves

Gerald Allen

Stuart Cohen

Robert A. M. Stern

Venturi & Rauch

Peter Eisenman

Mitchell/Giurgola—Romaldo Giurgola

George Ranalli

Roger C. Ferri

Allan Greenberg

Hardy Holzman Pfeiffer Associates

John Hejduk

Coy Howard

Frank Israel

Kliment & Halsband

Rodolfo Machado

Meltzer Oliver Solomon

Charles Moore

Jorge Silvetti

Stanley Tigerman

13

After the Modern Movement
1977–1978

Modern architecture as we know it is in disarray: though such leading architects of the Modern Movement as Paul Rudolph, I. M. Pei, and Kevin Roche continue to produce major new work using the language of the International Style, the forms as well as theories on which they are based are systematically being questioned—and often rejected—by a growing number of younger architects who are trying to forge a philosophical basis for architecture and a new language of form that is described, for want of a better term, as "Post-Modern."

Though the origins of the Post-Modern movement can be traced back to the mid-1950s, it is only now gaining a serious audience among critics and the public at large. A recent spate of books and articles by architects and critics, including Brent Brolin's *Failure of Modern Architecture* (1975), Peter Blake's *Form Follows Fiasco* (1977), C. Ray Smith's *Supermannerism: New Attitudes in Post-Modern Architecture* (1977), and, most provocatively as well as most importantly, Charles Jencks's *Language of Post-Modern Architecture* (1977), share a belief that the predominant philosophic and stylistic system in Western architecture in this century—the Modern Movement and its International Style (commonly referred to over-simply as modern architecture)—is really only a phase in the 500-year history of architecture in the modern age, and a waning one at that.

Jencks is the first to embrace the new mood and to begin to erect a scaffolding of theory for Post-Modernism, a term which he suggests is at best "negative and evasive," so much so that Charles Moore, one of the movement's leading architects, was heard to opine after Jencks delivered a lecture at Yale last spring (1977): "Why must I be post anything; why can't I be pre-something?"

Despite its shortcomings, the term "Post-Modernism" has caught on. It is pretty clear that in the context of the architecture of the present it is shorthand for "Post-Modern Movement" architecture; that is to say, it refers to a new phase of modern architecture, and not to an end of the modern period itself. It describes a desire to return architecture to a more "normative" or culturally inclusive course of development than that charted by the pioneers of the Modern Movement—a movement Charles Moore has described as modern architecture's "Puritan Revolution." Post-Modernism seeks to look backward in order to go forward. It should not be regarded as an attempt to jettison modern architecture itself, but rather to pick up the strands of theory and style that were cut by the pioneers of the Modern Movement, especially the concerns for architectural history and the visually comprehensible relationships between old and new buildings. It is opposed to an architectural theory based exclusively on utilitarian functionalism and technological determinism.

One must take the Post-Modernist position seriously when Philip Johnson, America's most eminent architect, and one long associated in the eyes of both the profession and the public at large with modernism, not only states that in his view the Modern Movement has run out of gas, but also proceeds to design a neo–Beaux-Arts façade for an apartment building on Fifth Avenue. This façade, which Ada Louise Huxtable, America's most widely read architecture critic, characterizes as "Post-Modern," is a wildly eclectic combination of moldings, faux-mansard roof, and Chicago school bay windows that ten years ago would have seemed unimaginable from an architect of Johnson's stature. Today, it is a testament to the pervasiveness of the so-called Post-Modern position among our most thoughtful architects. It also marks a return to architecture as discourse: once again architecture is a conversation across time rather than a monosyllabic battle of ideologies.

It is important to briefly review the history of the Modern Movement and to re-examine the targets that are under attack by the Post-Modernists. The new Post-Modern generation should be seen in relation to the three generations of architects who constitute the Modern Movement. The first is the so-called "heroic" generation of *form-givers,* Le Corbusier and Mies van der Rohe most especially, who believed in architecture as a primary force in culture, even as a way to save the world. The second is the *formalists,* the refiners and redefiners of canonical International Style form, exemplified by Philip Johnson, Eero Saarinen, and Paul Rudolph, among other Americans who struggled to resolve the misfit between the theory and the formal language they inherited, and the volatile, inconsistent, and less than ideal situation they lived in—a period characterized by world war, unprecedented commercialization of the architectural profession, and global and urban crises—which combined to assign architecture, and particularly the idea of architecture as a way toward utopia, to a less central role as a shaper of man's destiny than the founders of the Modern Movement had suggested it should and would enjoy. While the heroic form-making ambitions of some and the technological bravura of others among this group no longer hold the same mystique of power and progress that they once did, a market for this work still exists—particularly in those so-called "developing" countries whose vision of America remains rooted to the values that many Americans rejected the night Lyndon Johnson told the nation that it could have guns and butter—war in Vietnam, peace and prosperity at home. Yet as Jencks puts it rather bluntly, it is precisely because the "International Style has been accepted on a massive scale by those who build cities . . . [and has become] the conventional style of the ruling class and its bureaucracy (at least for its large-scale offices and civic buildings) . . . [that] its use hardly ensures the same sincerity which preoccupied the pioneers of the style."[1] Philip Johnson is one of the new members of this second generation to criticize it from within, claiming that the pioneering advocates of the Modern Movement won their case "too fast and too quickly, and ended up with a bunch of cheap towers. We hooked onto economics as a way of selling it—[we believed] that modern architecture could save the world."[2]

The third or so-called "New-Modernist" generation, represented by Richard Meier and Peter Eisenman, has emerged as much in reaction to the permissive inclusivism of the Post-Modernists (whom they oppose) as to the dilution by the second generation of the fundamental philosophical and formal values initiated by the founders of the Modern Movement. Third-generation modernism seeks to revitalize the Modern Movement by renewing the process of purification and returning to the forms, if not always to the philosophical idealism that motivated European modernism in the 1920s and early 1930s. The machine-form cubism of Le Corbusier is being revived by Richard Meier even though Le Corbusier abandoned it as too abstract after World War II; the expressionistic glass-architecture projects of Mies van der Rohe are at last being realized by Cesar Pelli even though Mies changed his style radically when he actually began to build tall buildings in the United States; and the rigorous, highly cerebral propositions of such architects as Hannes Meyer and Giuseppe Terragni now influence Eisenman's search for an autonomous architectural form that is free not only of the technological and functional determinism of the Modern Movement, but also of any reference to culture or history itself.

While the second generation continues to command important commissions for new buildings both in the United States and abroad, it remains aloof from the fray, that is, the battle between the "New Modernists" and the Post-Modernists—sometimes described as the battle between the "Whites" and the "Grays"—which occupies the pages of the professional journals and the platforms of the major universities and the prestigious Institute for Architecture and Urban Studies in New York. This battle of styles is not unlike the one that took place in America in the 1930s during the last great economic depression, when the advocates of the Modern Movement struggled to have their point of view not only recognized but accepted over the prevailing "traditionalist" modes of design. It is an open secret today that for most architects, especially the younger ones in their thirties and forties, there has been no real prosperity in the 1970s; that this decade has been almost as disastrous for practice as was that of the 1930s.

But the battle of the 1970s between New Modernists and Post-Modernists is not without irony: the brave-new-world modernism of fifty years ago is now seen by the insurgent Post-Modernists as orthodox, stifling, and not a little irrelevant, while the New Modernists find themselves reviving a style, even though its founders rejected revivals and nostalgia of any sort and above all else rejected the very idea of style itself (Le Corbusier insisted that "styles are a lie"). Unlike New Modernism, however, Post-Modernism looks back and recognizes the legitimate role of nostalgia in design. But it is not a revival style in the narrow sense; at the same time, it does not seek to dump the immediate past. Because it is inclusive, it depends on forms and strategies from both the Modern Movement and the architecture that preceded it, though it declares the pastness of both. It is *a* modern style but not *the* modern style, and in its recognition of the transience and multiplicity of styles within the historical epoch we call modern, it also rejects that emphasis on unity of expression that was so central to the Modern Movement and its International Style. Post-Modern Movement architecture accepts diversity, it prefers hybrids over pure forms, it encourages multiple and simultaneous readings in its effort to heighten expressive content. In its emphasis on meaning, it rejects the idea of a single style in favor of the view that there are already many styles (and that new styles will continue to emerge), each of which has a particular and not a universal meaning. It recognizes, for example, that the International Style may be the most viable style for certain building types: offices, factories, and hospitals, perhaps for the houses of those among the rich who are interested in abstract art, but that it is not universally applicable, as has been the claim of its founders. For example, it has proven abysmally unsuccessful for theatrical and concert halls, both technically and atmospherically, as anyone who has visited just one of dozens of examples built all over the world since 1945 can attest.

With the emergence of Post-Modernism it is no longer enough for an architect to analyze a building program and a constructional system to yield a building design without considering the issue of image and style. As a result, the Post-Modern architect must be something of a scholar. As Jencks observes, he "must master several styles and codes of communication and vary these to suit the particular culture for which he is designing." The Post-Modern architect is therefore eclectic in the best and proper sense of the term: self-consciously selective about the relationship between form and content, acutely sensitive to the relationship between the production of shapes and the context of history and culture.

The origins of Post-Modernism can be traced back to a number of trends of the mid-1950s: the publication of a succession of revisionist histories broadening the definition of modern architecture to include all buildings of distinction, whether or not they were technologically innovative or distinguished precursors of the Modern Movement; the about-face of Le Corbusier with regard to his earlier work, as symbolized by his sculpturally inventive and metaphorically charged design for the Chapel at Ronchamp; and the articulation by Eero Saarinen—the second generation's most maverick talent—of a design philosophy called "the style-for-the-job," which, in its frank embrace of the symbolic function of architecture, flew in the face of the antistyle biases of the Modern Movement.

Nonetheless, it was not until the publication in 1966 of Robert Venturi's book *Complexity and Contradiction in Architecture* that the first major Post-Modern chord was struck. In the years since its publication this book has established itself as one of the century's most influential architectural texts. With Denise Scott Brown and Steve Izenour, Venturi extended the discussion in a second book, *Learning from Las Vegas,* published in 1974. Venturi was joined in his extended attack on the orthodox modernism of the '50s and '60s by Charles Moore, whose important articles of the mid-'60s were finally collected in 1976 and made available as the book *Dimensions.*

Against the background of the zenith of American second-generation modernism and its underlying belief in the power of minimalism based on Mies van der Rohe's cryptic and improbable utterance "Less is More," Venturi proclaimed that "Less is a Bore," calling into question what he dubbed the "exclusivist" attitude of orthodox modern architecture. The exclusivist attitude has at its core a conviction that the design of buildings is responsible to nothing outside the process of programmatic accommodation and technological efficiency. It reduces architecture to a private conversation between clients, architects, and engineers instead of opening up a public one using familiar and widely understood forms in new ways to make new statements. Having become abstract and elitist, Venturi and others argue, orthodox modern architecture has become increasingly inarticulate; in abandoning its traditional iconographic role, it falls back on problem-solving and technological expertise, areas in which social scientists and civil engineers can and do effectively undercut the architect's power base. Modern Movement architects have been content to make things and let history assign meanings (which the marketplace and the man in the street have been only too happy to do: "poor man's style," "factory style," "hospital style" are well-known terms used to describe the most "advanced" production of the recent past). Venturi, Jencks, and others have suggested that this historically unprecedented act of cultural aloofness and formal narcissism has been the Modern Movement's very undoing.

In opposition to exclusivism, Venturi offered a point of view that, not surprisingly, he labeled "inclusivist." This point of view is at the heart of Post-Modernism. It seeks a redefinition of architecture through the acceptance of what Venturi has characterized as the "complexity and contradiction" of modern life. Again in response to Mies's minimizing dictum, Venturi says, "More is not Less."

Inclusivism rejects the Modern Movement's aloof and heroic stance with regard to the realities of day-to-day living in favor of a more modest and flexible position by which architecture embodies values that are supported by society and not just other architects. Inclusivist design struggles to approach each problem on its own terms and rejects the prototypical solution in favor of the individual case.

Post-Modernism also rejects the abstraction of the Modern Movement's International Style in favor of a return to "representational" as a key element in communication. Charles Moore, for example, states that his recent design for a fountain at the Piazza d'Italia in New Orleans is "shaped like the map of Italy (only very slightly abstracted), with the five architectural orders on the wall surrounding it rendered, not exactly standardly, but certainly quite specifically in stainless steel and water, [while] ten years ago, in parallel circumstances at Lawrence Halprin's Lovejoy Plaza, in Portland, Oregon, we had *abstracted* a mountain waterfall into a set of concrete steps over which the water splashed and would have found a more specific recall of the High Sierra unnecessary, and just a little tacky."

The importance of this shift from abstraction to representation cannot be overstated; with marvelous irony it has been in no small way reinforced by the exhibition of student drawings from the École des Beaux-Arts, which Arthur Drexler organized in 1975 at the very temple of abstraction, the Museum of Modern Art in New York. Drexler's show was at first greeted with confusion and suspicion by architects and critics; but, unlike most of the museum's architecture shows, which have been "box-office poison," this one was well attended—a sure sign of its special appeal to the public at large. And now even the critical establishment is coming to appreciate the powerful statement Drexler intended it to make. Philip Johnson, the founder of the museum's Department of Architecture and Drexler's predecessor as its director, states that in organizing the Beaux-Arts exhibition, Drexler "did a very stirring and controversial thing by showing that modernism isn't any longer the line that has to be followed."

Drexler's next exhibition, "Transformations in Modern Architecture," scheduled to open in 1979, promises to complement the historical emphasis of the Beaux-Arts show with a major reassessment of the state of modern architecture. Given that the museum introduced the Modern Movement and its International Style to the American public in 1932, and has consistently advocated its cause since, this exhibit could become a signal event in the unfolding of the new Post-Modern Movement.

It is now pretty clear that twenty years after its initial formulation, Post-Modernism has begun to take on the paradigmatic aspects of a style. As such it is not circumscribed by a narrow list of visual do's and don'ts like those of the International Style as enunciated by Hitchcock and Johnson in 1932, but one guided by three attitudes which, though they define an approach—a theory even—do not force the architect to adopt any particular set of formal tropes.

The three attitudes or principles of Post-Modernism are as follows: *Contextualism, Allusionism,* and *Ornamentalism.*

Contextualism recognizes that the individual building is a fragment of a larger whole.
Post-Modern architects prefer incomplete or compromised geometries to pure forms; moreover, they seek to make new buildings that "fit in" to their surroundings, whether natural or man-made, and they also seek to make them partly a commentary on the history of architecture itself; in so doing they extend the conversation of architecture across time. A key work illuminating the idea of contextualism is Venturi and Rauch's Guild House of 1960–65, a modest-sized apartment house that uses conventional elements in unconventional ways to yield a double reading between physical and historical context, thereby expressing the ambiguous relationship between the context of the place, the specifics of the program, and compositional ideals. At Guild House the contextual approach to design operates at both the level of high art and popular art: compositional strategies based on Michelangelo's handling of windows at the back of St. Peter's and Philibert de l'Orme's gatehouse at the Château at Anet are combined with those taken from ordinary 1920s apartment house plans. The use of common red brick makes an obvious connection with the surrounding nineteenth-century warehouses, as well as the mediocre public row housing which bounds the site and also characterizes it. Together these make for a building that is at once serviceable, matter-of-fact, and extraordinarily subtle.

Allusionism: architecture as an art of historical and cultural response.
Allusion is the means by which Post-Modernist architects achieve the visual aspects of contextualism. It is at the core of the new sensibility. Though it employs eclecticism—banished from "polite" architecture by the Modern Movement—it is not to be confused with that simplistic eclecticism of either style or taste that has too often in the past substituted pat, predigested imagery for more incisive analysis. Nineteenth-century eclecticism was often a process by which either a whole style or the work of a particular architect was evoked—sometimes to make a point, but just as often as not merely to look good. To be allusionistic—or radically eclectic, as Jencks calls it—demands more than that: it demands that architecture communicate meaning through metaphor *and* by direct reference

("quotation"); as Jencks puts it: "Various parts, styles or sub-systems (existing in a previous context) are used in a new, creative synthesis"; each part must find a "semantic justification"—that is, each part quoted or alluded to must mean something in terms of program, context, and the individual cultural aspirations of the client, as well as those acceptable to the community at large.

The Post-Modernist examination of and increasingly frequent deference to historical precedent grows out of the conviction that appropriate references to historical architecture can enrich new work and thereby make it more familiar, accessible, and visibly more meaningful to the people who use buildings. Charles Moore and Richard Oliver write:

> Modern architecture as purification rite seems to have run its course, and architectural historians (and even some architects) are urging us toward a "radical eclecticism" or a serious search for stereotype as a way of making architecture which communicates with (or better, is inhabitable by) possible users. At such a time as this a yearning to connect with these simpler pleasures seems not abnormal at all, but a way of finding ourselves. Nostalgia . . . may turn out to be a rough equivalent of tradition, a force so summarily (and so disastrously) dismissed by Modern architecture.[3]

So far, the use of quotation has been tentative, and sometimes a little obscure, as in Moore's use of wooden Tuscan columns to support his house at Orinda, California, and Venturi and Rauch's outrageously scaled neo-Ionic wooden column supporting one corner of their addition to Oberlin College's Allen Art Museum. But Moore's use of Mexican-style plastic patio tiles to pave the courtyard of the Lee Burns house in Santa Monica and Venturi and Rauch's use of a "Palladian" window to help transform what is a modest neo–fisherman's cottage to the status of "rich man's" summer house for the Trubek family in Nantucket are quite explicit examples and do not require a Ph.D. in art history to be understood.

Perhaps somewhat less accessible has been the use of a broad strategy of eclecticism to suggest earlier styles: the use of light yellow paint in combination with wood molding on the façade of the Lang House to evoke the owners' love for South German baroque architecture and the architects' love of Palladio's Villa Barbaro at Maser (though the moldings are based on an Eton College façade) while also distracting the eye from the exemplary ordinariness of the otherwise plain façade; the combination of an Italian garden in the form of a map of Italy, with a mock monumental column screen to give appropriately Italian embellishment to the forecourt of an undistinguished office tower in New Orleans (the project was commissioned by a group of Italian-Americans as a gift to the city). Moore does not give us the Italy of the history books but rather that of Hollywood: any minute now Ann Miller and eighty chorus boys from *Kiss Me Kate* could well be tapping their feet to the Cole Porter tunes.

Venturi and Rauch's two new houses for the Brant family, both designed and in construction at the same time, are in completely different styles in response to their different locations, directly refuting the Modern Movement's belief in universal solutions and the irrelevance of issues of style. Each combines literal quotation with mood. One, in Bermuda, is in the "Bermuda cottage" style; the other, a ski house in Colorado, looks like something a good Viennese Secessionist architect might have done with the commission in about 1910.

Ornamentalism: the wall as the medium of architectural meaning.

The Modern Movement became so obsessed with the idea of architecture as space that the art of designing vertical surfaces (walls) was given up and thereby became the realm of interior decorators who, as a result, rightly asked to be called interior designers. The enhancement of the vertical plane need not always be justified in historical or cultural terms. At the very least the embellished wall is a response to an innate need for elaboration and for the articulation of a building's elements in relation to human size. In the work of Michael Graves, chair rails, base boards, "false" and "real" windows and doors are all composed to achieve what might seem, at first viewing, an improbable marriage between cubist abstraction and humanistically based anthropomorphism: to a remarkable extent Graves makes Le Corbusier "talk" in the language of Soane.

Venturi first used applied ornament to give a large and appropriately public scale to a modestly scaled institutional building in Ambler, Pennsylvania. The introduction of supergraphics by Moore and his associates at the Sea Ranch Swim Club has already become a standard—a commercialized and now regrettably trivialized decorating response to the inarticulate Modern Movement interior. In his own house in New Haven, Moore used layered plywood panels to make ornament at a variety of scales and provide places for the inclusion of personal possessions, whether ancestor portraits or knickknacks one picks up at the flea markets of the world, things that may be ugly but are also meaningful, like wedding gifts from good friends, too often banished to attic storage in the service of modernist minimalism.

Venturi and Rauch's Brant House at Greenwich, Connecticut, is a veritable handbook of Post-Modern attitudes toward ornament: the very artfulness of the brick pattern declares frontality (though the house is freestanding, it is not an object-in-the-round; yet its "front" is not its entrance side); the grandness of the brick gives the house a proper "estate" image; the clapboarding de-emphasizes the rear and connects the house with New England cottages; the green color fuses the house and the landscape without sacrificing its integrity as a manmade object. This hybrid vocabulary is no more improbable than is the owners' diversified collection of early American and art deco furniture and pop art that is housed within.

I have written these words in the belief that the Modern Movement has run its course. Design is, in part, a process of cultural assimilation. Though it includes problem-solving, the functional and technological paradigms for the vast majority of situations with which we deal are established. Our task is to question the formal paradigms that dog us at what can be regarded as the close of the Modern Movement. Such questioning must come not only from the wellspring of an individual architect's "talent," but also from a knowledge of history, a concern for the state of the architectural art at a given moment, and a serious respect for the aspirations and intelligence of clients. It must be continuously reaffirmed that individual buildings, no matter how remotely situated from other works of architecture, form part of a cultural and physical context. What is more, architects are obliged to acknowledge these connections not only in their words, but also in their deeds—that is, in the combination of forms they establish and, perhaps too casually, call "design."

As a culture, as architects, we know so very much. What must be done is to face this knowledge squarely—and in so doing, face the world around us, taking it for what it is, incrementally adapting the objects and ideas in it to our needs while we in turn adapt to its demands. My attitude toward form, based on a love for, and knowledge of, history, is not concerned with accurate replication—though I believe that certain situations make this an appropriate strategy. It is eclectic and uses collage and juxtaposition as techniques to give new meaning to familiar shapes and, in so doing, to cover new ground. Mine is a confidence in the power of memory (history) combined with the action of people (function) to infuse design with richness and meaning. If architecture is to succeed in its efforts to participate creatively in the present, it must go beyond the iconoclasm of the Modern Movement and recapture for itself a basis in culture and the fullest possible reading of its own past.

14

Venturi and Rauch
Learning to Love Them
1978

It is ten years and a little more since the Museum of Modern Art's publication of Robert Venturi's book *Complexity and Contradiction in Architecture;* sixteen years have gone by since Venturi's very important project for the Franklin D. Roosevelt Memorial was first published by Thomas Creighton; and it is also sixteen years since Venturi's important early work was published in the "Philadelphia School" issue of *Progressive Architecture* and Vincent Scully selected him for inclusion in a group of talented young architects that he assembled for *Art in America*. Twenty-four years ago Venturi published his first article, an essay on the Campidoglio.[1]

I am listing these bits and pieces of chronology because they seem to suggest that the time is right—if not even overdue—for a monograph on the public work of Venturi and his partners: their work represents a solid if not necessarily consistent line of development over almost a quarter of a century. Theirs is one of the seminal contributions to the architecture of our time.

The quarter-century of thinking and making architecture that is mirrored, at least in some small part, in *Venturi and Rauch: The Public Buildings* constitutes the first systematic attack on orthodox modern architecture, which is more usually referred to in Europe as the Modern Movement (with all the moral and political urgency that such a label implies) and in the United States as the International Style (with all the emphasis on the appearance of things that the use of the word *style* suggests).

Venturi's 1953 article on the Campidoglio struck the opening chord of the Post-Modern Movement. Flying in the face of the object fixation of the late International Style, he wrote that "the architect has a responsibility toward the landscape, which he can subtly enhance or impair, for we see in perceptual wholes, and the introduction of any new buildings will change the character of all other elements in a scene." The subsequent books and essays written by Venturi and his associates have restored to architecture its role as a self-conscious communicator of ideas; the semantic dimension of Post-Modernism would be unthinkable without the example of their writings or buildings.

Venturi and Rauch stand for a number of things in American practice that were notably absent in the post–World War II building boom. The emergence of the firm must be seen against the irony of America's acceptance of the International Style as the appropriate expression for commercial and corporate projects, and its ultimate demise, which we are now witnessing, and which the commercialization of the Modern Movement surely hastened, as Venturi and partners point out in their essay "From La Tourette to Neiman-Marcus" in *Learning from Las Vegas*.[2]

Venturi and Rauch stand for art in relationship to commerce, rather than art in the service of commerce; they stand for architecture as an intellectual and artistic pursuit. They take and often they formulate polemical positions not for their own sake but in order to strip naked the pretentiously clothed insufficiencies of the architecture around us. Their praise for Co-op City, though exaggerated, offers significant observations about the relationship between production and style in housing, and their comparison of their own Guild House with Paul Rudolph's Crawford Manor is a rare example of frank (if a trifle belligerent) criticism by one architect of another's work. Together these essays present a comprehensive view of the issues revolving around housing as architecture, which includes a serious consideration of economics and available technologies but, in the final analysis, rests on the more profound consideration of the "content of the image" and the "method used to achieve image."[3]

Because Venturi and Rauch willingly express their ideas clearly and forcefully, they have exposed themselves to some of the most virulent attacks imaginable by their fellow professionals. For this alone, architecture is in their debt; together with the Smithsons and perhaps one or two others they have established a situation in which it is possible for architecture to become a pursuit of the mind as well as the crayon. They have made us see once again that our architecture must become an act of belief as well as an act of creativity: their work has been at once a rejection of the empty formalisms of mid-century practice and a reinvocation of the larger meanings which the history of architecture represents.

Venturi and Rauch stand for cultural pluralism in addition to, and at the service of, their polemics and their architecture. Denise Scott Brown has written convincingly about design as an act of research into what one sees, rather than what one wants to see. But more importantly, together with Robert Venturi she has mined the recent past and our contemporary scene in a thoroughly admirable and quite successful attempt to adumbrate a genuine body of precedent and theory upon which to rebuild our concept of architecture; in its inclusiveness, such precedent and theory must be contrasted with the idiosyncratic genealogy of the Modern Movement traced by Giedion and Pevsner and with the pseudo-theory of that movement—the spurious functional and technological determinism which has plagued the architecture of the rank-and-file modernists for the past fifty years.

Venturi and Rauch have undertaken what only a very few art historians and critics have attempted to do, even though, at least in theory, that is their job:

they have begun the arduous task of reweaving the fabric of modern architecture, putting back into place the threads that were pulled out because they did not fit into the grand, if rather too thin, fabric of the Modern Movement's International Style. As a result of their work, Lutyens and Le Corbusier, Nolli's Rome and Bugsy Siegel's Las Vegas, Irwin Miller's town and Mr. Levitt's subdivision—for too long seen as contradictory, if not opposed phenomena—can now be seen as complexly related parts of the culture of our time.

The work of Venturi and Rauch is the product of a collaboration. Seen from the outside, it would appear that, of the partners, John Rauch brings to the firm a certain realism; Denise Scott Brown, an impatient intelligence, a creative and seemingly perpetual state of moral indignation; while Robert Venturi brings to it one of the distinguished artistic talents of his generation. Together with their other close associates, especially Steve Izenour and their late partner Gerod Clark, the principals of the firm stand for something exceptional in American practice, now as ever: art and theory uniting behind a desire to build.

Despite the very real nature of the collaboration, I think it fair to say that Venturi is the firm's leader and a very fine architect in his own right. His is the design talent, the "eye" if you will, and not only the eye, but an eye connected to a superb intelligence. One need only read Venturi's early writings, the Campidoglio article, and, more importantly, *Complexity and Contradiction in Architecture,* and study the early buildings and projects to grasp his contribution to the firm and to architecture in general: the relationship between his wonderful observations about the history and theory of architecture, which occur on virtually every page of *Complexity and Contradiction,* and the early work, such as the Vanna Venturi House, the Guild House, and the projected houses for Millard Meiss, for D'Agostino and Wike, set extraordinary standards for any of us who would write and build.

So much has been made of the "theory" by critics and, I regret, sometimes by members of the firm—especially as it is articulated in *Learning from Las Vegas,* which is, for me, a bit overblown and supercharged—that on occasion the buildings tend to be regarded as "built-theory" rather than as "architecture." In recent work, the urge to make beautiful buildings has been permitted to give way to the urge to build theory. For example, at the Humanities Building at Purchase, the intended irony of the forms, which seem to make puns on the architecture of the typical middle-brow suburban International Style school building of the 1950s, is lost on many of the users, who are only too familiar with the "original" and who see the Humanities Building as just so much more of the same.

On the other hand, stylishness often overwhelms theory: the addition to the Allen Art Museum at Oberlin is a marvelous building in its own right, but its deference to the original Italianate design by Cass Gilbert is merely perfunctory. Careful readings of the Venturi and Rauch theory—for example, their discussion of eclecticism—lead one to think that a building that actually looked like the Gilbert design would have been the more appropriate and natural result of their process. As it now stands, the Oberlin addition is a comment on Gilbert's design but not a logical extension of it. In this sense it is a mannered example of late orthodox modernism and falls short of the radical eclecticism that may well be the hallmark of a renewed architecture seeking to recapture its semantic role and to reintegrate itself into the larger context of buildings and history.

Given the scope of their innovation, who can blame them if the work of the firm has not always been as much as one would hope for? They are the New Pioneers, to use an old label coined by Henry-Russell Hitchcock in a new context; that they have not yet become the "New Traditionalists," which so much of their theory suggests they might be, is troublesome but understandable. Too often, the architecture of Venturi and Rauch continues to speak in the private language that has plagued us since the time of the Modern Movement and which, it seems to me at least, an architecture that is truly dumb and ordinary must eschew.

15

New York, New York
Pluralism and Its Possibilities
1979

Unquestionably, New York is the center of architecture in the United States. Though this is not as true as it once was from the point of view of the volume of its production (before the depression of the early 1970s, there were almost as many practicing architects in New York as in the rest of the country), it is indisputably so in regard to the production of ideas and to the establishment of trends: architecture as an art thrives in New York; which is as it should be, given New York's role as the leading American cultural center.

In this essay I would like to concentrate on representative institutions and phenomena which characterize New York's role and which are unique to it. Not only is New York important because it is the home of some of the more provocative architectural formalists of our time, it also is the nation's architectural communications center, housing its professional press as well as two of the best among the handful of journalists who write architectural criticism in the newspapers; it is home to some key educational and cultural institutions; it is attractive to expatriated foreigners who guarantee to it a lively mosaic of conflicting ideologies; and its impact reaches out into neighboring smaller architectural centers such as Princeton, New Jersey, and New Haven, Connecticut. In attempting to capture the essence of the New York architectural scene I of course touch on the role key architects play, but it seems to me at this time that the work they produce would not be what it is were it not for their interaction with its institutions, and that, therefore, the latter should be the principal focus of my remarks.

Before beginning the main theme of the essay, a word or two about the nature of practice in New York and the role of the "big," "corporate" offices seems appropriate. The shift of ideology from "modernism" to what is now called "postmodernism" that characterizes the events of the past five or six years has left most of the larger firms in the lurch. It is not that they do not build; quite the contrary, they build as much if not more than before, exporting to the oil-rich Eastern world the painfully tired abstractions of the late International Style that have come to symbolize cultural ennui as well as environmental profligacy at home, if not yet abroad. How ironic that the commercialized modernism of the 1950s and '60s, which has lost virtually all its mystique at home, continues to represent power and wealth to the newly rich nations of the OPEC world seeking to establish their place under a capitalist sun.

A few of the larger firms continue to build important work at home. I. M. Pei and Partners is surely the most prestigious of these: yet the critical and popular success of their East Building for the National Gallery of Art in Washington, D.C., not unlike that of the hotels of John Portman and the Crystal Court in Minneapolis by Philip Johnson and John Burgee, seems not so much an endorsement of modernism as a reiteration of the public's continuing faith in public buildings that are obviously public in their character and frankly sensual in their effects. Nonetheless, as critics such as some of those writing in a recent issue of *Progressive Architecture* or in some of the art journals have observed, Pei's building—perhaps the last important "modern" building—is as conservative today as John Russell Pope's classical design for the original National Gallery was at its completion in 1941.[1] Its use of the diagonal geometry that emanated from Philadelphia in the early 1960s seems contrived; it is in many ways, to paraphrase the title of a sensational novel of the late 1950s, a 94.5 million dollar misunderstanding. The East Building is conceptually not very dissimilar from Carlin and Millard's Central Fire Station in New Haven, Connecticut, first published in 1961, with the service towers that house fire hose, fire stairs, and the like now housing galleries for the art, while crowds of visitors in the public concourse "stand-in" for the fire trucks in the apparatus room.[2] It will be interesting to see in which direction Pei proceeds in his native China, which has enlisted his services, a by-product of the new "normalization" of relations with the United States that has recently begun.

Of the large offices, the one that seems most provocative and polemical is that of Philip Johnson and his partner John Burgee. Johnson and Burgee have absorbed many of the ideas of the postmodernists into their work. Their most sensational proposal, the projected headquarters building for the American Telephone and Telegraph Corporation (AT&T), has received an unusually high level of publicity for a building that is, in terms of its program, merely a routine office building. Its overtly historicizing character and its self-conscious attempt to revive premodernist attitudes to the design of the tall building surely contribute to AT&T's notoriety. But its special relevance is the by-product of the role its principal designer, Philip Johnson, plays in the New York architectural scene. His recent "conversion" to the postmodernist sensibility—which owes not a little to his own earlier buildings and writings—has lent the argument on its behalf considerable credibility.[3] His statements in the press and his infrequent public lectures—for example, those at the architecture school of Columbia University in September 1975 and again in January 1979, at Yale University in October 1978, and at the Institute for Architecture and Urban Studies (IAUS), where he has participated in informal discussions at various times with Charles Jencks, Peter Eisenman, and myself—have not only brought the new sensibility to the public's attention but lent it prestige. His role in this

New York, New York

regard is quite similar to George Howe's in introducing the modernist sensibility to American practice in the late 1920s and early 1930s.[4]

Even without the issue of modernism's decline and the emerging postmodernism, the New York scene would surely be considerably dimmer without Johnson: by word and deed he has stood for an architecture that is at once pragmatic and philosophical, while so many of his peers have stood for a more conventional kind of success. Just as Johnson's support of the Museum of Modern Art in the 1930s was critical to the success of modernism in the United States, his patronage of the IAUS since its founding in 1967 has been decisive in the establishment of that unique force. (In fact, in 1965 and 1966, Johnson frequently spoke of retiring from architecture, and founding and directing such an institution himself.)

The IAUS has its headquarters at the top of a loft building in midtown, across from the New York Public Library and affording an unforgettable view of Raymond Hood's American Radiator Building. The Institute is a research and educational enterprise whose audience includes high school students enrolled in vacation-time summer courses, college and university students studying the history, theory, and design of buildings for academic credit, post-graduate architects keeping in touch with the shifting sands of ideology, and a substantial group of laypeople merely interested in learning about architecture. The Institute also publishes an important if sometimes somewhat esoteric journal, *Oppositions,* which is surely the preeminent American journal devoted to architectural ideas. Its exhibition program, though modest in scale, is stimulating and is becoming better known as a result of a new series of catalogs, the first of which has recently been published.[5]

The Institute has from time to time become involved in research projects of its own, such as its ambitious study of the street as a typology.[6] On one occasion it has engaged in an actual building project: the Marcus Garvey Village, built in a devastated urban battleground in the outer borough of Brooklyn. Marcus Garvey reflects the strengths and weaknesses of the IAUS in its social intentions: it is an admirably pragmatic response to conditions which are generic to most older Anglo-American cities; in its minimalist formal language, however, it is intractably modernist and leaves quite wide the gap between the finished product and the suburban aspirations of its inhabitants.[7]

The IAUS was founded by and is headed by Peter Eisenman, an architect whose strong personality and incisive intelligence continue to dominate it, despite the fact that others contribute to its day-to-day operation and to its programs: Peter Wolf, an urban planner, is the Institute's chairman; Charles Gwathmey, a practicing architect, has taken an active position in his capacity as president of its board; Kenneth Frampton and Anthony Vidler, Englishmen now based in New York, and Mario Gandelsonas, from Argentina, each an architect-theorist, edit *Oppositions* along with Eisenman and oversee the public lecture programs; Andrew MacNair, assisted by Craig Owen, edits *Skyline,* a brilliant newspaper devoted exclusively to architecture and the related visual arts and largely written by young architects and critics.

Two museums play a critical role in the New York architectural scene: the Museum of Modern Art and the Cooper-Hewitt Museum. Of these, the Museum of Modern Art, which established its Department of Architecture in 1931, is preeminent, although the Cooper-Hewitt, newly reestablished as the National Museum of Design under the auspices of the Smithsonian Institution and now located in the former mansion of Andrew Carnegie, is attempting to become an important rival.[8] MoMA's architecture department is headed by Arthur Drexler, who succeeded Philip Johnson, its first director. While Drexler's exhibition program of the late 1950s and '60s continued to explore the major themes of modernism and the work of such masters as Wright, Le Corbusier, and Kahn, his publication in 1966 of Robert Venturi's book *Complexity and Contradiction in Architecture* signaled a major shift away from the modernist ideology, which had been hitherto inviolate at the museum. This shift has since had as its principal manifestation the exhibition in 1975 of nineteenth-century drawings from the École des Beaux-Arts in Paris and the comprehensive catalog of that exhibition, which appeared in 1977.[9] The Beaux-Arts exhibition sent a mild shock wave through the profession as a discussion held at the IAUS in early 1976 suggests.[10] Equally importantly, it brought the issues of the shift of values away from modernism out for public and professional discussion. Interestingly, the Beaux-Arts show was the first architecture exhibition at MoMA ever to attract a wide audience outside the profession.

In 1977 and 1978, Drexler organized a series of small seminars at MoMA to which members of the profession were invited for discussion. Drexler also organized small exhibitions in the museum's Goodwin Galleries to reawaken interest in aspects of early twentieth-century architecture, which had been cast into near-oblivion by the Modern Movement's overwhelmingly successful bid for ideological and stylistic hegemony: Stuart Wrede was guest curator for an exhibition of the work of Gunnar Asplund, which revealed that the work of this minor master before and after his flirtation with the International Style in the early 1930s was far more interesting than had been remembered; Allan Greenberg was guest curator for an exhibition of Sir Edwin Lutyens's architecture, which impressed all but the most ideologically rigid modernists with the talent of this until recently ignored architect. Given Drexler's early support of Venturi's book, and his interest in nineteenth-century classicism, the exhibition of Lutyens's work should not have come as much of a surprise. Nonetheless, it provoked considerable consternation in the corridors of the IAUS, where some viewed it as a kind of reverse Stalinist revisionism; on the other hand, Greenberg was invited by the New York office of SOM to lecture to its designers about the new classicism he advocates.[11]

The culmination of Drexler's four-year revisionist process is the museum's current architecture exhibition, its first major effort since the Beaux-Arts show. This exhibition, called "Transformations in Modern Architecture," is extraordinarily comprehensive, illustrating over 300 buildings, largely from the United States, England, and Japan, although Germany, France, Spain, and Italy, among others, are also represented. While the variety of work in the exhibition may suggest to the casual viewer that there is no strong point of view, careful study of Drexler's text and of the juxtaposing of the exhibited buildings reveals a trenchant critique of late modernism and a sympathetic presentation of the postmodernist position. Those in search of a new doctrine will be disappointed, though the focus on Venturi's and James Stirling's work among living architects can be seen as a revelation of Drexler's biases. The extensive and isolated presentation of work using mirrored glass seems odd in the context of the show—though Drexler admits to a special fascination with this material (and the PPG Foundation lent the show financial support). Surprisingly absent from Drexler's written text is any specific recognition of the shift away from abstraction and nonrepresentation, and the semiological aspect of much current production is ignored; though many of the buildings presented are intended to contradict the hermetic, *l'art pour l'art* attitude that has characterized modernism (and the museum's ideology as well), the presentation of these buildings seems to ignore those messages.

The role and impact of the Cooper-Hewitt Museum are quite different from MoMA's. Richard Oliver, an architect and former associate of Charles Moore, is the Cooper-Hewitt's curator of design. The Cooper-Hewitt began to exhibit architecture only after its establishment in 1975 as the National Museum of Design in affiliation with the Smithsonian Institution. Because its architecture program is hampered by a minuscule budget and by its position in a museum largely devoted to the decorative arts, which itself has not yet developed much status among scholars, some see it as not a fitting complement to MoMA.

Surely the Cooper-Hewitt's recent exhibition "Ornament in the Twentieth Century," a comprehensive exhibition drawing on all aspects of the museum's collection, though very beautiful, did little to counter this criticism: no catalog was produced, and the material selected for display seemed equally divided between table settings, fabrics, and other ephemera on the one hand, and architecture and furniture on the other.

Nonetheless, in the more narrowly architectural exhibitions in which Oliver was able to build his themes on more solid theoretical foundations, he has accomplished a great deal, despite limited resources: the exhibitions "Resort Architecture," and "Place, Product, Packaging" introduced new talent and brought before the public such key issues as vernacularism in commercial architecture and historicism and eclecticism in contemporary design.[12] Oliver also organized a component of the exhibition "Drawing Toward a More Modern Architecture."[13]

The limited effectiveness of the critical establishment in New York, whether in the daily press or in the professional journals, lies in the journalistic, as opposed to historical or theoretical, thrust of its production. The presence of the professional press in New York, combined with the fact that the *New York Times,* the nation's most influential newspaper, employs two architecture critics—Ada Louise Huxtable and Paul Goldberger—who are each widely syndicated throughout the United States, sets New York apart from such other centers as San Francisco and Chicago, where there are fewer architecture critics and where those who do exist do not have ready access to a national audience. With local events likely to be reported nationally, the intensity of normal professional intercourse is increased, perhaps disproportionately. An article by Goldberger on the opening of a modest building in New York may well be picked up by newspapers across the country, yielding untold benefits to the architect who suddenly finds himself—at least for a moment or so, and of course only in a minor way—an item of national news. Similarly, to its great credit, the *Times* reports in depth on architectural developments both here and abroad. While Goldberger, who is quite young, is becoming an important figure, his senior colleague at the *Times,* Huxtable, now sits on the newspaper's editorial board and wields a powerful influence on the profession: in the field of historic preservation, which she championed from the first, she has marshaled the public on a number of occasions on behalf of threatened landmarks; in the area of new construction, she has taken strong stands against designs she disapproves of—even the formidable Museum of Modern Art, now planning a major physical expansion, has not escaped her critical scrutiny; neither have such leading architects as Philip Johnson or Ulrich Franzen, whose recent attempts to bring to commercial building programs a measure of contextual responsiveness and historical continuity have been found wanting. Nonetheless, careful examination of the positions she has taken over the years reveals an eclectic as opposed to a consistent point of view.

If one looks for a more theoretically based critical position, one must turn to the staffs of MoMA, the Cooper-Hewitt, and the IAUS, to the programs organized by the Architectural League of New York, and to the schools of architecture in the city and its two principal architectural "outposts," Princeton and New Haven, each a little more than 90 minutes by train from midtown.

The Architectural League is a venerable institution founded in 1881 to give expression to the ideas of younger architects. Though it has gone through a number of transformations, it has remained true to its original ideals and to its concern for the interrelationship between the various arts and architecture. The League's occasional exhibitions of the work of architects under 40 years of age has become something of a tradition: in 1940 and again in 1966, its "40 Under 40" exhibits marked the emergence of new generations of architectural talent. The League's support of such artists in the late 1960s as Alan Sonfist and James Lee Byars was critical to informing the public of the existence and intentions of conceptual art. In the 1970s the League has energetically satisfied the seemingly insatiable appetite of the New York architectural intelligentsia for debate: a succession of lectures, "conversations," and symposia has given a respectful hearing to virtually every important ideological position. In the past few months, for example, Philip Johnson, Peter Eisenman, and the author, in discussing the relationship between historicism, history, and practice, focused on the revival of interest in the work of Lutyens; Michael Graves and Susana Torre engaged in heated "conversations" about issues of meaning, representation, and abstraction in Graves's architecture; Jaquelin Robertson and Edward Larrabee Barnes discussed Barnes's impact on a younger generation of designers and his own earlier indebtedness to the example set by Marcel Breuer.

The League's exhibition program has also enjoyed considerable success, though it is hampered by its dependence on outside institutions for display space; "200 Years of American Architectural Drawing" (1977) was held at the Cooper-Hewitt and later toured nationally.[14] David Gebhard and Deborah Nevins served as curators for what was the first major scholarly effort of its kind and was an important factor in the rebirth of interest in architectural drawings; "Women in American Architecture" (1977), which opened at the Brooklyn Museum before travelling to other cities, was directed by Susana Torre.[15] Also a pioneering effort and an effective culmination of a five-year campaign to publicly redress prejudices against women within the profession, it revealed a hidden history of American architecture that had been shockingly ignored by historians and professionals alike. The League's current exhibition project, directed by Cervin Robinson, is concerned with the history of architectural photography. It promises to offer major insights into the effect the camera's eye has had on the design process.

Of the half dozen or so architectural schools in New York and close-in suburbs, The Cooper Union and Columbia University in Manhattan, Yale University in New Haven, and Princeton University in Princeton enjoy the most prestige.

The Cooper Union, under the leadership of John Hejduk, has become a kind of American equivalent of the more characteristically European *technische hochschule;* Columbia, under James Stewart Polshek's tenure as dean, has set out to reaffirm the role of graduate-level professional education within the context of a major university and, as such, is comparable in its intentions to Yale, where Cesar Pelli is now dean, and Princeton, where the dean is Robert Geddes.

Under Hejduk, Cooper has become a kind of academy in which the work of most studios bears the imprint of his unique architectural personality or that of Raimund Abraham, who has recently come to enjoy considerable influence over the curriculum.[16] Cooper has not been particularly effective as a forum for debate but rather for the establishment of a point of view. Columbia, as befits the idea of a university, with older students who have finished baccalaureate programs in the liberal arts before undertaking architectural studies leading to their first professional degree and a more diverse faculty—including Romaldo Giurgola, Ada Karmi-Melamede, Kenneth Frampton, Steven Peterson, and the author, as well as numerous visitors, who have recently included Piero Sartogo, Arata Isozaki, and Lauretta Vinciarelli—has sought to foster debate: Columbia sponsors weekly public lectures, which take advantage of its position in New York in order to further the relationship between the academic and professional realms and to introduce to the school ideas and personalities from other parts of the United States and abroad. It has a separate program in historic preservation and a program of publications that, though off to a hesitant start, now promises to rival that of the IAUS.[17]

Yale, which has traditionally relied on visitors to bear the burden of its studio teaching, has had James Stirling on its roster for ten years; other important recent visitors include Richard Meier, Stanley Tigerman, and Giancarlo di Carlo. Yale recently initiated a series of seminars in contemporary architecture, which are to be published and promise to be an important document of our time. Quite important also are Yale's semi-annual studio reviews, to which distinguished and articulate practitioners are invited to join with the Yale faculty to discuss the work, and by extension to comment on the general direction of architectural thought.[18]

Princeton is dominated by Michael Graves, whose distinct style affects much of the work that comes out of the design studio, as well as that of younger faculty colleagues such as Peter Waldman and Alan Chimacoff. Because of its small size, Princeton is more like Cooper Union than Columbia or Yale; Graves's painterly style has dominated much of the work of the students and the faculty as well; its increasing historicism seems inextricably intertwined with the university tradition.[19]

I focus here on the role of the schools—perhaps overly so—not so much for their inherent impact on the New York scene, but for what they do to make that scene possible and distinct from other cities: teaching positions give intellectual and financial support to young architects (or even older ones who wish to combine intellectual discourse with commercial practice); good schools attract the best young minds who often stay to work in the offices. Because each of the schools is small, their curricula can be flexible enough to adjust the emphasis of the studio work to the formal as well as pragmatic issues of the day.

For example, Hejduk's studio problems involving the nine-square grid and the use of Juan Gris's paintings as a source for architecture have had a tremendous impact on actual practice; Robert Venturi and Denise Scott Brown's Las Vegas and Levittown studios at Yale not only introduced radical new subject matter but also opened up an entirely new mode of perception; my own studios based on the continuity of the language of traditional form have contributed to the ongoing reassessment of the relationship between representation and abstraction in architectural design.

In the 1940s New York was enriched by the presence of a number of the leading modernist artists who, fleeing political events in Europe, settled in the city. Piet Mondrian, Max Ernst, Salvador Dalí were among many others who contributed to the transformation of the local rather provincial art scene to such an extent that by the time the hostilities had ceased in 1945, it was New York and not Paris that was the art capital of the world. In the 1970s, a similar phenomenon is occurring, though it is not war but political and economic uncertainty that causes so many Italians and Argentines to settle in New York. True enough, the inherent vitality of New York attracts these architects, yet their contribution to the continuity of that vitality occurs in a number of areas: they have brought with them a skill and passion for architectural drawing; a commitment to ideology that is not exactly characteristic of the more pragmatic American temperament; an interest in problems of typology and linguistics that is also somewhat alien to the native temperament; and finally, a continuing faith in the modernist belief in a new form-language, though not necessarily in its antirepresentationalism.

It used to be argued that the United States, and New York in particular, was a melting pot—a place where all racial and national traits liquefied and merged into one unique, distinctly American product. Such was probably never the case; but now the idea of the melting pot is no longer even an ideal. At the risk of confusion, we revel in the diversity of the scene, in the contradictory quality of our ideas. It is the thousand flowers blooming that defines New York—the presence of precious hothouse orchids together with tougher garden varieties that lends this place its unique vitality. One comes to New York to see architecture being made, and not so much to see it. How different from Chicago, where the products of Mies's talent and those of his followers are everywhere to be seen. Chicago is like Detroit or Hollywood—the product and the place are one; architecture is Chicago's dominant plastic art, just as film is Hollywood's chief artistic product; they are company towns, urban villages grown up to produce and market one or two things. New York is a metropolis, a world capital; architecture is dreamed here, realized everywhere. As one sits at one's drawing board in New York, if one is at all alive to ideas, their pressures on one's work are staggering; no one in New York can escape them. Who would want to?

16

The Doubles of
Post-Modern

1980

Cubism and superrealism [surrealism], far from being the dawn of style, are the end
of a period of self-consciousness, inbreeding and exhaustion. One thing seems clear
to me: that no new style will grow out of a preoccupation with art for its own sake.
It can only arise from a new interest in subject matter. We need a new myth
in subject matter. We need a new myth in which the symbols are inherently pictorial.
—Kenneth Clark, "Boredom Blamed"

What has been called modern architecture for the past fifty years is in disarray:
though such leading architects as Paul Rudolph, I. M. Pei, and Kevin Roche
continue to produce major new work, the forms as well as the theories on which
that work is based are systematically being questioned by a growing number of
younger architects who perceive the waning of modernism and who are questioning the prevailing philosophic basis for architecture and its form-language. This
questioning sensibility has come to be described, alternately and rather imprecisely, as "Post-Modern" or "Post-Modernist."[1]

Charles Jencks's book *The Language of Post-Modern Architecture* is the first
to explore the new mood and to begin to erect a scaffolding of theory for post-
modernism.[2] Jencks suggests that the term *Post-Modern* is at best "negative and
evasive." Nonetheless, it does enjoy some precedent in architecture.[3]

The terms *modernism* and *post-modernism* have been used in other disciplines
besides architecture, including political history and literary and art criticism. In
each of these disciplines, they suggest two different conditions resulting in related
sets of what I would describe as "doubles"—the doubles of modernism and of post-
modernism. Both grow out of the same two distinct but interrelated sensibilities

or conditions, and both fall within the modern—that is, Western humanist/post-Renaissance—period.

These conditions affect both modernism and post-modernism. Borrowing the term from Frank Kermode, I would label the first of these conditions *schismatic*. The schismatic condition argues for a clean break with Western humanism. I would label the second condition *traditional*, borrowing the term from Stephen Spender. It argues for recognition of the continuity of the Western humanist tradition. Traditional modernism can be "conceived of as a return, at once spontaneous and willed, to eternal values, long forgotten or buried but which a reborn or renewed historical memory makes once again present"; schismatic modernism can be seen as a sensibility in which "the new and the modern are seen in terms of a birth rather than a rebirth, not a restoration but … a construction of the present and future not on the foundations of the past but on the ruins of time."[4]

The two modernisms can be distinguished by their attitudes toward the past: traditional modernism, typified by the writings of Proust or T. S. Eliot or the paintings of Picasso, views the past as a source of order; schismatic modernism, typified by the work of Duchamp or Mondrian, views the past as a burden. Although the two kinds of modernism are distinct, they are linked by an apocalyptic view of the future and by recognition of Western humanism as an ongoing condition.

It is important to reiterate that the modern period as a whole encompasses a continuing tradition of humanistic thought and action, though some of its stylistic movements—for example, Dada and surrealism—regard humanism as a yoke.

Like the two modernisms, the two post-modernisms can be distinguished by their attitudes toward the past. While the schismatic Post-Modern condition posits a break with both modernism and the modern period itself, the traditional Post-Modern condition proposes to free new production from the rigid constraints of modernism, especially from its most radical and nihilistic aspects (as exemplified by Dada and surrealism), while simultaneously reintegrating itself with other strains of Western humanism, especially those which characterize its last pre-modernist phase, that of the Romanticism which flourished between 1750 and 1850.[5] Thus, schismatic post-modernism is a sensibility that considers itself not only beyond modernism but also outside the modern period, one that seeks to establish the mode of thought and artistic production that is as free from the 500-year tradition of Western humanism as that mode was free from the previous Gothic era of religious Scholasticism. Traditional post-modernism, on the other hand, is one that seeks to reintegrate or subsume modernism within the broad category of the modern period as a whole.

In post-modernism, the distinctions between traditional and schismatic conditions are useful in illuminating the distinctions between the work of John Gardner and William Gass in literature or of Peter Eisenman and Michael Graves in architecture. Though the term *Post-Modern* appears to be used to describe sensibilities and theories that share as common ground a reaction to the modernism that has dominated much of the cultural activity of the past 125 years, the traditional and schismatic conditions serve to distinguish between distinct sensibilities within the Post-Modern devolution; these distinctions have at their core the question of

the relationship between new work and the tradition of humanism that characterized the modern period itself.

Thus the doubles of the Post-Modern, two distinct but interrelated Post-
Modern sensibilities: a schismatic condition that argues for a *clean break* with
the tradition of Western humanism, and a traditional condition that argues for a
return to, or a recognition of, the *continuity* of the cultural tradition of Western
humanism of which it holds modernism to be a part.

> Somebody should write the history of the word "modern." The OED isn't very
> helpful, though most of the senses the word now has have been in the air since
> the 16th century, and are actually older than Shakespeare's way of using it to mean
> 'commonplace.'...The New is to be judged by the criterion of novelty,
> the Modern implies or at any rate permits a serious relationship with the past,
> a relationship that requires criticism and indeed radical reimagining.
> —Frank Kermode, *Continuities*

In order to clarify what is meant by the term *modern* in the neologism *Post-Modern*,
it is necessary to establish clear definitions for the related terms *modern* and *modernism*. Such a seemingly pedantic exercise is necessary because the distinctions
between the older terms have become blurred by daily use, and they have become
ineffective for discourse.

What can be called the "modern period" begins in the fifteenth century with the
birth of humanism. The renaissance of classicism in architecture is the first of
the modern stylistic phases: the baroque and the rococo are subsequent modern
styles. The International Style of circa 1920–1960 is also a modern style, often
thought to be *the* modern style in which the meaning of the word *modern* is trans-
formed and limited so as to represent only those values more properly described
as modernist, a term that describes the urge to produce new artistic work that
eschews all known form-language and, ideally, all grammar in favor of a new self-
referential (that is, in architecture, functionally and technologically determined)
language of form whose principal cultural responsibility is toward its moment in
time. Modernism sees art as a manifestation of the zeitgeist; it strives to reflect the
moment of its conception. Modernism, in the most oversimplified terms, represents a moralistic application of a superior value to that which is not only new but
also independent of all previous production.

Modernism views the present as a state of continuing crisis; it sees history
only as a record of experiences, a body of myth, but not as objective truth, and it
is apocalyptic in its relationship to the future. A person who believes in the sensibility of modernism is a modernist as well as a modern, the latter term being the
more general one and simply referring to someone who has lived in the modern
period and has contended with or at least recognized the issue of modernity but
who has not necessarily adopted a modernist stance.[6]

Modernism is not a style in and of itself in the sense that the Renaissance
and baroque were styles with unifying principles. It can be regarded as a succession of attempts to redefine the syntax and the grammar of artistic composition
(the poems of Mallarmé, the stream of consciousness of James Joyce and Virginia
Woolf, the buildings of Mies van der Rohe and Le Corbusier). As a result,
and rather perversely, to the extent that it has deliberately been made difficult and

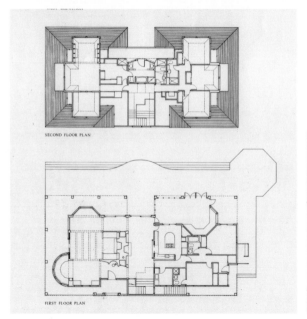

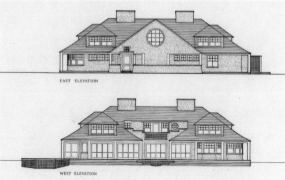

Fig. 1. Robert A. M. Stern, plans and elevations, Residence at Chilmark, Martha's Vineyard, Massachusetts, 1979–1983

inaccessible, artistic production has also shown itself to be modernist. In some cases there has been an effort to go beyond issues of syntax and grammar and to seek to establish new form-languages, which, because they are not culturally based (that is, familiar), are by necessity personal or self-referential.[7]

Modernism does not accept the appearance of things as they are in nature and in the man-made world; it seeks always to take them apart in order to discover their hidden and presumably essential character. Modernism seeks to close and ultimately to eliminate the distance between the object perceived and the person perceiving the object. It seeks to do this in two ways: by insisting that all experience and thereby all art exists in the present—Giedion's phrase was the "eternal present"—and by insisting that each work of art and each act of artistic production is a personal act.[8] This presentism and the self-referential aspect of artistic production are fundamental to any examination of the nature of modernism in relationship to the issue of an ongoing culture that we call the Western humanist tradition.

It has been argued that modernism can never be part of any tradition, that it is a thing apart, a parallel tradition to Western humanism. This issue of modernism as a sensibility apart from the modern has resulted in that plethora of modernist styles or *isms* which have made the history of the literature and art of the last 125 years seem so confusing and troubled.

While the term *modern,* as in the phrase "the modern period," is a term of historical description (like the Middle Ages), it is also a term of sensibility and style. Like the term *baroque,* it can be used with and without a capital letter. One can exhibit a baroque or a modern turn of mind while acting outside the Baroque or Modern period.

As a term describing a style, the use of the word *modern* opens up a veritable Pandora's box of confusion: for example, *L'Art Nouveau,* for a while known as *Le Style Moderne,* is a style in the modern period and, more specifically, was a modernist style in that it sought to stand free of the *historical continuum.* At the same time, insofar as it is the "fine art" manifestation of the bohemianism of the *fin de siècle,* it also represents a sensibility.

Another meaning for *modern* is up-to-date or "contemporary." The term *contemporary* cannot be used to describe a stylistic sensibility because it signifies merely the absence of any strongly defined period features. Thus, all current production is modern: "the specific claim of 'modernism' to be finally and forever open" is rendered preposterous by the history of the Modern Movement.[9]

As Susan Sontag has observed, this "notion of a style-less, transparent art is one of the most tenacious fantasies of modern culture. Artists and critics pretend to believe that it is no more possible to get the artifice out of art than it is for a person to lose his personality. Yet the aspiration lingers—a permanent dissent from modern art with its dizzying velocity of style *changes.*"[10] Harry Levin articulates what I believe to be a fundamental characteristic of the modernist era: "Now we are all contemporaries; about that we have no option, so long as we stay alive. But we may choose whether or not we wish to be modern" (by which I think Levin means modernist).[11]

Thus, one must be wary of the use of the term *modern* in architecture, as in most of the arts and in literature. It is not really a description of a style but, as Irving Howe has observed, "a term of critical placement and judgment."[12]

Contemporary historians and critics of modern architecture, perhaps even more than their counterparts in literature and the fine arts, seem to confuse the broad historical definition of the modern period with related but distinct ideas pertaining to modernism and to use the terms interchangeably. While this issue of historiography critically affects the seeming confusion of the current situation, it is too long and too complex to be dealt with effectively in this essay. Suffice it to say that until the impact of Hegelian and Marxist thought came to dominate the developing discipline of art and architectural history in Germany in the second half of the nineteenth century, historians undertook to define modern architectural history in broad terms and to regard the Renaissance as the first of a sequence of modern styles. Even as late as 1929, Henry-Russell Hitchcock, in his *Modern Architecture: Romanticism and Reintegration,* embraced a chronologically broad and relatively inclusive definition of modern architecture. Nonetheless, perhaps under the impact of his subsequent collaboration with the more polemical Philip Johnson on the book *The International Style,* and perhaps as a result of his subsequent contact with European modernist historians such as Giedion and Pevsner, Hitchcock has since drawn back from his earlier and more inclusive position.

In *Modern Architecture,* Hitchcock traces the origins of the modern period to the breakup of the Gothic style, regarding each phase since that time not as an "independent style" like the Greek or the Egyptian, but as a subsidiary manner of one modern style. Yet, even in *Modern Architecture,* Hitchcock was already under the sway not only of the emerging polemic of the International Style but also of the historical determinism that pervades so much German art historical writing of the period. In *Modern Architecture* Hitchcock claimed that a fundamental characteristic of the modern style is a "preference for formal experimentation," as if Egyptian and Greek architects in antiquity were never interested in trying anything new.[13] In his later books, by inference, and explicitly in the essay "Modern Architecture—A Memoir," Hitchcock has altered his original position, claiming that had he followed his initial plan to cover the whole range of time from the Late Gothic to the present, it would have been more or less analogous to the books of the nineteenth-century architectural historians such as James Ferguson [who] . . . dealing with the "modern styles" . . . interpreted "modern" in the old sense as the third portion of the relevant past: "Modern times," that is, the period from the Renaissance onward, in distinction to "Antiquity" and the "Middle Ages."

Hitchcock goes on to observe that

what is, at any given point, accepted more broadly as "modern architecture" can have no fixed beginnings—various historians and critics have set its start all the way from the early fifteenth century to the early twentieth. Nor, even more obviously, can it have a fixed ending. What is still properly considered modern architecture began, according to my present view, in the 1880s, not way back in 1750, nor yet later in 1900 or in 1920; it will be over only when we, or the next generation, have another name for it."[14]

Thus Hitchcock brings us to a fundamental issue of the moment: although at first glance it seems difficult to sustain as the broadest definition of modern architecture all the production of the post-medieval period, upon further reflection such a definition seems more workable than those later attempts to link the historical definition of the modern period in architecture too closely with specific economic, political, or cultural events that have occurred since the middle of the eighteenth century—that is, with the Industrial Revolution, and the political revolutions in the United States and France—or with prior positions taken on behalf of any particular manifestation of current or contemporary production that might seem more "advanced," "innovative," or "progressive." Such a broad view opens up the definition of modern architecture, enabling it to be understood not as a unified style but rather as a humanistic pursuit involving a continuous interweaving of diverse and often contradictory formal tendencies assembled, discovered, sometimes even invented through various processes, including eclecticism, modernism, and technological as well as functional determinism. Such a view would hold out 1750 as an important marker in time, as it would also note the decisive shifts that took place in the period 1870–90 (emergence of a dominant modernism) and again around 1960–70 (emergence of a dominant post-modernism). But this view, as I hope to demonstrate later, would not see decisive reasons why any of these phases should mark the conclusion of the modern period's larger themes, or their replacement by themes not already present in the formative stages of the modern period.

It is not Hitchcock but Giedion, Pevsner, and J. M. Richards who have exerted the greatest influence on the profession's and the public's view of what modern architecture was and should have been during the past forty years: much of the confusion about the character and chronology of the modern period in architecture can be attributed to their tendency to present the history of the architecture of the past 200 years as a series of morality tales involving heroic struggles between pragmatic materialism and high ideals, between "good guys" and "bad guys," "progressives" and "reactionaries," "constituent" and "transitory" facts. Whole careers and aesthetic movements have been cut off from the so-called "mainstream" of historical flow: Giedion's *Space, Time and Architecture* and Pevsner's *Pioneers of the Modern Movement* have been the most influential in

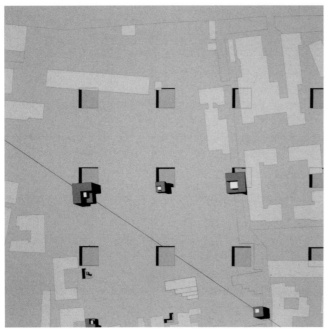
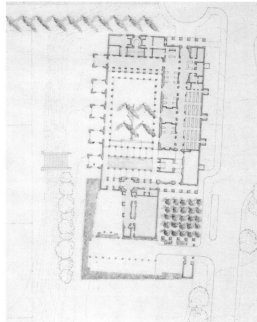

Fig. 2. Peter Eisenman, plan,
Cannaregio Town Square,
Venice, 1978

Fig. 3. Michael Graves, site
plan, San Juan Capistrano
Library, California, 1981–1983

the architectural profession and therefore the most troublesome. In these works, as Hitchcock has observed, much of the architecture of the nineteenth century has been treated "as constituent premonitions of [the] 'modern architecture'" of the 1920s and '30s and not as legitimate artistic production in its own right.[15]

Outside the architectural profession, most educated people now in their forties and fifties were exposed to this point of view in introductory courses in college, sometimes in the original text of Giedion and Pevsner, but more often in such popularizing work as Richards' *Introduction to Modern Architecture,* in which

> the words "modern architecture" are used here to mean something more particular than contemporary architecture. They are used to mean the new kind of architecture that is growing up with this century as this century's own contribution to the art of architecture; the work of those people, whose number is happily increasing, who understand that architecture is a social art related to the life of the people it serves, not an academic exercise in applied ornament. The question that immediately arises, whether there is in fact enough difference between people's lives as they are lived in this century and as they were lived in previous centuries to justify a truly "modern" architecture being very different from that of the past—and indeed whether "modern" architecture is quite as revolutionary as it is supposed to be.
>
> For whatever reason, modern architecture has been passing through a sort of "puritan" phase, in which the negative virtues of simplicity and efficiency have been allowed to dominate, and since 1939 a concentration on the essentials has also been necessitated in most countries by the overriding need to build cheaply.[16]

The revisionist architectural history of the 1950s and '60s, which owes a considerable debt to the example of Hitchcock's comprehensive *Architecture: Nineteenth and Twentieth Centuries,* sought to develop a broader characterization of the modern period, which would include the stylistic revivalism of the late eighteenth and nineteenth centuries as well as the self-referential modernism of the twentieth. But despite Hitchcock's influence, the determinist view of history typified by Giedion's *Space, Time and Architecture* seems to have prevented the revisionists, in their search for a broader view, from considering events earlier than the mid-eighteenth century. Thus, even the very important redefinition of modern architecture that Vincent Scully offered in 1954 and refined in 1961, though the first to free the stylistic analysis of architectural production from the futurist polemic of the Modern Movement of the 1920s, is not free from political determinism and is not, in the final analysis, sufficiently broad in its historical scope. Acknowledging a debt to Frank Lloyd Wright, Scully offered a definition of modern architecture as the "architecture of democracy," an "image of ourselves" emerging "precisely at the beginning of the age of industrialism and mass democracy [where] we first find it, in terms of fragmentation, mass scale, and new, unfocused continuity."[17] In this sense, Scully, seeking to reconcile the views of such early twentieth-century historians as Fiske Kimball with those of Giedion and Pevsner, brings us to the threshold of our current perception of the distinctions between the modern tradition and modernism.[18] As a result it is now possible to see the Modern Movement as an episode in the broad history of modern architecture itself.

Similarly, one can see modernism not as a style but as a strategy, one of a number of *isms* that have emerged in the modern era to help the artist express his attitudes toward the present in relation to his sense of the past and/or the future: in architecture, "eclecticism," "associationalism," and "technological determinism" are other attitudes that interact with modernism to help organize a theory upon which to base work. Thus, though modernism has had its period of hegemony, resulting in a univalent style whose abstraction rendered it difficult and uncommunicative from the first, it should not be seen as a style in and of itself. The International Style was the great modernist style, and modernism itself remains a modern sensibility. Yet there are those who would argue that it is a sensibility parallel to Western humanism and thereby outside it, that is, not at all part of the tradition that began with the Renaissance, and it is this issue that constitutes the crux of the current debate.

The idea of a Post-Modern age was introduced by Arnold Toynbee in his *Study of History,*[19] and it has been developed by a number of historians, most notably Geoffrey Barraclough.[20] The Post-Modern age discussed by Toynbee and Barraclough is one in which there is increasing recognition that co-existence is the *modus vivendi* of the pluralist condition of our time. This pluralism in turn forces a close examination of the validity of the proposition that the distinction between a single standard and competing standards sets the contemporary of the Post-Modern period apart from the Modern period as a whole. If, as Toynbee and Barraclough argue, the Modern period began at the end of the fifteenth century, when Western European culture began to exert its hegemony over vast land areas and cultures not its own (and Western European man found himself having to deal not only with the pluralist politics of European nationalism in its formative stages but also with the pluralism brought about by encounters with the "native" populations of the New World), then it perhaps can be argued that the Post-Modern or contemporary phase they describe is really just another stage in modern history, a "global" or "post-industrial" age following a "national" or "industrial" age, an

The Doubles of Post-Modern

era of "relativism" that at once accepts the inherent diversity of the present while seeking order and meaning through a connection with the past, especially with the Romantic era.

Post-modernism should not be seen as a reaction against modernism; it seeks to develop modernism's themes by attempting to examine them in relationship to the wider framework of the modern period as a whole.

The divided nature of modernism complicates our understanding of the Post-Modern devolution. At the beginning of this essay, I defined two kinds of Post-Modern sensibilities, which can now be seen as related to modernism: a traditional one and a schismatic one. But the complex nature of modernism itself, with its two distinct conditions or types united by an apocalyptic view of history—not to mention the claims that are sometimes made for modernism as a sensibility completely independent of Western humanism—complicate the situation with regard to post-modernism. As a result, it can be argued that there are not one but two sets of Post-Modern doubles: that there are *two types of traditional post-modernism* and *two types of schismatic post-modernism.*

Fig. 4. Arquitectonica, Palace Condominium, Miami, 1978–1981

The first type of traditional post-modernism—and the one which I would argue is the more viable of the two—argues for a break with modernism (where modernism is itself seen as a *break with* Western humanism) and a reintegration with a view of Western humanism that includes modernism among its many and sometimes conflicting conditions. The second type sees itself as a continuation of modernism (in which modernism is itself seen as a successor *sensibility* and *style* to the baroque and rococo, a sensibility and style that is contradictorily and inexplicably, in its present-ism, a contradiction of the very notion of style).

This second type of traditional post-modernism is somewhat dubious: at the very least it fails to account for the stylistic complexity of the Romantic era, and it leads us to a question of whether such a post-modernism is really different from modernism itself. For if traditional modernism is a condition in which all art is seen as being in the present, though not breaking with the values and symbols of Western humanism, then where can this second type of post-modernism stand in time? Is there a place beyond the present?

The first type of schismatic post-modernism—and the one which I would argue is the more viable of the two—argues for a *continuity with* modernism (in which modernism is itself seen as a *break with* Western humanism). This kind of schismatic post-modernism, like the second type of traditional post-modernism, is a continuing modernism, but the use of the prefix *post-* has meaning because it permits the designation of a condition that is distinct from modernism because it breaks with the Western humanist tradition. Schismatic post-modernism of this type marks the full flowering of a sensibility that has its origins in modernism's aspiration toward a clean break with the Western humanist tradition.

The second type of schismatic post-modernism is itself seen as a *continuing* tradition. This is the so-called "post-modern breakthrough to post-modernity," in which a totally new state of consciousness is achieved that insists on the obsolescence of modernism as well as the entire Western humanist tradition.[21] Attractive though such an image seems to those who view the current situation as unnecessarily confusing, it is difficult to make clear just exactly how this new condition will emerge. As Richard E. Palmer writes:

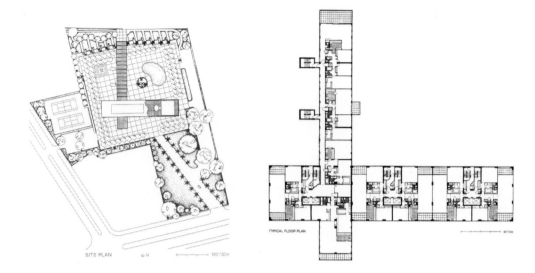

SITE PLAN   ⊾N   ⊢——————⊣ 100 / 30m

TYPICAL FLOOR PLAN

Postmodernity raises the question of a transition and transformation so radical as to change the fundamental views of language, history, truth, time and matter—so radical that "understanding" becomes a quite different process. It raises the possibility, in other words, of a "new hermeneutics."

    The hermeneutical problem of bridging the gap between modern and postmodern sets-of-mind goes in both directions: the problem of understanding a postmodern way of thinking when the assumptions and furniture of our thinking are themselves given by modernity, and the problem of a person who, having achieved a postmodern, postspatialized, postperspectival, or holistic framework, must then communicate it to someone who has not reached it.[22]

Fig. 5. Arquitectonica, site plan and typical floor plan, Palace Condominium, Miami, 1978–1981

Thus, though there are four conditions of post-modernism, it would seem that in the case of two, questions of considerable complexity remain unanswered at the present moment, thereby limiting the effectiveness of these conditions for artistic production if not for discourse. The difficulties raised by the second type of traditional post-modernism—that is, the notion of a continuing modernism—simultaneously claiming a position within humanism and apart from history, seems hopelessly contradictory. It seems to be a condition that, despite the Post-Modern label that might be applied to it, is no more or no less than that of the traditional modernism of Proust, of the Joyce of *Ulysses,* of Picasso, and of Le Corbusier.

    The difficulties of the second type of schismatic post-modernism—the postmodernist breakthrough—have already been discussed. It takes as its point of departure the work of such writers as Joyce, but, as yet, it has not found a truly convincing voice. Such critics as William Spanos and Ihab Hassan are attempting to articulate the nature of the post-modernist breakthrough.[23] Because this type of schismatic post-modernism is only schismatic, it doubles back on itself and reaches a dead end.

    Thus it becomes clear that the second type of schismatic post-modernism is not just a shift of emphasis within modernism; its relationship to modernism is not comparable to that which post-impressionism had to impressionism; schismatic post-modernism is radical in the extreme. In an essay on "Joyce, Beckett and

The Doubles of Post-Modern

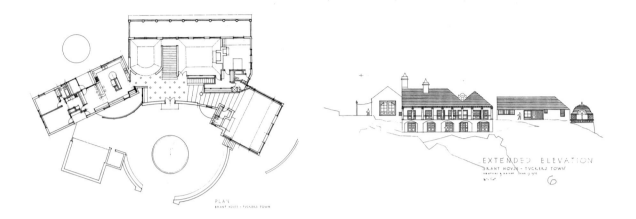

PLAN
BRANT HOUSE - TUCKERS TOWN

EXTENDED ELEVATION
BRANT HOUSE - TUCKERS TOWN

Fig. 6. Venturi and Rauch, first-floor plan and south elevation, Brant House, Tuckers Town, Bermuda, 1975–1977

the Postmodern Imagination," Ihab Hassan observes that though "one might be inclined to conclude that modernism is simply the earlier movement . . . and that post-modernism is the later movement, which began to dominate Western literature after World War II," one must finally see that "however jagged or ironic [modernism] allowed itself to be, it retained its faith in art, in the imaginative act, even at the edge of cultural dissolution. . . . Post-modernism, on the other hand, is essentially *subversive* in form and *anarchic* in its cultural spirit. It dramatizes its lack of faith in art even as it produces new works of art intended to hasten *both* cultural and artistic dissolution."[24]

The two conditions of the Post-Modern that are at this moment important, and the ones I should like to consider in some detail in the remaining pages of this essay, are: 1) the schismatic post-modernism that argues for a clean break with Western humanism and a continuity with modernism and 2) the traditional post-modernism that argues for a break with modernism and a reintegration with the broader condition of Western humanism, especially with the Romantic tradition. These seem the only possible categories because they are the only ones that contain in them the "double" sensibilities of continuity and change that are necessary to sustain generative cycles of creation.

The emergence of the Post-Modern sensibility can be seen as a logical result of the opposition between the Romantic and modernist sensibilities, the former reveling in diversity, the latter struggling to find a universal cultural voice. Post-modernism is not revolutionary in either the political or artistic sense; in fact, it reinforces the effect of the technocratic and bureaucratic society in which we live— traditional post-modernism by accepting conditions and trying to modify them, schismatic post-modernism by proposing a condition *outside* Western humanism, thereby permitting Western humanist culture to proceed uninterrupted though not necessarily unaffected.

Post-modernism, though a reaction to modernism, is not a revolutionary movement seeking to overthrow modernism. Modernism cannot be ignored. We cannot pretend that it never existed and that we can return to a pre-modernist condition (such is the folly of such neo-traditionalist architects as John Barrington Bayley or the theorist Conrad Jameson). Post-modernism is especially affected by that aspect of modernism, which derived from Romanticism itself, particularly the Romantic belief in the religious aspect of art. Most importantly, the Post-Modern

Fig. 7. Venturi and Rauch, Brant House, Tuckers Town, Bermuda, 1975–1977

condition arises out of the need to account for, and to continue to function under, the drastically altered circumstances that emerged from the political and cultural events of the 1920s and 1940s and which continue to condition action in this last third of our century. Thus it must be seen that post-modernism is a modern sensibility that includes modernism by virtue of its reaction to it; it is the manifestation of what Irving Howe describes as "the radical breakdown of the modernist impulse," which came as a result of the experience of the Holocaust, of World War II, of the use of the atomic bomb. At its root lies existentialism, an attitude toward history and the idea of time that has extended beyond our thought processes to the very mode of our consciousness.

Schismatic post-modernism can be seen as an outgrowth of the anti-intellectualism of the modernism of the 1920s and '30s. In philosophy and literature it is represented by such writers as Norman Brown, Herbert Marcuse, Marshall McLuhan, Donald Barthelme, Samuel Beckett, and William S. Burroughs. In architecture, Peter Eisenman is its leading advocate. It rejects the Western humanist tradition and, in the realm of aesthetics, it rejects Aristotelian composition. Though very much related to modernism, schismatic post-modernism is nonetheless a distinct sensibility. And it adopts the post-modernist label to differentiate itself from the modernist tradition.

Schismatic post-modernism separates itself from traditionalist post-modernism by suggesting that it is not simply the crises of mid-century life that have irreparably changed the relationship of men to each other and to their ideas, but that these events have rendered untenable that relationship between men, objects, nature, and the sense of the ideal (the deity) which has been accepted since the Renaissance. Schismatic post-modernism sees the relationship between men and objects as a competitive one, and God as dead or, at least, removed from the fray.

It is in this context that Eisenman's position can best be understood. His proposal to make architecture autonomous is anti-historical and anti-symbolic; his endeavors to produce an architecture that is autonomous and self-referential—that is, hermetically sealed from all concerns except the process of its own fabrication and fabulation—make his works virtually impenetrable. Eisenman's houses become symbolic of their own process of conception, but that process is so cut off from contemporary culture, history, and pragmatism that in the end, the effectiveness of the symbolic gesture ceases to be symbolic of anything outside itself; the building runs the danger of becoming merely an object that can, at best, make its appeal on a sensuous and hedonistic level. Although it struggles to free itself from all cultural references, by its very physicality it cannot but remind the viewer of some object previously seen or experienced.

Despite his belief in an autonomous architecture, Eisenman's ideology is culturally based. It draws extensively from the linguistic theories of Noam Chomsky and from the work of such literary critics as Roland Barthes and William Gass, who has himself written about one of Eisenman's buildings, House VI.[25] In basing his argument for an autonomous architecture on theories developed in relation to others in parallel but not necessarily related artistic disciplines, and in making comparisons with discoveries in the sciences, especially mathematics and physics, Eisenman seems caught up in a contradiction not unlike the one that characterized the justifications devised for modernist architecture by historians and polemicists such as Giedion, who sought to justify architectural modernism by connecting it with Einsteinian physics.[26] Schismatic post-modernist architecture, as represented by Eisenman (and I can think of no other architect who might be included in this category) buoys itself up with analogies to literary and linguistic theory.[27] But where modernism's connection to physics was ex post facto, schismatic post-modernism's connections have been established the other way around. As a result there seems to be in Eisenman's work what John Gardner has observed in the work of such schismatic post-modernists as John Cage and William Gass: a sense of "art which is all thought … art too obviously constructed to fit a theory."[28]

To sum up: Eisenman's work, in its dazzling extremism, brings into focus the fundamental dilemma of schismatic post-modernism, which, to paraphrase Kermode, is based on an inherent contradiction that can be seen in modernism itself: can one reconcile a cult of self-referential form-making with a denial of the existence of form itself? Schismatic post-modernism leaves us little choice: with all of previous culture removed in theory, at least, we are left with an aesthetic of unparalleled abstraction and hermeticism and without, as yet, even a hope for the emergence of an atavistic mythology to help crack the code. Eisenman leaves us terribly alone, naked.

John Gardner has written that the problem with the idea of art as pure language—which it seems to me is the basic concept of Eisenman's position as it is basic to Cage's and Gass's—is "that it shows … a lack of concern [on the artist's part] for people who care about events and ideas and thus, necessarily, about the clear and efficient statements of both." Gardner's phrase "linguistic opacity" suggests that the need to communicate is not a primary function of art. One might ask, what can this seeming "search for opacity" do for us? What are we to make of these "linguistic sculptures," which at best make, as Gardner writes, "only the affirmation sandcastles make, that it is pleasant to make things or look at things made, better to be alive than dead?"[29]

It may well be that the extreme position that Eisenman represents in architecture, Cage in music, and Gass in literature marks an end part in a cycle, and that a viable post-modernism must be one that opens up possibilities for new production rather than describes a situation that can be seen as ultimately futile and nihilistic.

Irving Howe has argued that although there is in modernist literature a "major impulse" to express "a choking nausea before the idea of culture," there is also "another in which the writer takes upon himself the enormous ambition not to reinvent the terms of reality."[30] It is this realistic, accepting aspect of modernism that is carried over in the second, traditional or inclusive post-modernist reactions.

Howe regards Saul Bellow, William Styron, and Bernard Malamud as "traditional" Post-Modern writers, in the sense that in their books, the action of individuals takes place in relationship to specific cultural conditions. Robert Gillespie, writing about the younger American novelists of the 1960s, states that the work of a considerable group, among them Wendell Berry, Scott Momaday, Larry McMurtry, Wright Morris, and the Ken Kesey of *Sometimes a Great Notion,* share a traditional post-modernist point of view. These writers accept "responsibility for the world's condition, and therefore of authority in managing it. Consciousness for them is less a curse than it is an act of conscience. They are eager to locate themselves in 'a place on earth' (the title of one of Berry's novels) and to merge their lives with that place. From such felt relation comes sustenance...so a region has its own mythology which may offer the only sustaining relation between past and future."[31] Traditional post-modernism is simultaneously inside contemporary society and critically detached from it; it uses art to comment on everyday life; it is at once "satiric" and accepting in its view of culture; in this sense it seeks to make telling interpretations of everyday life. Such a post-modernism begins to "restore that state of balance between unchecked fabulation and objective social realism" necessary to prevent artistic production from degenerating into trivial self-indulgence.[32]

In painting and in architecture, traditional post-modernism relies increasingly on representational as opposed to abstract or conceptual modes. Rackstraw Downes equates traditional post-modernism with a revived realism in painting. Critical of what he describes as modernism's "pictorial narcissism . . . a painting capable only of admiring its own nature," Downes's argument against modernist abstraction and in favor of pre-modernist representation hinges on his criticism of modernism's exclusivist principle of selectivity:

> While Old Master painting had allowed emphasis of the different aspects of form, its nature was holistic and embracing, whereas Modernist styles were partial. As were their means, so was their grasp on reality. Expressionism, Dada and Surrealism were associational styles which dealt respectively with emotions, ideas and fantasies. Hedonistic Impressionism, Cubism—a still life style—and Purism which dealt in Utopian absolutes, concentrated on particular properties of form. Modernism, then, constituted a rapid succession of specialized styles, each one supplying some deficiency of the rest; what they gained in intensity and concentration they lost in comprehensiveness and range.
>
> Modernism was indeed to excel in uncompromisingly personal triumphs and, likewise, fail to produce a syntax sufficiently limber and resourceful to be widely shared and passed along. In fact, that was one of its rules, that no manner should develop into an available language; because if it did so it would become transparent and the Modernist purpose would be lost.[33]

Downes notes that while the modernist looks to the examples of the past in a search "for lessons which it would not have known it could teach," the post-modernist looks back on history "in a spirit of empathy for its ostensible purposes." Nonetheless, traditional post-modernism does not advocate stylistic revival,

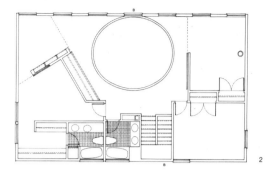
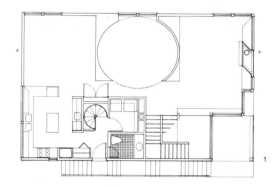

Fig. 8. Stuart Cohen and Sisco/Lubotsky, floor plans, Mackenbach House, Bloomingdale, Illinois, 1979

though it does support the concept of emulation. Traditional post-modernism looks back to history to see how things were done and to remind itself that many good ways of doing things, which were cast aside for ideological reasons, can be usefully rediscovered. Thus, for example, inclusive post-modernism can employ recognizable imagery in an abstract way—it can be at once pre-modernist and modernist.[34]

Traditional post-modernism opens up artistic production to a public role which modernism, by virtue of its self-referential formal strategies, had denied itself. In painting, as William Rubin has observed, "one characteristic of the modern period *seems* to be ending. That is the tradition of the private picture—private in its character and subject matter as well as in its destination—that is, for the small circle of collectors and friends of artists who sympathize with vanguard art."[35] In this sense, the current interest in photography should be seen as a last-gasp modernist stance.

Architecture, of course, is by definition a public art. Yet in its modernist phase, it often spoke the private language of painting—one need only recall the arguments advanced in Henry-Russell Hitchcock's book *Painting Toward Architecture*.[36] More importantly, as Suzannah Lessard points out: "Between the abstract beauty of technological principles and the underpinning of intricate solutions to innumerable minute problems, there is another kind of middle ground which was overlooked in the exuberant rush to modernity. Between man's desire to expand his ego and the needs of man as ant—I can think of no better way to express the dual preoccupation of the age of technology—the question of what human life would be like in the new world floated unasked, unnoticed."[37] It is this aspect of social and cultural responsibility—not in the narrowly simplistic sense of architectural do-goodism but in a broader and more profound sense of a genuine and unsentimental humanism—that characterizes traditional post-modernism's distinction from the abstract, self-referential schismatic post-modernism that we have already discussed.

Traditional post-modernism rejects the anti-historical biases of modernism; influences from history are no longer seen as constraints on either personal growth or artistic excellence. History, no longer viewed as the dead hand of the past, now seems at the very least a standard of excellence in a continuing struggle to deal effectively with the present. Modernism looked toward the future as an escape from the past; traditional post-modernism struggles with the legacy of that attitude, a world filled with objects whose principal artistic impetus often came from a belief that in order to be "modern" they must look and function as little as possible like anything

The Doubles of Post-Modern

that had been seen in the world before. The traditional post-modernist struggle, then, is not to free itself from the past, but to relax what has been characterized as "the stubborn grip of the values created by the rebellion against the past."[38]

Traditional post-modernism rejects what Charles Moore has described as the "obsessive normalization of the recent past, where we have drawn our expressive elegance out of poverty and ... our process out of crisis."[39] It argues that it is proper and sufficient to struggle with the problems of the present viewed in relation to the values continuing from the past, while leaving the future to those who will inherit it.

Traditional post-modernism recognizes that the public has lost confidence in architects (though it still believes in the symbolic power of architecture). Modernist architecture offered very little in the way of joy or visual pleasure; its conceptual basis was limited and disconcertingly materialistic. By once again recognizing the common assumptions a culture inherits from its past, traditional post-modernism is not only an announcement that modern architecture has emerged from its puritan revolution, its catharsis at last behind it, but also an avowal of self-confidence in contemporary architecture's ability and willingness to reestablish itself on a basis that not only can deal with the past but also match it, value for value, building for building.

Fig. 9. Stuart Cohen and Sisco/Lubotsky, Mackenbach House, Bloomingdale, Illinois, 1979

Traditional post-modernism seeks to look backward in order to go forward. It should not be regarded as a jettisoning of modern architecture itself, but as an attempt to pick up the threads of theory and style, which were cut by the pioneers of the Modern Movement, especially the concerns for architectural history and for visually comprehensible relationships between old and new buildings. In its inclusiveness, traditional post-modernism does not propose an independent style; it is a sensibility dependent on forms and strategies drawn from the modernist and the pre-modernist work that preceded it, though it declares the obsolescence of both. It is *a* modern style but not *the* modern style. In its recognition of the transience and multiplicity of styles within the historical epoch we call modern, it rejects the emphasis on unity of expression that was so central to modernism itself. Traditional post-modernism recognizes both the discursive and expressive meaning of formal language. It recognizes the language of form as communicating sign as well as infra-referential symbol: that is to say, it deals with both physical and associational experience, with the work of art as an act of presentation and representation. It rejects the idea of a single style in favor of a view that acknowledges the existence of many styles (and the likely emergence of even more), each with its own meanings, sometimes permanently established, but more often shifting in relation to other events in the culture.

In architecture, Robert Venturi and Charles Moore can be seen as the leading advocates among an older generation of traditional post-modernists; Michael Graves and myself, among others, from the point of view of age, though not from one of ideology, occupy a middle ground (that is, we are young enough to have been students of Venturi and Moore), and an even younger generation, including Stuart Cohen, Thomas Gordon Smith, and the Arquitectonica group, is beginning to make its positions felt as well.

Venturi and Moore are in many ways transitional figures: their theoretical positions are more "advanced" in the movement toward a position that includes modernist and pre-modernist values than is their built work, which as often as

Fig. 10. Thomas Gordon Smith,
Tuscan House, Livermore,
California, 1979

Fig. 11. Thomas Gordon Smith,
Laurentian House, Livermore,
California, 1979

not tends to be abstract and nonrepresentational (Venturi's Allen Art Museum and Hartford Stage; Moore's own house in Los Angeles) as it is representative of ideas that are contextually based (Venturi's three Brant houses and Benjamin Franklin house "restoration"; Moore's Burns House and Piazza d'Italia). This is not surprising since their education was modernist, and until recently theirs has been a virtually solitary struggle to integrate its ideals with the wider body of architectural culture.

The work of the other traditional post-modernists who have been cited can be characterized by a struggle to use traditional languages without falling into the presumed trap of revivalism. The heritage of modernism remains a problem for all: its impulse to "make it new," as Ezra Pound put it seventy years ago, conflicts with the sensibility to make it legible and make it appropriate; the preoccupation with traditional languages is often at the expense of the languages of modernism, which, no matter how abstract, have come to mean certain things in the culture at large, and the recognition of stylistic diversity can be viewed as *laissez-faire* permissiveness. Thus, in some traditional post-modernist work the grammar of architectural composition has not been explored with the same care as have the individual elements or the overall meanings; in other words, some traditional post-modernist work has become "picturesque."

Everywhere there are signs of an emerging cultural resynthesis: Richard Gilman sees a "new naturalism" in the drama; John Gardner pleads for a "moral fiction" based on a belief in an art dedicated to the "preservation of the world of gods and men"; Daniel Bell states that the "problem, then, is whether culture can regain a coherence, a coherence of sustenance and experience and not only of form."[40] Signs of the shift in sensibility in art and architecture abound. All this seems clear enough, and I hope that what I have written has shed some light on the nature of these shifts. If what I have written has any value, it is as a reminder that all which glitters in a new or different way is not necessarily golden, that the ranks of the avant-garde may no longer be the exclusive defenders of the holy grail of insight: that a shift in sensibility need have very little if anything to do with progress. The fact of the matter is that the reaction to modernism is not only a vote of "no confidence" in its ideology but also a recognition that its forms are exhausted. As Gardner observes:

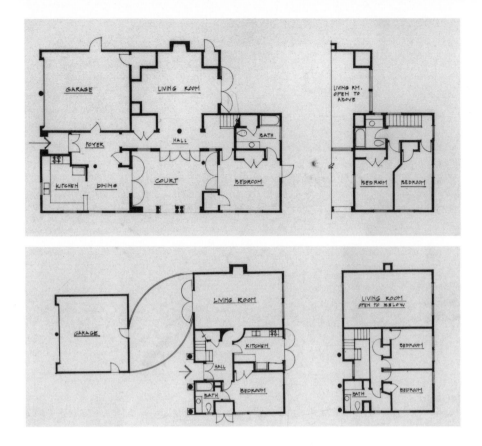

When modes of art change, the change need not imply philosophical progress; it usually means only that the hunter has exhausted one part of the woods and has moved to a new part, or to a part exhausted earlier, to which the prey may have doubled back.

Aesthetic styles—patterns for communicating feeling and thought—become dull with use, like carving knives, and since dullness is the chief enemy of art, each generation of artists must find new ways of slicing the fat off reality.[41]

Fig. 12. Thomas Gordon Smith, floor plans, Tuscan House, Livermore, California, 1979

Fig. 13. Thomas Gordon Smith, floor plans, Laurentian House, Livermore, California, 1979

The fundamental nature of this shift to post-modernism has to do with the reawakening of artists in every field to the public responsibilities of art. Once again art is being regarded as an act of communication as opposed to one of production or revelation (of the artist's ego and/or of his intentions for the building or his process of design). Though art is based on personal invention it requires public acceptance to achieve real value—to communicate meaning. An artist may choose to speak a private language, but a viewer must be willing and able to read the work, whether it be a book, a painting, or a building, for the work to have any kind of public life at all. To the extent that contemporary artists care about the public life of art, they are post-modernists (modernist artists make things for only themselves and/or for the gods); to the extent that an artist believes in the communicative role of form but is not willing to accept that such a role necessarily carries with it cultural meanings that are not inherent to the form, his is a schismatic post-modernism.

Modernism in architecture was premised on a dialectic between things as they are and things as they ought to be; post-modernism seeks a resolution between— or at least a recognition of—things as they were and as they are. Modernism imagined architecture to be the product of purely rational and scientific processes; post-modernism sees it as a resolution of social and technological processes with cultural concerns.

Post-modernism seeks to regain the public role that modernism denied architecture. The Post-Modern struggle is the struggle for cultural coherence, a coherence that is not falsely monolithic, as was attempted in the International Style in architecture, or by National Socialism in the politics of the 1920s and '30s, but one whose coherence is based on the heterogeneous substance and nature of modern society: post-modernism takes as its basis things as they are *and* things as they were. Architecture is no longer an image of the world as architects wish it to be or as it will be, but as it is.

17

Classicism in Context
1980

Just as the Post-Modern condition in architecture has been misinterpreted by journalists and others who see it as an independent style that is anti-modern (anti–Modern Movement/International Style), so too has the renewed interest in the classical language of architecture been misconstrued in a variety of ways. In this brief essay I would like to argue for the continuity of the classical language throughout "modern" (that is, post-Renaissance) architecture and to propound some strategies for its use which I believe to be valid for contemporary architecture.[1]

If one accepts the term *modern* in the broad way I have suggested, then it can be argued that what we have considered to be various independent and successive styles—the baroque, rococo, neoclassical, modernist, and Post-Modernist—are simple phases in a continuum and as such are useful for understanding the historical evolution of architecture in the "modern" period. Moreover, if one accepts the argument that the work of the modern period can be viewed as a continuum, one can then claim that the modern is as unified as the earlier Gothic or classical periods are now perceived to have been.

Further, one can argue that the continuum of modern architecture is characterized not merely by a succession of stylistic periods—though, as I hope to demonstrate, they play a key role—but by three paradigms for action. The interaction between these paradigms, on the one hand, and the compositional sensibilities initially characterized by the historian Heinrich Wölfflin as the four stages of style (the classical, mannerist, baroque, and rococo), on the other, establishes the particularities of individual work, as well as individual historical phases in the modern continuum.

The three paradigms of modern architecture are the classical paradigm, the vernacular paradigm, and the process or production paradigm. The classical paradigm is concerned with the grammar, syntax, and rhetoric of what is generally called the classical language—arguably *the* language and tradition of Western architectural culture. The classical paradigm takes the compositional methods and the basic forms of the Graeco-Roman world as the model for an architecture that attempts to be at once rational and humanistic (natural). The vernacular paradigm is based on a belief that the classical paradigm is elitist and that the architecture of the modern world should find a local basis for form. This paradigm uses the messy vitality of everyday life to combat the expressionless clichés into which an overdependence on the other two paradigms can lead, and supplies forms that are culturally highly specific. The process paradigm represents an attempt to establish a model for conditions which are distinctly those of the modern, and especially the industrialized, world. These conditions can be said to have had their greatest architectural impact in the revolutionary processes that have evolved for the making of building components. Since architecture, as opposed to mere building, is a representation and not a direct expression of reality, it is an art. Thus the relationships between actual architectural production and each of these traditions or modes—the classical, the vernacular, and the technological—are symbolic, and it is this symbolic relationship that gives the three modes their paradigmatic nature in the design process.[2]

Since the Renaissance, classicism, seen as a distinct mode, has been explored in two ways in architecture: syntactically, as an aid to composition, and rhetorically, as an aid to expression. Despite the impression given by the proponents of the Modern Movement, the pioneers of modernism were not only thoroughly grounded in classicism but also, as Colin Rowe, Reyner Banham, and others have suggested, preoccupied with its grammar (forms) while they struggled to free themselves from its rhetoric (content).

Much of the most satisfying "advanced" modernist work from this century represents a continuing search for a new rhetoric, based on production grafted onto the "eternal" or continuing principles of classical composition. In this sense Modernism and Post-Modernism are part of the same modern, pluralist tradition. Despite the claims of the polemicists for modernism, it now seems clear that the exploration of classical themes in the nineteenth century did not thwart architecture's ability to come to terms with either the processes of production or the new functional demands placed on it. Rather, the use of known models and the mastery of classical grammar made it possible for architects to conceptualize some of the most functionally and technologically complex works ever built and also to make those works comprehensible to the public at large. For example, innovative works at the beginning and end of this cycle of revival—Soane's Bank of England (1788–1830) and McKim, Mead & White's Pennsylvania Railroad Station (1906)—each combine Roman imperial formal elements with elements unique to the production processes of the nineteenth century (especially glass and iron roofs) to produce remarkably original and wholly modern works. Similarly, Frank Furness, in his Pennsylvania Academy of the Fine Arts (1871–76), combined the grammar of classical composition and the techniques of nineteenth-century constructional processes (glass and iron) with Gothic form (the vernacular paradigm) to produce a museum and art school which express the very modern idea that the making and viewing of art have come to enjoy a kind religious function in the modern world.

If one accepts the thesis that modern architecture appropriately represents the complex interaction between the often conflicting issues that characterize the modern world, then one must accept a hybrid or pluralist stance—in short, a humanist view of architecture. From this point of view it is difficult to sustain a belief in modernism's struggle to re-establish a monolithic style, because such a style would possess an intolerably inadequate palette with which to address the complexities of modern life.

Pluralism is the characteristic state of the modern world. In architecture it is represented by the interaction of the three paradigmatic modes of representation (the classical, vernacular, and process). When architecture tips too far in the direction of one or another of these modes and excludes the others, it runs the risk of becoming dry, dogmatic, dead, alienated. When the classical paradigm becomes dominant, as in the drawings of J. N. L. Durand, in some of the projects of Albert Speer (but not in his great searchlight architecture at Nuremberg), or in the work of the Soviets in the 1930s and 1940s, architecture is sapped of the vitality that almost inevitably grows out of the explicitly represented dialogue between what is real in the present and what is imagined from the past. Such a dialogue enriches and makes meaningful the architecture of Palladio, of the Shingle Style architects, and of Le Corbusier, but not that of Quinlan Terry, of SOM, or of Norman Foster.

At this moment, it seems possible once again to be more explicit in our use of traditional architectural language than we have been for fifty or so years. Suddenly classicism is everywhere discussed, its grammar and rhetoric everywhere explored. This current interest in classicism encompasses many attitudes, including a strict adherence to its grammatical rules but not to its forms (Leon and Rob Krier, Aldo Rossi), a sensuous joy in its most representative shapes (Thomas Gordon Smith), or a cool correctness with regard to both syntax and rhetoric (Allan Greenberg, Quinlan Terry). My own feeling is that these attitudes, and especially the last, which Robert Venturi and Denise Scott Brown have characterized as "too easy," are at the very least too hermetic—too sealed off from the pluralism of modern experience as represented by a concern for the process of building and for the relationship of high art to the vernacular. I would agree that, just as it has since virtually the inception of modern times at the beginning of the Renaissance, the hybrid composition truly bespeaks our moment. So it was in modernism, where Le Corbusier's or Mies's combinations of classical composition and machine form are surely more potent than Hannes Meyer's single-minded built ideology. The work of Alvar Aalto surely confirms this—his combination of natural and vernacular forms with the mechanomorphology of high modernism may have baffled narrow ideologues such as Sigfried Giedion, but it is surely this which gives his work its unique character.

We stand at an interesting point: everything seems free and open yet some are already arguing for "correctness," for a set of universally applicable rules. Classicism is once again beginning to reoccupy its "normal" place in modern architecture. But the seeming contradictions between its syntactical and rhetorical functions, as in the 1920s, threaten those who naively long for a singular style, a utopia of uniformity.

Not since the breakup of the Gothic has there been a singular style in the West; nor has there ever been a language—whether spoken or built—that did not change over time, that did not incorporate phrases from slang (the vernacular) and from the foreign sources to which it was exposed. An academy may try to keep language pure, but a vital civilization will inevitably confound that intent and in so doing keep it alive. Post-Modern classicism differs from modernist classicism in the value it sets on the classical tradition as a system of representation. We are not witnessing a rebirth of a universal classical style (like that of the Graeco-Roman world). Rather, we are witnessing a revitalization of the classical tradition in the context of other traditions. Through our better understanding of its inherent nature and through a process of cross-pollination with other traditions the classical language can again flourish. Left to stand by itself, isolated from the broader context of modern life, it cannot but again, as in the 1930s and 1940s, resonate with the implacable coldness of death.

18

Discontinuity and Continuity in Modern Architecture
Modernism and Post-Modernism
1981

> Modern artists (I don't mean all of them) who, through natural impotence
> or fear of walking down already traveled streets or out of misguided respect for
> the ineffability of life, refuse to give it a form; those who deliberately exclude
> every pleasant sound from music, every figurative element from painting, every
> syntactical progression from the written work, condemn themselves to this:
> to not circulating, not existing for anyone. Since there is no possibility for great
> communion between the public and the artist, they also reject the ultimate
> possibility of social significance which an art born of life always has: to return to
> life, to serve man, to say something for him. They work like beavers, gnawing
> at the visible, driven by an automatic impulse of an obscure need for an outlet or
> the need to build themselves a dark, ever darker, ever more hidden shelter.
> But they will never save themselves if they lack the courage to come into the light
> again and look other men in the eye; they will not save themselves if, coming
> as they have from the street and not out of the museums, they do not have the
> courage to speak words that can go back into the street, into circulation again.
> —Eugenio Montale

Modern architecture as we know it is in disarray: though leading architects of the late phase of modernism continue to produce new work, the forms as well as theories on which that work is based have been seriously challenged by a new, "Postmodernist" generation of architects. These architects are forging a philosophical basis for architecture that expands the "subject matter" of design. The inherent pragmatism of architecture fetishized by the modernists as technological

Fig. 1. Charles Moore, Rodes
House, Los Angeles, 1979

Fig. 2. Charles Moore, Piazza
d'Italia, New Orleans, 1978

determinism and functionalism has been brought into a more balanced relation-ship with neglected historical and cultural issues.[1]

In architecture, the decade of the 1970s has been characterized by the debate between those who continued to advocate values which can be described as "modernist" and those who can be described as "Post-modernist." This debate is in many ways parallel in its intensity to the battle in the 1920s and 1930s between "progressive" traditionalism and "revolutionary" modernism. Yet it is important to keep in mind the wider framework of the political and cultural malaise of the 1970s, from the blunder and hypocrisy of Vietnam to the broken dreams and harsh reality of the West's "gas crunch."

Although the ideology of modernism is intertwined with a belief that art is shipwrecked in a commercial society, those pioneers of the modernist revolution of the 1920s who immigrated to the United States quickly found commercial (capitalist) society to be quite useful for getting their ideas built. Mies's great work in Chicago is his corporate work; much more the social idealist, Le Corbusier, who remained in France, also remained almost totally aloof from commercialism and became endlessly bitter about his meagre production. In any case, the decade of the 1970s opened with the leaders of the second generation of modernists in full flood of prosperity building at a vast scale in their respective countries and in the oil-rich enclaves of the so-called Third World. And it is clear that, despite the misgivings about technology those of us living in industrialized nations have, we continue to be fascinated with the technological bravura of the work of the late modernists such as I. M. Pei, John Portman, and Norman Foster. While we may be dismayed and even appalled by this aspect of the production of our own era, we cannot help but understand why this work continues to have such appeal in the so-called "developing" countries, where it has come to symbolize the most "progressive" and "modern" aspects of our society.

The Postmodernist generation does not suggest that the end of modern architecture is at hand, but rather that its modernist phase, characterized by the antihistorical catharsis of the *Neue Sachlicheit* in the 1920s and continued into the urbanely sophisticated, but rather less tragic, late modernism, is at once aes-thetically hidebound and alienated from many issues raised by pluralist culture.

In comparison with the monism of orthodox modernism, Postmodernism seeks to embody in architecture appropriate representations of the diversity of

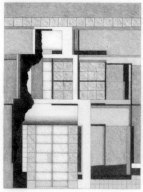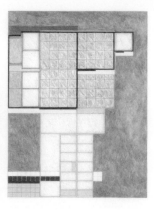

cultural experience. In so doing, it does not reject the technology and programs of our own time—it is not anti-modern or anti-contemporary—but seeks to represent experiences from history as well as from the vernacular of the everyday and the most advanced technology of the present.

Fig. 3. Michael Graves, drawing for warehouse conversion, Princeton, New Jersey, 1977

I have earlier suggested that Postmodernism is not a movement against anything, not a revolution, but a devolution; that is to say, Postmodernism, like the modernism it is in reaction to (but not simply against), is yet another phase in the ongoing continuum of modern architecture taken in the broadest sense—the tradition of Western humanist architecture that has prevailed since the Renaissance. This definition of the term *modern* was the one shared by architectural historians in England and America until the impact of German art history became dominant in the 1930s, and it parallels the definition of modern history in general.

If one accepts the term *modern* in this broad way, then it can be argued that what we have considered to be various independent and successive styles—the baroque, rococo, neoclassical, modernist, and Post-modernist—are simply phases in a continuum, and as such are useful for understanding the historical evolution of architecture in the modern period. Moreover, if one accepts the argument that the work of the modern period can be viewed as a continuum, one can then claim that the modern is as unified as the earlier Gothic or classical periods are now perceived to have been.

Further, one can argue that the continuum of modern architecture is characterized not merely by a succession of stylistic periods, though as I hope to demonstrate, they play a key role, but by three paradigms for action. The interaction between these paradigms on the one hand and the compositional sensibilities initially characterized by the historian Heinrich Wölfflin as the four stages of style on the other (the classical, mannerist, baroque, and rococo) establishes the particularities of individual work as well as individual historical phases in the modern continuum.

The three paradigms of modern architecture are 1) the classical paradigm, 2) the vernacular paradigm, and 3) the process or production paradigm. The *classical paradigm* is concerned with the grammar, syntax, and rhetoric of what is generally called the classical language—arguably *the* language and tradition of Western culture. The classical paradigm takes the compositional methods and the basic forms of the Graeco-Roman world as the model for an architecture that attempts to be at once rational and humanistic (natural). The *vernacular paradigm* is based on

Fig. 4. Venturi and Rauch, Dixwell Fire Station, New Haven, Connecticut, 1974

Fig. 5. Venturi and Rauch, Guild House, Philadelphia, 1964

a belief that the classical paradigm is elitist and that the architecture of the modern world should find a local basis for form for many of its tasks. The vernacular paradigm uses the messy vitality of the form of everyday life to combat the expressionless cliches into which an overdependence on the other two paradigms can lead, and supplies forms that are culturally highly specific. The *process paradigm* represents an attempt to establish a model for conditions that are distinctly those of the modern, and especially the industrialized, world. These conditions can be said to have had their greatest architectural impact in the revolutionary processes that have evolved for the making of building components. Since architecture as opposed to mere building is a representation (therefore, an art) and not a direct expression of reality, the relationship between actual architectural production and each of these traditions or modes—the classical, the vernacular and the technological—is symbolic. It is this symbolic relationship that gives the three modes their paradigmatic nature in the design process.

From this theoretical position, it can be further argued that in the early part of the modern era, that is, before the industrial age of the late eighteenth century, the issues raised by the vernacular and process paradigms were largely ignored by architects (with the exception of Palladio, whose combination of the classical and vernacular modes is a notable early manifestation of the modern sensibility). As a result, it is possible to understand why the architecture of the first 250 years of the modern period has been regarded not only as more unified than that which came after (that is, as concerned only with one paradigm, that of the classical) but also as distinct from that which followed. This is the position taken by the leading historians of modernist orthodoxy, especially by Sigfried Giedion, Nikolaus Pevsner, and others who have traced the origins of what they too narrowly describe as modern architecture only to the mid-eighteenth century.

While it is true that modern architecture did not begin to struggle with the issues raised by the process paradigm until the late eighteenth century, it continually dealt with the contradictory impulses raised by a struggle for universal order implicit in the academic model and for the need to respond to local traditions implicit in that of the vernacular. In relatively simple cultural terms this struggle can be seen in Palladio's villa architecture; at a more complex level, it gives the work of the Spanish and Portuguese in the Americas that solemn and almost obsessional quality that distinguishes sixteenth- and seventeenth-century

Fig. 6. Allan Greenberg, model of Building for Best Products, Venice Biennale, 1980

Hispanic-American work from the much less interesting comparable work at home, and therefore represents in a natural way the struggle outside Europe for hegemony between the Western and the indigenous/vernacular cultures, a struggle that is a political hallmark of the modern era from its inception. Thus, while the European succession of styles, insofar as they are applied to public work, can be seen as each wholly classicist (Renaissance or normative classicism, mannerist classicism, baroque classicism, etc.), once the architectural issues become more utilitarian, as in the design for villas for working farms, or the styles applied north of the Alps (as in Germany or rural France) or beyond Europe itself (as in the new world), the vernacular tradition interacts with the classical almost from the inception of the modern era.

After 1750, as a result of new pressures brought on by the revolution in production techniques, the issues become still more complex and even more related to utilitarian issues. The interaction between the three paradigms begins with a vengeance (rampant eclecticism), leading to the confusion of styles and modes that the modernists of the 1920s, looking back nostalgically to the monism of the Gothic era, sought to recapture. The succession of compositional modes in the nineteenth century (the so-called "Battle of the Styles") is usually characterized as the by-product of a desperate confusion. But it can be argued that the restatement of the classical styles from neo-Renaissance classicism (Ledoux, Boullée) through neorococo classicism (the so-called "modern-French" style of the Beaux-Arts typified by the work of Victor Laloux at the end of the nineteenth century) is a natural result of the cyclical functioning of Wölfflin's four stages of style in relationship to the interaction of either the classical or the vernacular paradigms, with the paradigm of process leading to a new synthesis, which we call Romantic. For example, complex works at the beginning and end of this cycle of revival—Soane's Museum at Lincoln's Inn Field of circa 1820 and McKim, Mead & White's Pennsylvania Railroad Station of 1906—each combine Roman imperial formal elements with those unique to the production processes of the nineteenth century—especially glass and iron roofs—to produce a remarkably original and wholly "modern" work. Similarly, Frank Furness, in his Pennsylvania Academy of the Fine Arts (1871–76), combines the grammar of academic composition and the techniques of nineteenth-century constructional processes (glass and iron) with Gothic form (the vernacular paradigm) to produce a museum and art school that express the

Fig. 7. Robert A. M. Stern, New York Townhouse, New York, 1974–1975

very "modern" idea that the making and viewing of art have come to enjoy a kind religious function in the "modern" world.

If one accepts the thesis that modern architecture appropriately represents the complex interaction between often conflicting issues that characterize the modern world, then one must accept a hybrid or pluralist stance—in short, a humanist view of architecture. From this point of view it is difficult to sustain a belief in modernism's struggle to reestablish a monolithic style, because such a style would possess an intolerably inadequate palette with which to address the complexities of modern life: the single reading of modernism is one that is rooted neither in history nor in indigenous traditions but solely in the processes of production, and in its extreme form as represented in painting by Malevich or in architecture by Hannes Meyer, who deliberately tried to overthrow a humanist viewpoint. In its more traditional forms, represented in painting by Mondrian and in architecture by Le Corbusier, modernism tried to carry on humanist values while breaking with traditional modes of representation and substituting new subject matter (the processes of painting per se, the processes of machine production).

As such it was not necessarily doomed; what caused modernism's decline was its unbending utopianism based on a substitution of the values of technology for those of man. A rather more plausible attitude to the relationship between the real and the ideal is taken by Postmodernism, which calls for an architecture that represents the complex dialogue between man as he wishes to seem (the classical humanist), as he lives from day to day (the vernacular), and the rational processes of the objective world—that is, the technology man has produced and which continually threatens to overwhelm him.

If modernism is another stage of the modern period, it follows that its evolution can be analyzed in Wölfflinian terms as well. But the cycle of modernism is different from the preceding Romantic cycle in its attempt to hold on to the syntactical aspects of classicism but not its forms, and in its belief that those forms can be replaced by a new vocabulary based on the processes of production. Yet its evolution as a style conforms to the traditional pattern: such modernist works as Frank Lloyd Wright's Imperial Hotel or Mies's Reichsbank or Crown Hall can be labeled as Renaissance classicizing modernist; Wright's Midway Gardens or Le Corbusier's Unité at Marseille or Paul Rudolph's Art and Architecture Building at Yale as baroque; Piano and Rogers's Pompidou Center as rococo modernist. Similarly, it can be argued that certain high modernist buildings combine the process paradigm with vernacular forms: Le Corbusier's work with *béton brut* in the 1950s and his earlier de Mandrot and Mathes houses are notable examples of this tendency, as are most of Wright's smaller houses in which wood is treated as a machine product (Wright's essay "The Art and Craft of the Machine" makes this point quite explicitly). In the work of late modernist architects such as Norman Foster, any concern for the inherent ordering of classicism or a sense of the organic basis of form implicit in the vernacular is so outstripped by a worship of the paradigm of process that the buildings take on meaning purely as objects and not as architecture. That is to say, they appear more as containers for than as representations of human activity; they are emblems of a technology unchecked by human intention. It is this dehumanization of late modernism that triggers the Postmodernist reaction.

It cannot be overemphasized that the Postmodernism of our time is not a new style outside modern architecture, or even a revolutionary movement within

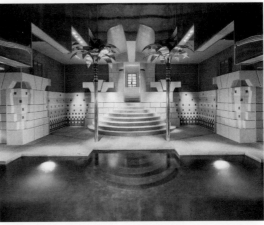

the modern against modernism. Postmodernism is a reaction that, as it grows, takes on its own characteristics within the continuum of the modern. It is not revolutionary at all; in fact, it can be seen as devolutionary, an ameliorative artistic movement within the modern, one that seeks to restore the balance between tradition and innovation within current architectural production after the puritanical, exclusivist revolution of modernism. Postmodernism is a return to a more "normative" or "inclusive" state. It should be regarded not as an attempt to jettison modern architecture but rather as an attempt to pick up those threads of theory and style that were deliberately cut by the proponents of modernism.

Postmodernism brings into question one of the principal issues of modernism, and of architecture itself—the relationship of form to ideology and, more particularly, to the "ideology of humanism." Le Corbusier, Mies, and Gropius were humanists, and therefore modern men as well as modern architects (as I have attempted to define modern), and their formal experiments (no matter how anti-historicist and anti-populist) were always involved with humanism (as explicitly manifested in Le Corbusier's investigations of proportion). Nonetheless, there was within the modernist attempt to establish a revolution in architecture (as in the Modern Movement in the other arts) a distinctly anti-humanist strain. A real attempt was made to operate beyond or outside the modern tradition as a whole. This can be seen in diverse experiments, such as James Joyce's late writings or those of Samuel Beckett, and in the idea of "non-objective" painting. This attempt to move beyond modern humanism has emerged in the post–World War II era as a kind of Postmodernism as well. Arnold Toynbee first used the term *post-modern* in the mid-1950s to characterize the new conditions brought about by the atrocities of the war and other dehumanizing events. Elsewhere, in an essay called "The Doubles of Post-Modern" (Chapter 16), I have characterized in some detail the distinctions between the two positions, and have attempted to demonstrate the inherent futility of the attempt to establish a condition of postmodernism outside the humanist tradition. Nonetheless, it is important to note that such an alternate position exists in the arts and in literature and that it is brilliantly represented in architecture by Peter Eisenman.

The definite break between the religious and the secular order of things, which marked the transition from the Gothic to the modern world in the late fourteenth and early fifteenth centuries, was not paralleled by any new set of circumstances

Fig. 8. Robert A. M. Stern, New York Townhouse, New York, 1974–1975

Fig. 9. Robert A. M. Stern, model of pool house, residence in Llewellyn Park, New Jersey, 1979–1981

Discontinuity and Continuity in Modern Architecture

Fig. 10. Venturi and Rauch, houses on Nantucket Island, Massachusetts, 1971

Fig. 11. Stanley Tigerman, House with a Pompadour, Ogden Dunes, Indiana, 1978–1979

in this century. Virginia Woolf may have felt that the world changed radically in 1910, but for most people then, as well as for us now looking back, it seems hard to see any break at that time as momentous as the shift of values that marked the transition from the theocraticism of the Middle Ages to the humanism of the modern era. The pluralism of the modern world, represented in architecture by the interaction between the three paradigmatic modes of representation that were initiated at the beginning of the modern period, is not effectively countered by the extreme modernist alternative that the Postmodernism of Eisenman and others proposes. Man still continues to measure the values of production against his own: Hiroshima and Three Mile Island represent severe challenges, which thus far are being met in a convincing, humanistic way.

An aspect of the dissatisfaction with modernism that became crystallized in the 1970s can be seen perhaps somewhat simplistically as the result of the realization that, while its proponents sought to dislodge architecture from the past by substituting materialist values (functionalism and technological determinism) for cultural ones, their intentions have been endlessly confounded by the inherently cultural basis of function. It is at the popular level that modernism's shortcomings have been most acutely perceived: the attempt to substitute a new language of form based solely on the material aspects of contemporary culture was constantly challenged by those who support that materialist culture, yet do so unquestioningly.

The intentions of modernism's proponents to establish a democratic style based on production are nowhere more seriously challenged than in the democratic marketplaces of the West. High-style modernism of the 1920s and '30s has become a fashionable style of architecture reproduced for rich clients, much as the various Louis styles are reproduced and sold in the best shops. Ironically, the truly democratic style in America as well as elsewhere is not modernist but modern: it is a robust if vulgar mixture of the three paradigms, and finds its expression in the leaning towers of pizza, split-level ranchburgers, and neo-Georgian gas stations of the suburban townscape. In the U.S., where the freestanding suburban single-family house and the commercial roadside shopping strip continue to be dominant building types, the paradigms of classicism and the vernacular flourish side by side with those drawn from the realm of technology. True, each is debased not so much by commercialism as by an absence that can be attributed to the lack of interest in traditional themes on the part of architects who might have supplied appropriately thoughtful models. The split-level raised-ranch neo-Georgian colonial houses and

Discontinuity and Continuity in Modern Architecture

Pizza Huts of consumer society are only a few of many hybrid building types that have emerged to meet the public's seemingly insatiable need to accommodate human aspirations, to the perils of technology left entirely to its own devices.

The transition of the 1970s from modernism to Postmodernism raises profound ideological issues; it cuts across traditional lines of artistic taxonomy (naïve art vs. academicism, high art vs. vernacular art, etc.) to address the culture as a whole. In Postmodernism, architecture struggles to recapture a sense of its own capacity to function as language and not merely as a process, to deal with different modes of behavior differently, to speak in guttural as well as refined dialects, to reflect upon and to represent the world as it is—a place for Parthenons and Pizza Huts, Le Corbusier and Levitt.

As the 1970s began, architecture was abstract, most architects content with the representation of the facts of a building's own making, the process of building having become the only subject symbolized in the design. The syntax had become the meaning. Today architecture is once again not only a matter of syntax but also one of rhetoric—the past is seen as somehow present, a necessary ingredient in the continuing evolution of architectural language. Classic and vernacular modes as well as an ongoing pleasure in the processes of production continue to dazzle us with new possibilities for meeting our challenges; we have a modern architecture still.

Fig. 12. Michael Graves, Snyderman House, Fort Wayne, Indiana, 1972

Fig. 13. Allan Greenberg, addition and renovation, seventeenth-century residence, Guilford, Connecticut, 1968–1972

19

Notes on Post-Modernism
1981

Author's Note: This essay is a distillation of two of the four seminars in which I participated at Yale in January and February 1978. Though the editorial work on the transcripts of the sessions leading to the published text was not completed until early 1979, and though many of the ideas initially stated in the seminars had been reformulated in the intervening months, I have tried to stay close to the tone of the original discussion. I ask that the reader bear with the seeming anachronisms of this strategy.

I think it appropriate to start with some comments on the term *post-modernism* and my use of it.[1] I adopted the term as a result of some discussions with Peter Eisenman in 1975. Eisenman pointed out that while it was perfectly clear that he and I were both against the same things, we were not in favor of the same things. That is, we were both concerned with the breakup of the seemingly monolithic Modern Movement, and we were both contemptuous of the kind of stylish, appliqué modernism that we saw around us, as well as the anti-architectural philistinism that was the unfortunate by-product of the student movements of the late 1960s. I was only too familiar with the latter, as much from teaching experiences at Columbia as from my own student days at Yale, where its earliest manifestations could be seen in the back-to-the-woods, architecture-as-act movements of the 1960s. Though Eisenman and I approached the situation from quite opposite points of view, we each saw the so-called revolutionary conditions of architecture of the sixties as ideologically confused, artistically debilitated, nihilistic, and anti-intellectual. Although these student movements supplied a necessary criticism of the then-current scene and made obvious the hypocrisy that afflicted our national political attitudes toward the war in Vietnam and the situation of minorities at home, they hadn't led to anything positive in terms of architectural production. What had begun as a useful critique of a situation proved unable to develop a positive direction of its own; it had no firm commitment in form-making or even a coherent political or social program. It was against things but not for things.

By 1975 Eisenman had evolved a point of view that was positive in its insistence that the ideals of utilitarian functionalism and technological determinism had hopelessly compromised the formalist intentions of the initiating architects of the Modern Movement and reduced that movement to a commercial exercise. He labeled his position "post-functionalism" and suggested that my position, which was, of course, an outgrowth of the work of Charles Moore and Robert Venturi, was post-modern. By post-modern, I believe Eisenman really meant anti-Modern Movement; moreover, I think he hoped it might also be against the Western humanist tradition. But as I hope to demonstrate, and as I see it, the term *postmodern* really describes a condition that comes after and is in reaction to the Modern Movement, and attempts to effect a synthesis between it and other strains of the Western humanist tradition.

In any case, I adopted the term as a useful label, only to find, just after I went "public" with it at an *Oppositions* forum in January 1976, that Charles Jencks was bringing out a book, *The Language of Post-Modern Architecture,* which dealt with the same subject.[2] This discovery, though initially annoying, was in the long run consoling: I was no longer the only person to believe that modernism was finished and that a new synthesis, a devolution and *not* a revolution, was well under way.

Though Jencks's book is quite wonderful in many ways, it fails to define very precisely, if at all, just what post-modernism is; it also does not make any connections between post-modernism in architecture and the use of the term to describe similar (but by no means identical) movements in the other visual arts, in music, or in literature. Its weaknesses and its strengths helped me to define my position and to outline a course of action; as a result, I undertook a cross-disciplinary investigation of post-modernist tendencies that resulted in my essay "The Doubles of Post-Modern" (1980) [Chapter 16 in this volume].

Arnold Toynbee appears to have made the earliest significant use of the term *post-modern* in his *Study of History* of 1954 (although Joseph Hudnut used it in 1943 in a once quite widely known essay, "The Post-Modern House"). Toynbee's argument on behalf of a post-modern period was developed by Geoffrey Barraclough in his book *An Introduction to Contemporary History.*[3] For Barraclough, the post-modern period, the origins of which he sets at about 1870–90, marked a radical break with the modern, or Western humanist, tradition; and a new "contemporary" history replaced the existing modern history which he believed had begun in the modern period, which, though imprecisely defined in architectural historiography, I accept as having begun around 1450.

I believe the post-modern/contemporary phenomenon described by Barraclough does not represent a break from the modern tradition but rather is a new phase within it. The modern period still exists and thrives. Culturally and politically we have not yet arrived at that state of true pluralism in which the Western humanist value system is only one among others of equal importance in the world—a state that Barraclough claims as essential to the definition of the new post-modern period. And in architecture I would say that the same is true. So what we have is architecture still grounded in the modern tradition but with the existence of two phases: modernism and post-modernism, each quite different from the other. Modernism was an attitude toward the making of things that sought to free itself from any reference to the past, but went further by rejecting historical values and advocating change at all cost. For modernism, the past merely served to define a negative condition: new is better. Having cut the thread of historical continuity insofar as artistic production is concerned, the modernist had no sources for his art outside the circumstances of its commissioning and the wellspring of his own perceptions. As a result, modernist art is at once materialistically determined and self-referential. Modernism's rejection of historical retention set each new work of art adrift to make its own independent iconic claim. Post-modernism, on the other hand, does not reject modernism and its monuments, especially not the way modernism rejected all previous stylistic movements—romanticism in particular, but also the Renaissance, baroque, and rococo—but post-modernism does reject the anti-historical stance of modernism and its cult of newness. Post-modernism in architecture argues that the modern period is characterized by competing ideas that co-exist: eclecticism, associationalism, representation, abstraction, and nonrepresentation.

Ours is a culture torn between the urge to jettison the past and start anew and the urge to link up in as many ways as possible with the past in order to ameliorate the impact of the radical changes science and technology have thrust upon us. Post-modernism accepts this seemingly contradictory condition, whereas modernism does not. Post-modernism holds out the possibility of a truly inclusive philosophy of action that will accommodate the condition of the present to the values society believes were embodied in the past and that it wishes to carry forward. As a philosophical condition, post-modernism is difficult to describe because one always wants to define things by saying what they are not. But to define a philosophical condition by saying that it represents an acknowledgment of everything, that it is, in essence, permissive and not restrictive, opens one up to the jibes of those who confuse permissiveness with moral and intellectual laxity. For Eisenman, for example, *permissive* is a nasty, pejorative term. He argues that he is the first true modernist, and in a certain way I think he's right. Eisenman has really thrown out everything from architecture except the object, and in his own work meaning comes from a confrontation between the viewer and the object.

You wouldn't include early de Stijl architecture as a source for Eisenman's work, then?

The work of such de Stijl architects and sculptors as Georges Vantongerloo is, of course, a source, but its implications for architecture as opposed to sculpture are not so extreme. It does not go nearly so far as Eisenman's—it isn't nearly as abstract. Next to Eisenman's House VI, Rietveld's Schroeder House looks like a sales model for National Homes: It's a real house! Or at least it comes close to being one, with a bottom and a top, a front and a back, and all kinds of literal flexibility—and it doesn't have a slot severing the conjugal bed. It's positively accommodating, primitively functionalist from Eisenman's point of view, I suppose.

Do you feel that Eisenman's is a valuable gesture to make at this time and place?

I think it's an interesting last gasp, an extreme cry in behalf of modernism, a splendid yawp just before the ever-receding modernist apocalypse. But it poses a dilemma for Eisenman: what to do next? House X, which is not going to be built, seems just a further complication of the ideas explored in House VI. An important question that Eisenman's work raises, and one that is implicit in the reductionism that is part of modernism, remains: what is the value of the object after all concern with utility and commodity and representation is omitted from the design process, when architecture is left naked and pure? Eisenman's last-gasp modernism comes at a time when modernism in the other arts is already under considerable attack.

In art criticism, for example, the term *post-modernism* has been used since the 1960s, principally to describe a direction of thinking that rejects the absoluteness of Clement Greenberg's claims about what he believes is the inherent nonrepresentational nature of painting and sculpture. Brian O'Doherty, Gregory Battcock, Calvin Tompkins, and Rackstraw Downes each use the term *post-modernism* in important ways. Though none of them has defined it precisely, Downes, in his essay in *Tracks* on behalf of realism brings the argument quite close to my own.[4] Modernism's anti-representational stance has reduced painting and sculpture to gestural arts in which craft has disappeared; as a result it has become very difficult to distinguish the empty gestures from those that are redolent with meaning. The seeds of the post-modernist "devolution" in art were sown in the late 1950s in the work of Robert Rauschenberg and Jasper Johns: not only is their use of recognizable imagery important, but their mixing of media represents a rejection of modernism's search for the essence of any given art form—pure painting, for example, as Greenberg defines it.

Are you suggesting that it's even more difficult to achieve the Greenbergian goal of purity or essence in architecture because you rely on buildings to serve some function, some external purpose outside themselves? And that Eisenman's search for pure architecture is a step backward? Might it also be true that if Eisenman were pursuing Greenberg's goal, he is going in the wrong direction? His buildings don't strike me as notable titillations for the architectural eye because they ignore so much of what architecture needs to do.

Greenberg's rigid and exclusivist insistence on modernist painting as the essence of painting, as pure painting, represents an extreme point of view that is sustained in the work of only a very few artists, most of whom I think are decorative but dull—Jules Olitski, Barnett Newman, Stuart Davis. Most modernist painters cling to some form of representation—whether it is Mondrian's syncopated grids that depict the boogie-woogie or Jackson Pollock's calligraphic gestures, which render visible the processes of art. Representation in painting and in the other arts is at once a source of pleasure (if only in what Edmund Wilson described in another context as "the shock of recognition") and a way to communicate meaning. Modernist architecture tended to substitute utopianism for representationalism; it focused its energies on the world as it might be and often lost sight of and interest in the world as it is.

While I would agree that architecture has to have a utopian ambition, I do not think it needs to be as single-minded a vision as it was. A post-modernist utopia would be one in which the various cultures would co-exist while each would retain its meaning and character. Frank Lloyd Wright, Le Corbusier, and Ebenezer Howard, three major utopian speculators of this century, were pretty explicit about how people should live, what they should do, where they should brush their teeth, everything. I think many views of utopia are wall-to-wall impossible, tyrannical in the most basic sense. I don't mean to throw out idealism, but an idealism that is based not on an improvement of what exists but on a radical imposition of something new is a form of totalitarianism. Progress is not really so dead as the philosophy of progress has made it appear to be. I think that it is part of the human condition to have an ameliorative urge, a progressive urge. But I think the idea of progress as its own reward, which was a pretty hot idea in the late nineteenth century, is probably dead. We know that some kinds of progress bring almost as many problems as possibilities. Modernism failed to recognize the retrogressive implications of material progress. Post-modernism attempts to measure progress relative to its absence.

Post-modernism has been described as a naïve throwback to nineteenth-century positivism. This is not so: the nineteenth century believed in progress as its own reward; the post-modernist sees progress as a relative process. The idea that small is beautiful is a post-modernist one. One of our contemporary dilemmas is that an intelligent person cannot act outside of history. The concept of history is really a concept of the modern period. It is the background against which we operate; modernity is the condition by which action in the present is measured in relationship to similar actions in the past. Modernism tries to escape from history but not from modernity. Despite their rejection of history, the advocates of modernism knew that history was closing in on them. They felt its terrible weight and they couldn't get away from it. I don't believe you can ever escape history; as Philip Johnson ruefully pointed out to architects at Yale in the 1950s: you cannot not know history.

Post-modernism is a frame of mind. It's a phase of history, a mood. And it's definitely here. Maybe it would be better if we called it "blue," or something you know. But it is a phase, and though someday it may have a proper name of its own, we're stuck with this "post-modern" one, at least for now.

Post-modernism embodies a kind of relativist position, an inclusive position, a permissiveness in the sense that everything can find its own level and its own expression, that each thing has its own value, and that the architect's job or society's job is to weigh and balance these things to make relationships. The very fact that today we can talk about buildings having meanings apart from those specifically related to functional accommodation and technological resolution—without anyone screaming in agony—confirms that our architectural culture has shifted from the modernist to the post-modernist: modernist architects would never acknowledge that buildings had built-in meanings. Gropius said that buildings were basically constructs to solve functional problems in relationship to technology, that they took on a style as a result of observation made from without. We recognize that when we make something, we consciously manipulate existing meanings, and that in the act of making we understand that the meanings might or might not change, that our work might add or subtract from them or modify those meanings. We think about meaning; we do not wait for society to assign meanings to our work, though on the other hand, we recognize that it will do so in time and that those meanings will become part of the meaning of the building we have designed.

One thing that bothers me is the dilemma that seems to arise from our need to make distinctions and our inability to really believe in those distinctions.

I think your dilemma is part of our inheritance from modernism: we're all trained in modernism, though this is much less true for the students in this room than for the teachers in this room. For example, the way we study art history is affected by modernist dialectics: two slides, this one or that; one slide usually represents one set of values and the other represents its opposite. We are programmed to see art as a dialectic when it isn't that simple. The urge to make categories is a modern obsession; the codification of knowledge in terms of values—good guys and bad guys—is modernist.

A movement is not really a style. The Modern Movement (which I consider to be the polemicizing arm of modernism) was about a lot of ideas that found their most complete expression in the International Style, which was the classicizing formal language that emerged in the 1920s. There were other styles that were equally involved in the ideas of the Modern Movement, but they were not as expressive or as potent; more importantly, they were considered anticlassical, and the classical taste is the dominant one in Western humanism. The origins of post-modernism in architecture can be traced to the 1950s. Important milestones include the publication of Henry-Russell Hitchcock's history of nineteenth- and twentieth-century architecture, which revealed the complexity of the period under discussion and shattered many myths fostered by Giedion and Pevsner; Reyner Banham's *Theory and Design in the First Machine Age,* which drew open the curtain that the polemicists of CIAM had dropped over certain modernist experiments in the 1920s that did not conform to their conception of what the new architecture should be; Vincent Scully's Shingle Style, which represented a stylistic movement in the modern period that was as clearly articulated and as pervasive, as inventive and as responsive to tradition as the rococo or the baroque, but which integrated classicism and the vernacular in a way that only the example of Palladio provided a precedent.[5] Post-modernist design was anticipated by Eero Saarinen, who sensed the limitations of the minimalism and nonrepresentationalism of the International Style. Saarinen was misunderstood by his contemporaries, including Minoru Yamasaki and Edward Durrell Stone, who parodied his intentions. Yet Saarinen's TWA Terminal at Kennedy Airport, the Dulles Airport outside of Washington, D.C., Bell Labs, and the Stiles and Morse Colleges at Yale are each an embodiment of Saarinen's belief in the "style for the job," and as such the buildings are important precursors of post-modernism. Intimations of post-modernist design can also be seen in the writings and some projects of Matthew Nowicki, who worked with Saarinen on the early proposals for Brandeis University. Nowicki was a Pole who was stranded here as a result of the Second World War. He was to have designed Chandigarh but was killed in an airplane crash in Egypt on a trip to the site. Like Saarinen, Nowicki had begun to question the presumptions of the Modern Movement. I think most of us do not now find Nowicki's architecture and sketches to our taste. The buildings are late 1940s structural handstands. Even his writings are probably more important in the context of their historical position than on their own terms.

So much for the precursors of post-modernism and its broad premises. What are its beliefs? How are they expressed in bricks and mortar? The article "Drawing Towards a More Modern Architecture" in *Architectural Design* was my first attempt at establishing a definition for post-modernism that would be neither prescriptive, nor proscriptive (as Hitchcock and Johnson's was for the International Style), nor so vague and amorphous as to render the term meaningless or permissive in the pejorative sense.[6] In my *Architectural Design* article I listed three hallmarks of the post-modernist sensibility: contextualism, allusiveness, and ornamentalism are each strategies for reintroducing into architecture qualities that modernism had deliberately thrown out. These hallmarks are culturally and perceptually oriented, unlike those of modernism (functionalism, technological determinism, utopianism), which are pragmatic and ideological.

How can you argue that there's any more validity in the cultural function of architecture than in its pragmatic function?

Virtually all buildings in the history of architecture have been pretty much based in pragmatism—that is, in problem-solving. Whether it is a pharoah in need of a tomb or a nineteenth-century robber baron in need of a palace, a building begins with a program. But utilitarian programs repeat themselves. More importantly, despite the emergence of so many new programs and problems, most building types of our time have been largely carried forward from antiquity with only a very few innovations: the dome set on top of the basilica at Florence, the solid mass interrupting the basilica, as in the Prairie House of Frank Lloyd Wright, the skyscraper, the giant shed uninterrupted by internal supports, as at the Galerie des Machines. In any case, I don't think you can base a style on issues of function. Though style is not based on utilitarian pragmatism, it is a utilitarian device; style has function. It is the culturally responsive part of design.

This is in regard to another issue. Something you said yesterday seemed a little curious to me, and I was wondering if you would explain it further. In talking about the British Art Center you said that one of the ways you might go about judging whether it was a good or appropriate building was how closely it conformed to what was expected of a given type of building for its utilitarian and cultural purpose. What exactly do you mean by that?

The BAC is a very interesting case in point at this time (fig. 1). When I was in architecture school Louis Kahn's work exemplified a number of ideals, principally the one concerning the integration of structural and spatial concerns to make spaces of great integrity. Kahn also reintroduced historical architecture as a direct source of inspiration in the design process. But Kahn's use of history was abstract and personal; his buildings never looked like their models. For Kahn, history was meaningful on a personal, as opposed to a cultural, level. The history of the cultures that permitted him to build bore no particular role in his process of design. You remember that when Kahn learned that brick was the most suitable material for building in India and Pakistan, he asked brick what it wanted to be and it revealed to him that it wanted to be an arch. It is interesting that after this conversation Kahn did look at brick architecture, articulated or otherwise, but not at the brick architecture of the Indian subcontinent. Kahn turned to examples from Ostia Antica, which is part of the Western European tradition that he related to, but which is quite exotic for the ultimate users of the buildings he was about to design.

The self-referential aspect of Kahn's work characterizes the design of the BAC as well. On the exterior the building makes no effort to represent any aspect of

Fig. 1. Louis I. Kahn, Library Court, Yale Center for British Art, New Haven, Connecticut, 1974

its purpose; only the process of its making. Inside, the character of the display rooms is quite removed from the kinds of rooms that existed when the art in the permanent collection was originally made. Our expectations for a building that would establish an appropriate context for the work of George Stubbs and his contemporaries is only barely acknowledged by the use of wood paneling, which is treated as though it were a finer form of plasterboard and not as though it were a part of the tradition of Grinling Gibbons. Stubbs wants to be hung cheek by jowl with others, not isolated inside a white cube like Mondrian.

I am arguing for an architecture that is at once timeless and timely. Kahn's building is universal in its intentions; I am arguing for one that is specific and universal, one that deals in the eternal verities of light, structure, and space, which Kahn understood so well, and that also deals in the responsive or communicative aspects of style—not personal style but cultural style. The BAC is as it is because Kahn's ideas about architecture were as they were, not because of the purposes of the building—the sympathetic presentation of a significant collection of historical art. The BAC is a marvelous building, a key work of modernist art. In its way, it is perfect and wonderful, but is its way our way? In its search for rules broad enough to fit all exceptions, as Louis Sullivan put it, is it subtle enough to mark the distinctions and differences that make each situation, each work of art it contains, a unique moment to be savored for its own sake?

The wooden paneling was supposed to be referential to a certain time and place. Do you think that it was just not sufficiently characterized?

I've never been in an English country house in which Alvar Aalto had done the paneling.

Do you think the art really suffers?

Yes. The best place to see the art in the BAC is in the storerooms up at the top, where the paintings are hung on racks one next to the other and one atop the other. Images are jumbled up and the result looks quite like a picture gallery in a country house of the eighteenth and early nineteenth centuries, as depicted in paintings from the period. You can't put a dinky little picture of a dog on a vast wall and expect it to have the iconographic importance of a Raphael or a Mondrian. As an artist, Stubbs accepted the fact that his paintings would be hung as part of a "mosaic" of painted images; that his was an intimate, incidental art, not a transcendent one.

But do you think you could extend that argument and say that one of the ways of judging buildings in general is to see how much they conform to what is expected of them?

Yes.

Do you think that such a standard would be a kind of strange version of functionalism?

Cultural functionalism, not utilitarian functionalism.

Could it be that Kahn was not trying to make the universal kind of modernist space, but maybe was trying to make an atemporal thing? In other words, might it be possible to disassociate the building from how it is outfitted for a particular performance?

But why do that? In Kahn's gallery in Fort Worth, the Kimbell Art Museum, which is a marvelous building housing an eclectic collection of art from all periods, the universal space is functional from both the utilitarian and cultural point of view. The BAC, with its relatively fixed collection, suffers from Kahn's unwillingness to shift from the general to the particular; or rather, to include both the general and the particular. Probably this issue didn't occur to Kahn. Though he professed interest in the circumstantial, the ideal of the particular was outside Kahn's view of architecture. Take another case from the Yale campus—the display of American chairs from the eighteenth, nineteenth, and twentieth centuries in the Garvan Collection of the Yale Art Gallery. In this display (which I think was designed by Ivan Chermayeff), all the chairs are exhibited as though contemporary with one another. The exhibit seems to say that a chair is a chair is a chair ... and while this is true in the generic sense, it trivializes the role of the chair in a cultural sense. The same could be said of the human bottoms that the chairs support; it is true that an ass is an ass is an ass . . . but the differences of heft and carriage across time, not to mention from person to person, are what is really interesting. *Vive la différence!*

But it seems to me that if you go beyond that and extend the argument to other things, then at some point you have to start dealing with the question of what value is the unexpected and what could be reasonable grounds for using it.

The way you say the word *unexpected* brings us back to the modernist idea that a work of art is good if it is shocking; that somehow it is better if the viewer doesn't know what a work of art is about, if the viewer has to learn to understand it and therefore to admire it.

You're guilty of it.

Oh, I may be—yes, that's perfectly true.

I'll bet you don't like surprises.

Well…there are all kinds of surprises. There's the kind of surprise you get when you go to a movie expecting to see a musical with fabulous dancing and it turns out to have been even more fabulous than you had ever imagined. And then there's another kind of surprise you get when the marquee proclaims a musical but the film turns out to be an Ingmar Bergman musical, not very musical.

There's a distinction between shock and surprise.

We have now had a hundred years of the self-perpetuating avant-garde. Harold Rosenberg called it the "tradition of the new."[7] The idea of perpetual shock has become an institutionalized phenomenon in art, not without some jeopardy to the production of meaning. If an artist always feels he has to do something new, then what's the point of studying history, or of being educated at all except insofar as to master a craft, and even that is not very important when the shock value of novelty is held in higher esteem than the refinement of the object itself. Donald Judd has designed sculptures that he has had constructed over the telephone. What's the point of ever looking around? Why not go home and stare at your navel and wait for art to erupt from your inner self? This cult of the new, in which the new is defined as the difficult, is exactly what some of us have been struggling to overcome in the last twenty years. I think the hardest part is to admit that when confronted with the task of producing a building for a collection of eighteenth- and nineteenth-century horse and dog pictures, you might make rooms very close to the kinds of rooms architects of the late eighteenth century made, as close as you can get, in fact…

I think you could make an argument, though, that you have to design from what you know. And if you don't know anything, then I wonder what happens? You're just sort of in a vacuum as opposed to being in a situation where you have all this historical information to draw on.

I don't think it's enough to design from what you know unless you know everything. As an architect you must become a scholar; you must make the effort to find out what is expected of a building as well as what the point of origin is of a given set of circumstances that cause a building to be commissioned.

What is the point of departure then?

You have to find out what's expected of you by the client, by society, by history. As an architect you must not rest on a concern for the plumbing or the latest technological innovation or whatever. You should find out what the culture expects of a particular building.

I think what's bothering people is that doing precisely what is expected of you sounds entirely too much like feeding your mother.

What's wrong with feeding your mother? Can't you please your mother and still grow up? Why on earth has it come to be accepted that if you please your mother you don't grow up, but if you don't please your mother you do grow up? I think that's ridiculous. I think the problem is that you are preoccupied with originality. Why don't you get it right out on the table. You are nervous because you believe that in order to make it, you need to come forward with an unexpected, unprecedented, unfamiliar, idiosyncratic formal statement.

What you are saying has a lot to do with the word you were using. To me at least, you can change the word *unexpected* into such words as *new, startling, bold*. To me, unexpected needn't mean new.

I agree. So say a new thing by combining the words of the language in a new way. To make a subtle modification of what had been thought to be a closed issue is to do the unexpected. To shout an obscenity or to ignore all known rules of grammar and syntax is to shock.

To shift to another building type, another aspect of the problem, I was wondering about what one should do, what *you* do, when people expect (as I think they do) a certain kind of building, say a bank, to be new and sleek and modern even when it is to be built in a charming historical district.

The modernist styles, and especially the International Style, have already acquired meanings. The International Style now has a firmly established set of meanings and it can be used with as much deliberateness and self-consciousness as the Gothic or the Doric or whatever. The bank is a particularly interesting case in point. From the time of Soane through that of McKim, the urban bank was almost exclusively associated with the traditional, classical language of architecture, and especially with a strict representation of the orders on the principal façade. Since the time of Gordon Bunshaft's Manufacturers Hanover Bank in New York, the language of banks has been modernist classical, and especially associated with a Miesian vocabulary. This is particularly interesting given the anticapitalist intentions of many of the progenitors of modernism in architecture; but since the time of Bunshaft, that is, since the emergence of the second and largely American generation of modernist architects, the original associations of the language have been cast out in favor of a new and opposite set of values. I shall not go into the trivialization of Miesian form that accompanied this process, and which led one wag in the late 1950s to label Bunshaft's firm of Skidmore, Owings and Merrill as "Three Blind Mies."

The case of Edwin Lutyens's Westminster Bank on Piccadilly in London offers some interesting comments on the issue of a new building in a historical context. Lutyens's bank is located on a site adjoining Sir Christopher Wren's St. James Church. In deference to Wren's work, Lutyens designed the bank in the style of the church; it flanks the churchyard in a harmonious way, yet it is a fresh design that is remarkably interesting in its own right. Now, if one of us were to get the commission for the Westminster bank today—say it had been destroyed by bombs during the Second World War—how would we handle it? I would say that one would have to find a way to design a bank that satisfied the bank's image of itself as efficient, approachable, "up-to-date," while at the same time satisfying the culture's demands that Wren's building be honored. I would even suggest that the memory of Lutyens's building be honored too, not only because its (hypothesized) destruction is a monument to the folly of war, but also because the building represented something fine in its own right. To do this, one would have to be eclectic in the best sense. One would have to be able to speak of Wren and Lutyens and Mies; one would have to be something of an architectural linguist—that is, a scholar, which used to be the model of the architect before the romantic era's emphasis on personal invention.

So to those who worry about making things that look "modern," that is, contemporary, new, particular to our time, or whatever, I say relax. Take care of architecture and let the zeitgeist take care of itself. While it is folly to imagine that the past can be brought into the present, one can quite productively imagine what the past might have been like and include those imaginings in the formulations of the present. A building of our time is automatically a representation of our time.

Do you think that this kind of elaborate sensitivity to context is a fairly recent phenomenon or one that existed prior to modernism?

I think good architects have always responded to the context of their work. Even in modernism, despite its iconoclasm, the references, as in Le Corbusier's use of pipe rails and other machine products, to cite a typical example, were from outside architecture.

It seems you are saying that the culture of the present is tending to foster the establishment of a compound style. Do you think this tendency toward hybridization is only an aspect of our time, or is it characteristic of the bigger modern continuum?

The modern period is characterized by the production of art in relationship to the past; it is characterized by an eclectic process that is not known to have existed before the Renaissance. Modernism eliminated historicism, but it did not eliminate eclecticism; it chose its icons from outside architecture. The shingle style and free style architects of the late nineteenth century were not interested in the literal use of historical language, but they were in favor of historical influence. These styles drew upon earlier architecture just as has virtually every important architectural style since the classical language was revived in the fifteenth century on the basis of an eclectic integration of elements from the past. As a design strategy, eclecticism becomes increasingly difficult and interesting the further along we come in history. There is so much more to learn from and so many more meanings that it is more difficult to determine what to choose or at least what to relate to. Because we have access to so much past, we may become surfeited by it. This happened in the 1920s, and the purgative that was the Modern Movement, though possibly necessary, was a bit harsh. Its perpetuation for fifty or more years was surely disruptive to the natural processes of digestion.

Well, the reaction to the contextual brutality of modern architecture has tended to bring into the picture more incredibly soft attitudes toward things like preservation, such as, "That building is seventy years old or ninety years old, and it's just got to be there—and God help what we do if we ever start to tear it down." I think that is a kind of peculiar attitude, though perhaps it can be seen as a kind of overreaction to the excess of modernism. I'm wondering if forms of contextualism are also an overreaction, a kind of guilt over the lack of contextual sense in modern architecture?

I think the preservation movement is very much a post-modern phenomenon. Preservation would have been unimaginable twenty-five years ago. One reason preservation has become so popular is because people so distrust what might be built as the replacement for an old building, or have various grave and perfectly reasonable doubts that anything ever will be built at all. New Haven is a fine testament to the wisdom of these popularly held suspicions. The Hill neighborhood might have become horribly run down, but it was certainly better than the empty land that replaces it at the edges of downtown New Haven. The public is concerned that even an ordinary building from the past (but one at least built of nice materials) will be replaced by something that will be both ordinary and junky (built of absolute ersatz), or perhaps even worse, it might be replaced by something so offensively extraordinary that it looks like a building doing a handstand. Another thing about preservation is that, from an architect's point of view, and from the point of view of style, it brings us back in another way to the issues raised by Lou Kahn's building. We save these old buildings and then we proceed to remodel them in a way that is brutalizing to their inherent qualities. For example, the newly resuscitated Quincy Market in Boston causes one to ask, "For this they saved it? To sell wax candles?" And the renovation of the interior of H. H. Richardson's railroad station in New London, Connecticut, is absolutely illiterate.

Your school, the Art and Architecture Building, with its millions of faults, did not deserve the brutal renovations it has undergone. It is a work of art that has been outrageously trashed.

Part of the problem of "preservation architecture" lies with architects who have been brought up in the tradition of "zeitgeist determinism." These architects feel they must do something different because the times are different. So though they may argue that Richardson's station is great and that Richardson was a great architect, they are unwilling to subsume their own talents to the master's. We should measure the accomplishment of a work of historic preservation by a yardstick that takes into consideration our best and most scholarly estimate of what the original architect would have done, given the new program (but not necessarily given the new moment of history). It's easy to joke about the new international preservationist style of exposed brick walls, butcher block, ferns, and candles, but who will save our buildings from these preservers?

You seem to suggest that contextual responsiveness requires stylistic reproduction, or at least hybridization. Yet many of our most coherent urbanistic groupings incorporate buildings in many different styles.

Architecture can be contextually responsive in many ways. In addition to stylistic coherence, there is compositional congruence. If you're Hugh Hardy and you are designing a bit of infill in a Greek revival row in New York, is it appropriate to introduce a skewered bay window on the façade, even if you have quite faithfully otherwise reproduced the formal language of the row? If you're H. H. Richardson and you're building in Harvard Yard, can you make a new building that is at once a direct restatement of the original Georgian dormitory buildings in the Yard and a new statement that responds to a different functional program as well as to your own personal style? In this light it is interesting to compare Richardson's Sever Hall in the Yard with his Austin Hall for Harvard's Law School, which is located on what was in the 1880s a newly opened portion of the campus outside the Yard. Sever Hall is a work of contextual responsiveness; Austin is a far more abstract statement. Sever is for me the greater work. It is personal and contextual; it is a revival and a survival and in these ways a true innovation. I think it is true that in certain great cities buildings relate to each other by a sense of proportion and materials; relationships that are more abstract than representational. But if one part of the Rue de Rivoli were blown up, would you come in and rebuild it in a new way or would you rebuild the façade in the traditional style? The latter would be the only thing I could do. It's absurd to think otherwise.

The Rue de Rivoli is a special case. That's a kind of a set piece thing.

Well, the Greek revival streetscape on 11th Street, where Hardy is building, is also special; it is virtually the only one of its kind remaining in Manhattan.

If you build on a typical suburban street where all the houses have front lawns and little walks and garages and pitched roofs and shutters, and maybe one house is Georgian and so on, to me you don't come along and build a Villa Savoye—not so much because it does not fit in stylistically but because it does not fit compositionally. On the other hand, how do you add on to the Villa Savoye? What can one do? I think the courteous thing to do would be to make something sympathetic, even deferential. That's a good studio problem, right? It goes with my other wonderful fantasy, which is that one add on to the Villa Savoye because the family has gotten a divorce and there are now more kids and Mrs. Savoye (who kept the house) is remarried. The point is, instead of the monolithic attitude of the Modern Movement's International Style, which argued that we have a way of building, that the zeitgeist has us all sewn up, can't we say that there are many ways?

The overt reference to a particular style sometimes seems to recall not so much that style as other overt references. For example, period rooms in some museums remind one more of model rooms in department stores, where they're trying to sell period furniture, than interiors of the period intended to be illustrated.

Some department stores do things very well.

I'm not questioning that they do. I think that they do it well and that fast food and popular culture people also do their thing well.

What I think you're getting at is what I would describe as the "how are you gonna keep 'em back in Oxford and Cambridge after they've seen Yale's Branford College" syndrome. You can't do it "straight" anymore. You can't go back. It's impossible. You can't go to Cambridge or Oxford and see them fresh once you have been to Branford College. It's so much better at Branford: it's cleaned up, it's perfect, spatially regularized, marvelous. You can never look at the original straight, and that's one of our modern problems. But how, also, can you look at the International Style anymore after you've taken a drive down Route 66? After you've seen it used for gas stations and Caldor's? The point is, we must draw back and think about what architecture means again. This is a true crisis, a perpetual ongoing crisis in our society. Williamsburg, Virginia, looks like the Harvard residential houses of the 1930s because the same architects who were restoring Williamsburg were also building the Harvard houses.

As an architect I am not offended by commercialism; I am only offended by the disjunction between the moralizing modernist ethos and its rather cynical accommodation to commercial realities. By this I refer to the situation that occurred in the 1950s, when Gropius and other pioneer modernists began to build large-scale commercial buildings and to assign holy values to their work. Gropius's defense of his role in the design of the Pan American building in New

York, in which he claimed that by virtue of his intervention New York was spared a vulgar product of crass commercialism, was self-serving to say the least. Scully has shown us in an article in *Perspecta* (1963) that Gropius's interference actually made the project worse![8] And Marcel Breuer's arguments in defense of his proposals for a tower atop Grand Central Terminal in New York are, if possible, even more appalling.

Do you eat at McDonald's?

Yes, sometimes. The great thing about a pluralistic world is that you can eat McDonald's at lunch and go to La Grenouille at night and not feel hypocritical. Craig Claiborne can write an article about the qualities of fast food one day in the *Times,* and the next day he can write about something as esoteric as truffles, and you don't think he's sold out. But can you imagine Walter Gropius talking positively about the pleasures of McDonald's architecture? I can't. And so I'm encouraged. We don't have a way of doing things. That's the wonderful thing about our time. And like it or not, you can't escape its pluralism. And personally, I don't see why you would want to. There is always room for any position. But I think you would be naïve to believe that there ever really was a way: Gropius's great frustration was that it never all came to pass. White Dusenbergs, or Adlers to be more precise, didn't take over the world. I don't know what Gropius thought when it was all finished, but there is quite a shift of intentions from the high ideals of the Bauhaus to the work of The Architects' Collaborative. He must have thought a little bit about this shift. It's pretty sad, it seems to me.

You said that right now there's no one way to do anything. What interests me was you said "right now." Do you think you're going to live out your life with what you're saying now being valid?

I don't believe there has ever been one way of doing architecture in what I define in the broadest terms as the modern period, and certainly not since the eighteenth century. So there is no particular reason to believe there is going to be one way until there is some radical change in the nature of our culture or our world in the broadest sense.

Well, do you think, for instance, that the articles we read in preparation for these seminars will be useful except as historical documents ten years from now, twenty years from now, thirty years from now?

I like to think so, yes. I like to believe that, given how long it has taken architectural ideas to unfold and take root in the past, this post-modern phase is to be with us for the rest of this century. The Modern Movement had its origins in the 1830s and reached a peak in the 1920s; and it's still going to be creaking along for quite a while. Paul Rudolph is about to begin to build the new New Haven City Hall, hardly a post-modern building. It's probably going to be a very nice building in its way, yet a lot of people are going to be very irritated by it because it will not embody certain attitudes that one believes in today. On the other hand, it is a building that was conceived ten or more years ago, and that looked pretty good to the people who were thinking about buildings then. So all these ideas we're talking about—modernist and post-modernist alike—are going to haunt us, for better or for worse, for quite a while to come.

Notes on Post-Modernism

At the moment, I am interested in the problem of literalness in architecture. The jokey use of Doric columns and other pieces of the classical language, as in Venturi's Allen Art Museum at Oberlin College (fig. 2) or in Charles Moore's Piazza d'Italia in New Orleans, is one thing, but what about the straightforward use of this language? The traditional classical language exists, just as do the languages of the International Style and Art Deco. They are all interrelated, and the distance of time between us and the battles of the 1920s may well give us enough breathing room to permit a synthesis to take place between them, comparable to the birth of English out of the Anglo and Romance languages of the Middle Ages.

Fig. 2. Venturi and Rauch, Ironic Column, Allen Art Museum, Oberlin College, Oberlin, Ohio, 1976

I went to Yale in the 1960s. It took me a long time to figure out that what I was taught I shouldn't do. We are all trapped by our education. I am attempting to "brainwash" you just as I was brainwashed by my teachers. I can talk faster than I can design. Everybody else in this room can too. But it's awfully hard to teach clients. It is interesting that when they come to architects like me, and like most of you will be when you are practicing, they expect me to produce buildings that Arthur Drexler won't show anymore at the Museum of Modern Art. You see, modernism has become a fashion, a style with cachet. Many clients want their buildings to look like what modern architects are supposed to produce.

So really there's a gap between what you think and what you design now and what people expect you to design.

I am always struggling to close those gaps.

Notes on Post-Modernism

20

On Style, Classicism, and Pedagogy

1984

An architect cannot escape style. I have never seen a building divorced from style, no matter how banal or inarticulate its expression. Every work of architecture represents an attempt to transcend mere shelter and accommodation. Building is specific, the literal translation of a program into bricks and mortar. Architecture is general, raising building to a poetic level by embracing the cultural continuum: form and style, syntax and expression—they are the "otherness" that lends building the resonance of art.

Every architect worthy of the name resorts to some chosen set of aesthetic rules. For these rules to function in a culture they must respond to circumstances beyond the issues of budget, materials, function, and—as important—the architect's own personality, and speak through a generally understood language. Form is the language of architecture. Style is interpretation.

Before the modernist period, architectural style was the product of a *rapprochement* between building technology and classicism; that is, between the particular requirements of a given program and the general traditions of fine building. Matters were complicated by the at least partial replacement of the craft tradition with industrialized production. Technology, hitherto the means of localizing the general principles of classicism through craft, became universal, and a new, more self-conscious balance has had to be struck between principles and circumstance. Style can now be said to represent the interaction between elemental forms (classicism) on the one hand and technology and the vernacular on the other—the vernacular representing the sense of a specific place. This interactive process is at the heart of architectural narrative—for me, the essence of architecture.

Architecture is a narrative art, and architectural style is analogous to poetic diction. Simple writing may literally communicate, but it ordinarily does not give much pleasure. Storytellers since the Greek tragedians have therefore embroidered their tales with references to, and even direct quotations from, works of the past in order to connect with tradition. The complexity of a narrative, its allusiveness, resonance, and aggrandizement of the reader's own experience, raises the statement of a simple literary theme to the realm of art.

One of the basic tenets of the Post-Modernist reaction to modernism is the reaffirmation of this narrative aspect: even so seemingly nonobjective an architect as Peter Eisenman is preoccupied with storytelling. It is interesting to note that with Eisenman now building for more than one person his narrative is moving from interior monologues to historical commentary, as in the castellated mock ruins of his project at Ohio State. Contextual commentary has always been central to the communication of an architectural message, and I see no reason to abandon it now.

Enduring art cannot be founded on a negative statement. Art requires an assertion of belief. The initial impulse of paradigmatic modernism was as much an iconoclastic attempt to destroy the concept of associative meaning in architecture as it was a positive glorification of the machine. But in actual practice, a crisis of style arose almost immediately. For Le Corbusier the traditional styles did not speak to the tumultuous issues of the day but were ingrained in a bourgeois culture, which he abhorred. Yet in banishing historical representation he left himself little with which to evolve a new style. At first he replaced the character of handicraft with that of machine production. Retaining the grid system of classical composition he subverted it with diagonal and curved plan forms that were intended to represent the randomness of everyday life; the free plan was the antithesis of the Beaux-Arts *marche* and its connotations of hierarchy and stratification. Le Corbusier's initial vocabulary for the "new architecture"—the ramp, the strip window, the pipe rail, etc.—was simply a set of elements that were preferred because they flouted classical convention. By the 1930s, even Le Corbusier was frustrated by the restrictive "purism" of his vocabulary and conscious of the futility of an art that refused to represent its past. His work thereafter sought to reconnect his art with the past. While it never satisfactorily came to terms with the monumental buildings of the classical tradition, it does explore the vernacular of the Mediterranean.

The typical architect today builds all over the country and must vary the character of his buildings to suit the place. Frank Lloyd Wright varied his style, and in doing so was not above making direct references to local historical styles. His buildings in Los Angeles are explicitly Mayan, a reflection of his desire to evolve an architecture appropriate to Southern California while avoiding what he would have called the trap of Spanish colonial. Yet he recognized in his writings the aptness of Spanish colonial for that climate, with its courtyards, arcades, and simple openings in unmodeled walls that capture the play of sunlight. His own work in the area was as historically referential as Bertram Goodhue's—where Goodhue turned to the evolved classicism of the Spanish colonial era, Wright went further back, to a near-mythic time before Columbus.

Wright's career represents an attempt to subsume classicism into an intensely personal vision. The Imperial Hotel in Tokyo was his most extended dialogue between classical composition and vernacular detail. Its rigorously symmetrical, hierarchical, and sequentially organized plan, complete with traditional *cour d'honneur*, was a masterful essay in academic formalism. Designed for Westerners visiting Japan, the hotel drew upon Tuscany for inspiration; its low massing, tiled hipped roofs, and careful placement of representational ornament on a vernacular field reflect the influence of Wright's recent stay in Fiesole far more than any drive toward technological expressionism or study of local building traditions. The entrance pavilion in particular—in its proportions, its framed setting within a courtyard, and its straightforward use of rhetorical elements to transform a mundane box—preserved a distant, far-off echo of Brunelleschi's Pazzi Chapel.

The Larkin Building was a similarly distilled meditation on an Italian *palazzo*, which intensified the typology's introverted focus on a glazed-in *cortile*. The ornament was rendered in Wright's own geometrical style, but its placement at the capitals and bases of piers was thoroughly classical. All of Wright's successful public buildings save the Guggenheim Museum reflected the same command of classical composition even as they rejected classical details. After he lost the commission for the McCormack House to Charles Platt, Wright's major domestic designs sought the same synthesis. His project had called for a series of episodic, disconnected pavilions, which failed to organize the extensive program. Despite Wright's bitterness over the loss, I suspect he realized that Platt had succeeded where he had failed. Thereafter his large houses were classically composed suites of biaxially symmetrical rooms; the most significant innovation was the ubiquitous placement of hearth masses in the center—a vernacular integration.

Wright's individualism was disciplined by his knowledge of tradition, demonstrated both by his Milwaukee Public Library project and his study of Lutyens. While one cannot study to become a highly personal talent like Wright (a common mistake of students in my generation), such a talent might emerge if one works from a tradition. Wright understood this perfectly. At Taliesin he set up a school in which students studied a tradition—not one culturally evolved of classicism, but the personally willed tradition of his own work, which he hoped to impose on the American people.

Classicism, as I see it, *is* the formal expression of modern (that is, post-Gothic) secular institutions in the West. Classicism inherently represents the public and institutional realm, and the vernacular may be said to represent that which is private and temporal. Classicism has traditionally been used to transcend or modify the vernacular in order to draw people together in their diversity; it brings the republican spirit of Washington to the county courthouses of the South and Midwest, just as it in turn brought the authority of Rome to cities meant to symbolize a nation—Leningrad, New Delhi, Paris, and Washington. The public realm, however, extends beyond great squares, museums, and seats of government to encompass all levels of shared space. Classicism is not inherently identified with or tainted by any particular ideology but has served rather as a distillation of the best that society can achieve. It is a tradition and a point of view. If, as some have suggested, even Monticello's classicism is marred by the memory of slaves, what of Bacon's Lincoln Memorial, whose testament to emancipation draws strength from a particular but nonetheless compelling interpretation of Greek democracy, and is further sanctified by memories of Martin Luther King and Marian Anderson, each of whom chose it as a forum? Great works of architecture—as surely as those of literature, painting, and music—transcend the particular social or political situation in which they were created. To say otherwise requires that we dismiss all art of the past, and indeed the present moment, and idly wait for social conditions to improve.

Classicism is the only codified, amplified, and perenially vital system of architectural composition bringing order to the process of design. It is also the only codified, amplified, and perennially vital language of architectural form. Gothic is equally representational and widely admired, but it was a short-lived system, inextricably connected to a narrower set of associations, and without a fully developed compositional system of its own. Modernism—that is, functionalism—set out to do away with both associative meaning and the very concept of architectural grammar. It therefore possesses only the most minimal of resources to establish or vary character, and its compositional technique was based on behaviorism and a literal-minded interpretation of construction. Classicism is at once a tradition and a language incorporating rules of syntax and rhetoric; it provides a methodology to establish composition and character.

Classicism, as Lutyens argued, is "the high game" of architecture. It presents the designer with a system of symphonic complexity for relating the smallest detail to the overall structure. It is the most abstract and complex language an architect can speak, but it has that virtue Ruskin termed "superabundance": it is at once a source of intellectual pleasure to the initiate and of sensuous delight to the layman. A fundamental concern with the relationship of public and private space to human scale is inherent in classicism and in no other architectural tradition. That concern enhances the sheer beauty of moldings and ornament, which provide classical buildings with layers of detail, enriching people's experience as they pause for second and third moments to appreciate the play of light on carved surfaces, the formalized naturalism of acanthus leaves, wreaths, and garlands, the literary text of inscriptions, or the empathetic thrust of a column. Classicism—taken as a language of form—embraces all that richness; moreover, it embodies it: it has it built in.

The teaching of architecture today is, I think, tragically haphazard. Students drown in the modishness of magazines and the faculty. In the absence of any structured pedagogy they lack any organizational tools with which to tackle a project. The only modern system of architectural education that succeeded in producing a large and diverse corps of skillful, confident, and often inspired designers was the French academic method, and it is time to consider emulating rather than merely nostalgizing its achievements. Students should learn the grand tradition of classicism with all its myriad permutations and its history of anticlassical movements, including modernism, through both historical research and investigative design. It is neither an accident nor a testament to declining intelligence that so many of modernism's finest achievements were those of its first generation. Le Corbusier grew out of the classical tradition, even if his experience of it was largely provincial, and Mies and Gropius knew it cold. Their iconoclastic attitude toward classical rhetoric was balanced by their profound knowledge of classical systems of composition and proportion, which disciplined their work no matter the expression. Modernism's success in dismantling the classical system of education was suicidal; it reduced the rules of architectural composition and proportion to those of intuition and structural framing, condemning generations of students to a veritable Dark Ages of ignorance.

Every form of learning is based on models—we cannot, indeed must not, expect each student to reinvent the discipline of architecture within a three-year program of study or even within a full professional life. When I went to architecture school in the 1960s our models were not so much stylistic as individual: the heroes of contemporary architecture were our gods, either rising stars like Louis Kahn and Paul Rudolph or the established but still creative masters like Mies and Le Corbusier. Designing in the style of a particular architect was certainly better than basing one's work on the flow patterns of bubble diagrams and achieving only a diagram masquerading as a plan.

One architect does not a tradition make. A single person's oeuvre inevitably presents an interpretation too narrow and finite to sustain architecture's continued evolution; imitation of a hero quickly degenerates into parody. Kahn is the perfect exemplar of an architect working through tradition to achieve a personal interpretation of style. He was trained in the classical tradition. Like most of his generation he rejected that tradition under the initial impact of modernism, and his early work was thoroughly banal. It was only when studying at the American Academy in Rome in 1949 that he was directly exposed to the panorama of classicism, stretching from antiquity past the Gothic interlude into the 1930s, and the rest of his career represents an attempt to turn back, reidentify himself, and become a good architect through classicism. I would rather see Mario Botta and countless other less gifted, if sincere, imitators of Kahn emulate that struggle to recapture the clarity and hierarchy of classical composition than remain trapped in Kahn's much less convincing designs.

It is hardly restrictive or close-minded to suggest that we expose architectural education to twenty-five hundred years of history. Now that modernism is dead as a creative force and it is fashionable to turn to the more distant past for inspiration, it behooves us to teach the past in a logical and structured way. If we do not, the creative energies of the present moment will have the same meteorically short career as those of modernism. A new chapter in architectural history cannot sustain itself on a superficial understanding of the past or the faddish slickness of architectural magazines.

The Beaux-Arts method used precedent as a springboard for invention; it taught precedent not only through classroom lectures but also first-hand, through measuring and drawing buildings that were models of excellence. Most importantly, it required students to solve new problems with traditional styles. That is the only process by which an architect can truly begin to experience form, to comprehend its evolution, to accept it as data—and then to decide for himself whether, as such, it is to be copied, developed, eroded, or discarded.

In our own day the rediscovery of classicism has led Allan Greenberg to a scholarly "correction" of prototypes; for Leon Krier it entails a romantic primitivism with revolutionary social implications. Throughout history classicism has given order and form, composition and character to the most violently opposed concepts of architectural beauty. Whatever one's personal interpretation of the past, architecture must now go backward in order to go forward. As T. S. Eliot remarked, "Art never improves, but the material of art is never quite the same."[1]

The Renaissance cast its vision back beyond the Gothic to the presumed Golden Age of the ancients. Bramante and his colleagues measured the ruins of Rome, excavated and pillaged what they could, and debated the meaning of Vitruvius to recapture a lost theory of architecture. In the process classicism evolved into a far more subtle, systematic, and expressive language than their ancient ancestors would have thought possible. It became the language of modern times: the convincing expression of a man-centered secular culture. In 1876, American architects, glutted with the incoherencies and vulgarity of Victorian architecture, set out along the back roads of New England to document the fast vanishing vernacular and Georgian classical buildings of the colonial period. Their research evolved into the Shingle Style, an ineffably American synthesis that referred to, yet transcended, its prototypes as it reflected its moment in time and defined an enduring typology. We are at such a turning point again, but it remains to be seen whether we turn to the past with the same acute critical vision that guided the Renaissance and the École des Beaux-Arts. In 1923 Le Corbusier offered the challenge, "architecture or revolution." For our moment I would propose something different and more conciliatory: tradition *and* modernity.

21

The Continuity
of Post-Modernism
1988

Post-Modernism is not a style but a condition, a condition that began to be recognized in architecture in the 1960s in reaction to the conventional wisdom of the ahistorical, acontextual, self-referential, and materialist modernism that prevailed in the post–World War II era. To talk of Post-Modernist art is not only to recognize the complexity of human experience but also to revel in it. Today, it is easy to forget the circumstances of architecture in the 1950s and early 1960s, when everyday modernism had congealed into an aesthetically reductive, unremarkably simple-minded approach to the complex practical, cultural, and aesthetic programs posed by the creative process that is all too casually called "design."

When architects began to question modernism's premises in the mid-1960s, the more pessimistic among them questioned the very act of architecture itself.[1] The establishment of a new, ideal urban order of modernist buildings and towers, which had been considered a predestined responsibility by mid-twentieth-century architects, came to be seen as an arrogant act of cultural imperialism. Out of the ashes of the political and cultural upheaval of the late 1960s, Post-Modernism emerged as a civilized alternative to both the nihilism of the radical left and the arrogance of the modernist establishment: architecture reemerged as a cultural act. The reshaping of the environment was no longer an inalienable right of the professional, but a privileged collaboration involving the larger community. Those with a more profound and fundamentally optimistic point of view realized that the nature of the art of building had to be rethought in terms other than the dogmatic functionalism and technological and historical determinism that the complex modernism of the 1920s had been reduced to by the 1950s. For these optimists, building still had the capacity to affirm the human spirit, marrying material needs with enduring psychological values and not merely limiting itself to the programs of the present moment. Some of these architects advocated a philosophical and aesthetic stance that saw architecture and aesthetics in broad, historical terms as deeply rooted cultural languages, inaugurating a new era of the modern. This approach, first interpreted as "inclusivist," was after the late 1970s generally known as Post-Modernism. Robert Venturi's contribution was critical: his *Complexity and Contradiction in Architecture,* first published in 1966, was the definitive polemic for a modern architecture that was not linguistically and culturally reductivist as high modernism had become, but rather sought to enrich twentieth-century modernism by reintegrating it with the grand historical traditions of the modern as a whole.[2]

In 1977, with more than a decade of debate and some provocative if sometimes naïve work behind me, I identified three principal tenets of architectural Post-Modernism, which I believe are still valid: 1) contextualism: the individual building regarded no longer as an isolated self-referential object but as a fragment of a larger, essentially urban whole; 2) allusionism: architecture not merely an act of utilitarian problem-solving and technological expression but also an act of historical and cultural response; and 3) ornamentalism: buildings not manifestations of "pure form," but essential types decoratively embellished to represent a variety of issues, from construction technique to iconographical themes.

The issue of ornamentalism was and remains the most controversial; with architecture's mandate to participate in a specific context and convey meaning, buildings are necessarily involved with a process of ornamentation. For all of these reasons, Mies van der Rohe's neutral *beinahe gar nichts,* the "almost nothing" of thin-skin canonical modernism, could not be the basis for an architecture that was content merely to communicate exclusively with an elite audience.[3] Ornament is the key concept in an approach that sees architecture as more than an undifferentiated, infinitely repeatable expression of program, construction, or building type. Ornament is the essential extra that allows a building to extend construction into a broad realm of culture.

In my 1980 essay "The Doubles of Post-Modern" [Chapter 16], I attempted to further define the complex nature of this hybrid phenomenon by pointing out that in its reaction to the singular modernism of the mid-century, Post-Modernism contained within itself its own contradictions: the traditional strain and the schismatic strain. Traditional Post-Modernism proposes not only to free new building from the rigid constraints of the orthodox modernism of the 1950s and 1960s, but also to reintegrate or subsume modernism within the broad category of the modern as a whole by seeking syntheses—or at least reconciliations—between classicism, traditional local handicraft vernaculars, and the new "modern" vernacular of the machine. The schismatic strain seeks a complete repudiation of the modern, pursuing instead an intellectual and aesthetic anti-ideal that proposes as well a complete break with modernism. To the schismatic Post-Modernist, even the seemingly radical modernism is a failure because it was too involved with the Western humanist tradition; because it took as its standard of measure the achievements of the past, even as it sought to break with the past. (Le Corbusier's contrasts between the Delange Grand-Sport car and the Parthenon are particularly galling to the schismatic Post-Modernist.) Thus schismatic Post-Modernists argue that they are not Post-Modernist after all, but fully Post-Modern, fully free of the past and of traditional humanism. They argue, in essence, that a new, noncentered system of belief has emerged, necessitated by extraordinary mid-twentieth-century scientific events like the splitting of the atom and extraordinary mid-century political events such as the Holocaust, which rendered the traditional, centered humanism of the West invalid. While traditional Post-Modernism sees these events as the very reasons why traditional human values—which presumably would include those of aesthetics—have to be reaffirmed, schismatic Post-Modernism goes the opposite way toward a theory and an aesthetic that are not merely subversive but finally anarchic.[4]

I believe in the continuing viability of modern culture and its capacity to absorb new ideas and even to come to terms with seemingly uncontrollable, even irrational scientific and political phenomena without sacrificing its essential humanism. I see traditional Post-Modernism as a crucial integrative synthesis that has returned architecture to its proper role, not only as the embodiment of traditional cultural values, but also as an affirmation of an enduring humanity.

In their effort to break with tradition, schismatic Post-Modernists have struggled to articulate an approach that seeks late twentieth-century "avant-garde" equivalents to the plethora of modernist polemics and modernist styles of the 1920s. But in so doing, they have revealed themselves moderns and traditionalists after all—only theirs is the tradition of the avant-garde, the tradition of the self-proclaimed new, the new for newness' sake, the tradition of art as provocation.

The new modernism is as valuable today as it was in the 1920s, and it holds a position virtually the same as the modernist one of the 1920s: it is the "other," the "anti." But as such, while it does not seem to have the capacity for internal growth, it does have the power to enrich traditional work through synthesis. True, in the new modernism, as in the modernism of the inter-war period, there will be the occasional one-off masterpiece. But most of all, the new modernism serves as a critique, as the necessary other. In its way, its role is akin to that of the Gothic in the post-medieval era. The "Gothic" has been classicism's "other" throughout the modern centuries; it is a mystical presence that admonishes and even astounds architecture's inherent conventions.

There is much talk of revitalized Modernism, of neo-modernism, and deconstructivism, much of it premised on a trumped-up argument that the Post-Modernist point of view has closed the doors to the modernist experience. Post-Modernism is not anti-modernism. It is a corrective action, not a repudiation; a step in evolution, not a revolution. Traditional Post-Modernism does not seek to be exclusive, while by contrast it seems that the neo-modernists are already closing the gates to debate, praising their own work as progressive and condemning everything else as reactionary.[5] This represents an unfortunate narrowing of perspective, because there is plenty of room for Modernist-inspired ideas in traditional Post-Modernism. The powerful ideas of Modernism and the forms that express them are regularly brought into play by the leading Post-Modernist architects, contributing to an enhanced, public meaning of the buildings, rather than the titillation of a few bored architects, critics, and a communications media always hungry for the newest fashion.

However, the debate between a traditional and a schismatic approach to the modern tradition is no mere tempest in the aesthetic teapot. There are some very serious differences between the two approaches despite the shared values of an overall Post-Modern intention: I cannot allow myself to be lulled into a false sense of security that the urban spaces and buildings proposed by the schismatic "neos" and "decons" are simply different because they look different. There is a deep gulf between these one-off, anticontextual architectural set pieces and the contextually integrated work of traditional Post-Modernism. Architecture is a public art: it cannot confuse itself with off-the-wall gallery art or postlinear literature if it is to survive as a discipline. To advocate an architecture intent on showing that every text (every building type, every architectural language, every city) contains a subtext, and that the subtext often runs in a contrary direction, is undoubtedly valuable to our understanding of the complexity of architectural art. It may even lead to work that thrills our eyes with superb shapes and spaces. But it does not seem to lead to particularly satisfying buildings or particularly livable cities. And much of this work fails on its own terms, being based on an aesthetic derived from studio painting and sculpture and from techniques of literary criticism, which regrettably fail to measure up to the qualities of its sources, probably because the public nature of architecture is fundamentally and profoundly incompatible with the private world of the art studio and the scholar's study. To design a building as a decentered, dissociated, nonhierarchical layering of conflicting systems is to deny architecture its characteristics, and thereby to offer a critique of nothing at all. The attempt to "de-center" an architectural "center" that isn't there (surely it doesn't exist in the forms of purism, de Stijl, or constructivism) trivializes the genuine achievements of the architectural modernism of the 1920s, which far more successfully achieved architectural parity with easel painting.

Most valuable of all, then, is the critique of architecture that the new modernism offers; for me, if only by inverse means, that critique reaffirms the inherent vitality and validity of architecture as an independent medium of expression, not as a by-product or stepchild of technology or of studio art. By pursuing the subtexts and, in fact, eliminating the principal reading, the leaders of the recent "isms" follow as self-destructive a mode as those extreme modernists who careened from architectures of pure technology to architectures of pure function in order to avoid the wider, deeper, and more difficult reality of architecture as a complex mirror of culture. The extreme "isms" of 1920s modernism and today's 1980s modernism each fail for their lack of complexity and their lack of contradiction.

Though in many ways today's new modernism is a revival of the high modernist sensibility of the 1920s and 1930s, it must be considered apart from its spiritual ancestors. Unlike the canonical modernists who rejected the continuity of history, the new modernists do not; if anything, they see Post-Modernism as a break with history, albeit a truncated history that begins with modernism. So, in effect, their view is Post-Modernist in a critical way: they deal with history as reality and with history as an ideal. Not until the past is no longer considered as an ideal can the modern be said to have run its course. By reasserting that a work of architecture is an act of culture and, more to the point, by placing such acts within an historical argument, all of today's interesting work is Post-Modernist in the most profound way.

Selected Bibliography

Books by Robert A. M. Stern

New Directions in American Architecture. New York: Braziller, 1969; rev. 2nd ed., 1977.

George Howe: Toward a Modern American Architecture. New Haven: Yale University Press, 1975.

Editor, with Peter Eisenman. *Philip Johnson: Collected Writings.* New York: Oxford University Press, 1979.

With Deborah Nevins. *The Architect's Eye: American Architectural Drawings from 1799–1978.* New York: Pantheon, 1979.

With John M. Massengale. *The Anglo-American Suburb.* London: Academy Editions, 1981.

With Thomas P. Catalano. *Raymond Hood.* New York: Institute for Architecture and Urban Studies and Rizzoli, 1982.

With Clay Lancaster and Robert Hefner. *East Hampton's Heritage: An Illustrated Architectural Record.* New York: Norton, 1982.

With John M. Massengale and Gregory Gilmartin. *New York 1900: Metropolitan Architecture and Urbanism, 1890–1915.* New York: Rizzoli, 1983.

Editor. *International Design Yearbook.* New York: Abbeville, 1985.

Editor, with David G. DeLong and Helen Searing. *American Architecture: Innovation and Tradition*. New York: Rizzoli, 1986.

Pride of Place: Building the American Dream. Boston: Houghton-Mifflin/American Heritage, 1986. Companion to the Public Broadcasting System series.

With Gregory Gilmartin and Thomas Mellins. *New York 1930: Architecture and Urbanism Between the Two World Wars*. New York: Rizzoli, 1987.

Modern Classicism. New York: Rizzoli, 1988.

The House That Bob Built. Illustrated by Andrew Zega. New York: Rizzoli, 1991.

With Thomas Mellins and David Fishman. *New York 1960: Architecture and Urbanism Between the Second World War and the Bicentennial*. New York: Monacelli, 1995.

With Thomas Mellins and David Fishman. *New York 1880: Architecture and Urbanism in the Gilded Age*. New York: Monacelli, 1999.

Editor, with Peggy Deamer and Alan Plattus. *Re-Reading* Perspecta: *The First Fifty Years of the Yale Architectural Journal*. Cambridge: MIT Press, 2005.

With David Fishman and Jacob Tilove. *New York 2000: Architecture and Urbanism from the Bicentennial to the Millennium*. New York: Monacelli, 2006.

The Philip Johnson Tapes: Interviews by Robert A. M. Stern. Edited by Kazys Varnelis. New York: Monacelli, 2008.

Notes

Chapter 1. Pepsi-Cola Building

1. Ernst Danz, *Architecture of Skidmore, Owings and Merrill, 1950–1962* (New York: Praeger, 1963), 119.
2. Quoted in Reyner Banham, *Theory and Design in the First Machine Age* (New York: Praeger, 1960), 162.
3. Vincent Scully, Jr., "The Death of the Street," *Perspecta: The Yale Architectural Journal* 8 (1963): 91–96.

Chapter 2. Secrets of Paul Rudolph

1. Paul Rudolph, "Paul Rudolph," *Perspecta: The Yale Architectural Journal* 1 (1952): 18–25.
2. Ibid.
3. Vincent Scully, "A Note on the Work of Paul Rudolph," in *The Work of Paul Rudolph* (New Haven: Yale University Art Gallery, 1963).
4. Paul Rudolph, "The Six Determinants of Architectural Form," *Architectural Record* 120 (October 1956): 183–90.
5. Ibid.
6. See "House in Florida," *Architectural Forum* 89 (July 1948): 97–103.
7. Rudolph, *Perspecta* 1.
8. Paul Rudolph, "Revere House Grouping," letter to the editor, *Architectural Forum* 89 (December 1948): 28.
9. "One-Story House on the Second Floor," *Architectural Forum* 95 (October 1951): 186–89.
10. John Knox Shear, "Walker Guest House, Sanibel Island, Florida, 1953, Paul Rudolph," in "Houses Since 1907," *Architectural Record* 121 (February 1957): 204.
11. Paul Rudolph, "For Perspecta," *Perspecta: The Yale Architectural Journal* 7 (1961): 51–64.
12. "Cocoon House Uses the Navy's Moth-Balling Material to Weatherproof Its Catenary Curved Roof," *Architectural Forum* 95, no. 6 (June 1951): 156–59.
13. James Gowan, "Notes on American Architecture," *Perspecta: The Yale Architectural Journal* 7 (1961): 77–82.
14. "Excerpts: The Enigma of Katsura," *Architectural Forum* 113, no. 4 (October 1960): 175–79.
15. Rudolph, "The Six Determinants of Architectural Form."
16. "Modern Architecture and the Rebuilding of Cities," Panel Discussion, *Arts and Architecture* 79 (February 1962): 16–17, 30–32.
17. "Rudolph Calls Students to Task of Urban Design," *Architectural Record* 135, no. 5 (May 1964): 23–26.

Chapter 3. Stompin' at the Savoye

1. *Five Architects: Eisenman, Graves, Gwathmey, Hejduk, Meier* (New York: Wittenborn, 1972). Robert Venturi, Denise Scott Brown, and Steve Izenour, *Learning from Las Vegas* (Cambridge, Mass.: MIT Press, 1972).
2. Robert Venturi, *Complexity and Contradiction in Architecture* (New York: Museum of Modern Art, 1966). MoMA papers on Architecture, no. 1.
3. See *The New City: Architecture and Urban Renewal: An Exhibition at the Museum of Modern Art, New York, January 23–March 13, 1967* (New York: Museum of Modern Art, 1967).
4. "What you should try to accomplish is built meaning. So get close to the meaning and build." Aldo van Eyck, in "Team Ten Primer, 1953–1962," *Architectural Design* 12 (December 1962): 559–600.
5. Kenneth Frampton, "Notes from the Underground," *Artforum* 10 (April 1972): 40–46.

Chapter 4. Current Work/Persistent Preoccupations

1. Typical of Stern's lectures, the language that accompanied the slides of his work was not written; only his preliminary and concluding remarks, which set a framework for the office's work, were written in advance. Hence the "essay" here includes photographs without text.

Chapter 5. Post-Modern Architecture

1. Stuart Cohen, "Hardy Holzmann Pfeiffer on America," *Progressive Architecture* 56 (February 1975): 54–58.
2. Norman Mailer, "The Big Bite," *Esquire* 60 (August 1963).
3. Talbot Faulkner Hamlin, "The International Style Lacks the Essence of Great Architecture," *American Architect* 143 (January 1933): 12–16.

Chapter 7. New Directions in American Architecture

1. Robert A. M. Stern, *New Directions in American Architecture* (New York: George Braziller, 1969). The new edition was published by Braziller in 1977. The use of the term *post-modernism* seems to have been initiated by Joseph Hudnut in his essay "The Post-Modern House," *Architectural Record* 97 (May 1945): 70–75, which was reprinted as chapter nine in Hudnut's *Architecture and the Spirit of Man* (Cambridge, Mass.: Harvard University Press, 1949), 109–19. Its earliest influence, however, was Arnold J. Toynbee, *A Study of History* (New York: Oxford University Press, 1954–59), 8: 338.
2. Rosemarie Haag Bletter, "The Grey and White Architects: False Polarization in Recent Architectural Criticism." Lecture, 29th Annual Meeting of the Society of Architectural Historians, Philadelphia, May 19–24, 1976.
3. Donlyn Lyndon, "Philology of American Architecture," *Casabella* 281 (November 1963): viii–x, 8–40.
4. Douglas Davis with Mary Rourke, "Real Dream Houses," *Newsweek,* October 4, 1976, 66.
5. Richard Pommer, "New Architectural Supremacists," *Artforum* 15 (October 1976): 38–43.
6. Robert Venturi, *Complexity and Contradiction in Architecture,* with an introduction by Vincent Scully (New York: Museum of Modern Art, 1966). Robert Venturi, "Complexity and Contradiction in Architecture: Selections from a Forthcoming Book," *Perspecta: The Yale Architectural Journal* 9/10 (1965): 17–56.
7. William Ellis, "Forum: Beaux," *Oppositions* 5 (Summer 1976): 131–34.
8. George Baird was another speaker in the symposium that constitutes the first Preston Thomas lectures.

Chapter 8. Over and Under Forty

1. Henry-Russell Hitchcock, *Perspecta: The Yale Architectural Journal* 1 (1952).
2. Adolf K. Placzek, "Youth and Age in Architecture," *Perspecta: The Yale Architectural Journal* 9/10 (1965): 300–302.
3. Robert A. M. Stern, *New Directions in American Architecture* (New York: Braziller, 1969).
4. See Vincent J. Scully, *Louis I. Kahn* (New York: Braziller, 1962).
5. See Robert A. M. Stern, *George Howe: Toward a Modern American Architecture* (New Haven: Yale University Press, 1975).
6. See Allan Temko, *Eero Saarinen* (New York: Braziller, 1962).
7. See Henry-Russell Hitchcock, "Introduction," Yukio Futagawa, ed., *Work of Roche/Dinkeloo* (Tokyo: A. D. A. Edita Tokyo, 1975).
8. Saarinen's remark is quoted in Ian McCallum, *Architecture USA* (London: Architectural Press, 1959), 152. McCallum's book is an excellent record of the work and ideas of the second generation of American modernists as they stood at the brink of first maturity and international recognition.

9. See John Jacobus, *Philip Johnson* (New York: Braziller, 1965); also, Philip Johnson and Henry-Russell Hitchcock, *Philip Johnson: Architecture, 1949–1965* (New York: Hold, Rinehart and Winston, 1966).

10. See Sibyl Moholy-Nagy, *The Architecture of Paul Rudolph* (New York: Praeger, 1970); see also Robert A. M. Stern, "Secrets of Paul Rudolph: Paul Rudolph and His First Twenty-Five Years," *Kokusai-Kentiku International Review of Architecture* 32 (April 1965): 55–58 (in Japanese).

11. Paul Rudolph, "New Directions: Paul Rudolph," *Perspecta: The Yale Architectural Journal* 1 (1952): 18–25.

12. See Paul Rudolph, "The Six Determinants of Architectural Form," *Architectural Record* 70 (October 1956): 183–86.

13. See Hitchcock, "Introduction."

Chapter 10. Some Notes on the New "40 Under 40"

1. Architectural League, *40 Under 40* (New York: Architectural League, 1941).

2. "Goodbye Five: Work Done by Young Architects," *Progressive Architecture* 56 (November 1975): 200–221.

Chapter 11. The Beaux-Arts Exhibition

1. *Modern Architecture: International Exhibition, New York, February 10 to March 23, 1932, Museum of Modern Art* (New York: Museum of Modern Art, 1932), and Henry-Russell Hitchcock and Philip Johnson, *The International Style: Architecture Since 1922* (New York: W. W. Norton, 1932).

Chapter 12. Drawing Towards a More Modern Architecture

1. See Charles Jencks, *The Language of Post-Modern Architecture* (London: Academy Editions, 1977). See also Robert A. M. Stern, "At the Edge of Post-Modernism: Some Paradigms at the End of the Modern Movement," *Architectural Design* 47, no. 4 (April 1977): 274–86.

2. David Gebhard and Deborah Nevins, *200 Years of American Architectural Drawing* (New York: Whitney Library of Design, 1977), 21.

3. Joseph Rykwert, "Ornament Is No Crime," *Studio International* 190 (September–October 1975): 91–97.

4. Sir Kenneth Clark, "Ornament in Modern Architecture," *Architectural Review* 94 (December 1943): 147–50.

5. The Cooper Union for the Advancement of Science and Art, School of Art and Architecture, *Education of an Architect: A Point of View. An Exhibition for the Cooper Union School of Art and Architecture at the Museum of Modern Art, New York City, November 1971* (New York: The Cooper Union, 1971). This is the catalogue of an exhibition of student work over a decade (c. 1961–71), in which about sixty students were featured, including John Hejduk. "Architectural Studies and Projects," Museum of Modern Art, March 13–May 11, 1975. Informal exhibition. See related article, "Paper projects al MoMA, NY. Architectural Studies and Projects à New York, au Musée d'Art Moderne," *Domus* 546 (May 1975): 32.

Chapter 13. After the Modern Movement

1. Charles Jencks, *The Language of Post-Modern Architecture* (New York: Rizzoli, 1977), 84–85.

2. Barbaralee Diamondstein, "Pushing Future Directions in Modern Design," *ArtNews* 76, no. 7 (September 1977): 43–45.

3. Charles Moore and Richard Oliver, "Magic, Nostalgia and a Hint of Greatness in the Workaday World of the Building Types Study," *Architectural Record* 161 (April 1977): 118.

Chapter 14. Venturi and Rauch

1. Thomas Hawk Creighton, *The Architecture of Monuments: The Franklin Delano Roosevelt Memorial Competition* (New York: Reinhold, 1962). Jan C. Rowan, "Wanting to Be …the Philadelphia School," *Progressive Architecture* 42, no. 4 (April 1961): 130–63. Vincent J. Scully, Jr., "New Talent USA: Architecture," *Art in America* 49, no. 1 (1961): 62–67. Robert Venturi, "The Campidoglio, a Case Study," *Architectural Review* 113 (May 1953): 333–34.

2. Robert Venturi, Denise Scott Brown, and Steven Izenour, *Learning from Las Vegas* (Cambridge, Mass.: MIT Press, 1972), 96.

3. Ibid. See Part 2, "Ugly and Ordinary Architecture, or the Decorated Shed."

Chapter 15. New York, New York

1. "P/A on Pei: Roundtable on a Trapezoid," *Progressive Architecture* 59, no. 10 (October 1978): 49–59.

2. I am indebted to John M. Dixon, who clarified my thoughts on this relationship. See Robert A. M. Stern, "The Office of Earl P. Carlin," *Perspecta: The Yale Architectural Journal* 9/10 (1965): 183–98.

3. Johnson's collected writings have been published as *Philip Johnson: Collected Writings* (New York: Oxford University

Press, 1979). The book includes a preface by Vincent Scully and an introduction by Peter Eisenman; I have supplied commentary for each essay. For Johnson's role as pivotal figure in the New York architectural scene, see Robert Hughes, "U.S. Architects: Doing Their Own Thing," *Time* (January 8, 1979): 52–59.

4. See Robert A. M. Stern, *George Howe: Toward a Modern American Architecture* (New Haven: Yale University Press, 1975), esp. chapter 6.

5. Kenneth Frampton, *A New Wave of Japanese Architecture* (New York: IAUS, 1978).

6. Stanford Anderson, *On Streets* (Cambridge, Mass.: MIT Press, 1979).

7. "UDC/IAUS Publicly Assisted Housing: Low Rise, High Density," *Progressive Architecture* 54 (December 1973): 56–63.

8. Russell Lynes, *Good Old Modern* (New York: Atheneum, 1973).

9. Arthur Drexler, ed., *The Architecture of the École des Beaux-Arts* (New York: Museum of Modern Art, 1977).

10. William Ellis, ed., "Oppositions Forum: The Beaux-Arts Exhibition," *Oppositions* 8 (Spring 1977): 160–63.

11. Françoise Bollack and Tom Killian, Letter to the Editor, *Skyline*, March 1979, 2.

12. Richard Oliver and Nancy Ferguson, "Place, Product, Packaging," *Architectural Record* 163, no. 2 (February 1978): 115–20.

13. Robert A. M. Stern, ed., "America Now: Drawing Toward a More Modern Architecture," *Architectural Design* 47, no. 6 (1977).

14. David Gebhard and Deborah Nevins, *200 Years of American Architectural Drawing* (New York: Whitney Library of Design, 1977).

15. Susana Torre, *Women in American Architecture* (New York: Whitney Library of Design, 1977).

16. The Cooper Union, *Education of an Architect* (New York, 1971). Kenneth Frampton, "Notes from Underground," *Artforum* 10 (April 1972): 40–46; "Renovation: Foundation Building," *Domus* 551 (October 1975): 11–15.

17. Columbia University School of Architecture and Planning, *Working Paper I, The New York Federal Archive: A Proposal for a Mixed Re-Use* (New York: Columbia University, 1976).

18. Robert A. M. Stern, "Yale, 1950–65," *Oppositions* 4 (October 1974): 35–66.

19. Antoine Quatremiere de Gutman, pseud. (Robert Gutman), "Princeton's Beaux-Arts and Its New Academicism from Labatut

to the Program of Geddes," *Oppositions* 9 (Summer 1977): 117–21.

Chapter 16. The Doubles of Post-Modern

Epigraph: Kenneth Clark, "Boredom Blamed," *Art Digest* 10 (November 15, 1935): 13. I am indebted to Peter Eisenman, Kenneth Frampton, and Vincent Scully for reading and commenting on portions of this manuscript in a much earlier stage of its development; Suzanne Stephens has read it more recently. What is written here is much the better for their advice. Nonetheless, as I am sure they will be relieved to learn, I take full responsibility for the final product.

1. Portions of this text are based on material I introduced previously: See my "Postscript: At the Edge of Modernism," in *New Directions in American Architecture*, 2nd ed. (New York: Braziller, 1977), 117–36; "Five Houses," *GA Houses* 1 (1976): 36–77; "Something Borrowed, Something New," *Horizon* 20, no. 4 (December 1977): 50–57.

2. Charles Jencks, *The Language of Post-Modern Architecture* (London: Academy Editions, 1977); see also Jencks, "Post-Modern History," *Architectural Design* 48, no. 1 (January 1978): 11–62.

3. The term seems to have been initiated by Joseph Hudnut in his essay "The Post-Modern House," *Architectural Record* 97 (May 1945): 70–75, which was reprinted as Chapter 9 in Hudnut's *Architecture and the Spirit of Man* (Cambridge, Mass.: Harvard University Press, 1949), 109–19. Its earliest influential use was in Arnold J. Toynbee, *A Study of History* (New York: Oxford University Press, 1954–59), 8: 338.

Peter Eisenman and I discussed the term and its probable definitions at considerable length in the summer of 1975. I first "went public" with a definition for the term in relationship to architecture in 1976, using it to characterize a shift in mood represented by an event—the Beaux-Arts exhibition at the Museum of Modern Art—and a shifting of alliances among the architects who constituted the "White" and "Gray" groups of the mid-1970s. See my "Possibly, the Beaux-Arts Exhibit Means Something After All (with Apology to Clement Greenberg, Rosalind Kraus and the Month of October)," a paper delivered at the *Oppositions* Forum, Institute for Architecture and Urban Studies, January 22, 1976, and published in William Ellis, ed., "Forum of the Beaux-Arts Exhibition," *Oppositions* 8 (Spring 1977):

169–71. See also my "Gray Architecture as Post-Modernism, or, Up and Down from Orthodoxy" ("Gray Architecture: Quelques Variations Post-Modernistes Autour de L'Orthodoxie," L'Architecture d'Aujourd'hui," 186 [August–September 1976]: 83–98). [Chapter 6 in this volume.]

4. Renato Poggioli, *The Theory of the Avant-Garde,* trans. Gerald Fitzgerald (Cambridge, Mass.: Harvard University Press, 1968), 217. See also Daniel Bell, *The Cultural Contradictions of Capitalism* (New York: Basic Books, 1976), 34; Frank Kermode, *Continuities* (New York: Random House, 1968).

5. See Stephen Spender, *The Struggle of the Modern* (Berkeley: University of California, 1963), passim.

6. See ibid., 8, 13; Kermode observes that "the fact that defining the modern is a task that now imposes itself on many distinguished scholars may be a sign that the modern period is over," 28. See also Bell, *Cultural Contradictions of Capitalism,* 40–52.

7. See Clement Greenberg, "Modernist Painting," in Gregory Battcock, ed., *The New Art* (New York: Dutton, 1973, rev. ed.), 100–110; William Jordy, "The Symbolic Essence of Modern European Architecture of the Twenties and Its Continuing Influence," *Journal of the Society of Architectural Historians* 22, no. 3 (October 1973): 177–87.

8. David Watkin writes that "an art-historical belief in the all-dominating *Zeitgeist,* combined with a historicist emphasis on progress and the necessary superiority of novelty, has come dangerously close to undermining, on the one hand, our appreciation of the imaginative genius of the individual and, on the other, the importance of artistic tradition." *Morality and Architecture* (Oxford: Clarendon, 1977), 115. See also John Alford, "Modern Architecture and the Symbolism of the Creative Process," *College Art Journal* 14, no. 2 (1955): 102–23; see also Bell, *Cultural Contradictions of Capitalism,* 13, 20, 46–52.

9. David Antin, "Modernism and Post-modernism: Approaching the Present in American Poetry," *Boundary* 2, no. 1 (Autumn 1972): 98–133.

10. Susan Sontag, *Against Interpretation* (New York: Delta, 1966), 17.

11. Harry Levin, "What Was Modernism?" in *Refractions: Essays in Comparative Literature* (New York: Oxford, 1966), 271–95; see also Robert Martin Adams, "What Was Modernism?" *Hudson Review* 31, no. 1 (Spring 1978): 19–33. Adams's title and themes are deliberately based on those raised by Harry Levin in his earlier essay of the same title. See also Malcolm Bradbury and James McFarlane, eds., *Modernism,* 1880–1930 (New York: Penguin, 1976).

12. Irving Howe, *Decline of the New* (New York: Harcourt Brace, 1970), 3.

13. Henry-Russell Hitchcock, *Modern Architecture: Romanticism and Reintegration* (New York: Payson and Clarke, 1929), xvi.

14. Henry-Russell Hitchcock, "Modern Architecture—A Memoir," *Journal of the Society of Architectural Historians* 27, no. 4 (December 1968): 227–33; the broad view was taken by Montgomery Schuyler, for example, who stated that "modern architecture, like modern literature, had its origin in the revival of learning. The Italian Renaissance in architecture was inextricably connected with that awakening of the human spirit which was the beginning of modern civilization." "Modern Architecture," *Architectural Record* 4 (July–September 1894).

15. Hitchcock, "Modern Architecture—A Memoir," passim; Robert Venturi and Denise Scott Brown first used the good-guy, bad-guy analogy in their "Learning from Lutyens, or the Case of the Shifting Zeitgeist," *RIBA Journal* 76 (August 1969): 353–54.

16. J. M. Richards, *An Introduction to Modern Architecture* (Harmondsworth: Penguin, 1960), 9, 12. See Watkin, *Morality and Architecture;* Peter Collins, *Changing Ideals in Modern Architecture,* 1750–1950 (London: Faber and Faber, 1965).

17. Vincent J. Scully, Jr., "Modern Architecture: Toward a Redefinition of Style," *College Art Journal* 17, no. 2 (Winter 1958): 140–59; see also Scully's *Modern Architecture* (New York: Braziller).

18. Fiske Kimball and George H. Edgell, *A History of Architecture* (New York: Harper, 1918). Chapter 12, "Modern Architecture," was written by Kimball. See also James D. Kornwolf, *M. H. Baillie Scott and the Arts and Crafts Movement* (Baltimore: Johns Hopkins, 1972).

19. Toynbee, *Study of History;* see also Toynbee, *The Present Day Experiment in Western Civilization* (London: Oxford University Press, 1962), 26–37.

20. Geoffrey Barraclough, *An Introduction to Contemporary History* (New York: Basic Books, 1965).

21. Gerald Graff, "The Myth of the Postmodernist Breakthrough,"

TriQuarterly, no. 26 (Winter 1973): 383–417; see also Bell, *Cultural Contradictions of Capitalism.*

22. Richard E. Palmer, "Postmodernity and Hermeneutics," *Boundary* 2, no. 5 (Winter 1977): 363–93. This is the strain of post-modernity that Daniel Bell, in *The Cultural Contradictions of Capitalism,* disapprovingly characterizes as "the psychological spearhead for an onslaught on the values and motivational patterns of 'ordinary' behavior, in the name of liberation, eroticism, freedom of impulse and the like … it means that a crisis of middle-class values is at hand" (52). Bell also writes that in the 1960s a "powerful current of post-modernism developed which carried the logic of modernism to its farthest reaches. In the theoretical writings of Norman O. Brown and Michel Foucault, in the novels of William Burroughs, Jean Genet and, up to a point, Norman Mailer, and in the porno-pop culture that is now all about us, one sees a logical culmination of modernist intentions. They are, as Diana Trilling put it, 'the adventures beyond consciousness'" (51). "Traditional modernism, no matter how daring, played out its impulses in the imagination, within the constraints of art. …Post-modernism [of the breakthrough variety] overflows the vessels of art. It tears down the boundaries and insists that *acting out,* rather than making distinctions, is the way to gain knowledge" (52).

23. William V. Spanos, "The Detective and the Boundary: Some Notes on the Post-Modern Literary Imagination," *Boundary* 2, no. 1 (Autumn 1972): 147–68.

24. Ihab Hassan, "Joyce, Beckett, and the Postmodern Imagination," *TriQuarterly,* no. 34 (Fall 1975): 179–220. See also Hassan, *Paracriticisms: Seven Speculations of the Times* (Urbana: University of Illinois, 1975), 55–56.

25. William Gass, "House VI," *Progressive Architecture* 58, no. 6 (June 1977): 57–67.

26. Sigfried Giedion, *Space, Time and Architecture* (Cambridge, Mass.: Harvard University Press, 1941).

27. Mario Gandelsonas, "On Reading Architecture: Eisenman and Graves, an Analysis," *Progressive Architecture* 53, no. 3 (March 1972): 68–88.

28. John Gardner, *On Moral Fiction* (New York: Basic Books, 1978), 9.

29. Ibid., 69, 71.

30. Howe, *Decline of the New,* 7.

31. Robert Gillespie, review of *Beyond the Waste Land: The American Novel in the Nineteen-Sixties,* by Raymond M. Olderman, *Boundary* 2, no. 3 (Winter 1975): 473–81.

32. Gerald Graff, "Babbitt at the Abyss: The Social Context of Postmodern American Fiction," *TriQuarterly* 33 (Spring 1975): 305–37.

33. Rackstraw Downes, "Post-Modernist Painting," *Tracks* 2, no. 3 (Fall 1976): 70–73. See also Hilton Kramer, "The Return of Realism," *New York Times,* March 12, 1978, D1, D25; Robert Berlind, "Artist's Choice: Figurative Art," *Arts Magazine* 51, no. 7 (March 1977): 23; Bell, *Cultural Contradictions of Capitalism,* 104. Peter Collins argues that the idea of "precedent" offers a way beyond the blockage of the art historical concept of "style." See his *Architectural Judgement* (London: Faber and Faber, 1971), 28–32.

34. Traditional post-modernism should not be confused with the neo-traditionalism of Henry Hope Reed, John Barrington Bayley, Conrad Jameson. For Bayley and Reed, see Henry Hope Reed, *The Garden City* (New York: Doubleday, 1959).

35. Rubin is quoted by Douglas Davis, "Post-Modern Form: Stories Real and Imagined/Toward a Theory," in *Artculture: Essays on the Postmodern* (New York: Harper & Row, 1977). See also "The Post-Modernist Dilemma," a dialogue between Davis and Suzi Gablik, *Village Voice,* March 27, April 3, April 10, 1978.

36. Henry-Russell Hitchcock, *Painting Toward Architecture* (New York: Duell, Sloan and Pearce, 1948).

37. Suzannah Lessard, "The Towers of Light," *New Yorker* 54 (July 10, 1978): 32–58.

38. Ibid. James D. Kornwolf makes the interesting observation that "Le Corbusier's generation was misguided not to recognize that the nineteenth century's struggle with the past was also its struggle, and that a new understanding of the past, not a denial of it, was what was needed." *M. H. Baillie Scott,* 513.

   Peter Collins observes that "the *idea* of an 'International Style' was a product of the Renaissance. In fact, the so-called 'battle of the styles' might be more realistically and meaningfully interpreted as an attempt to refute the concept of an 'International Style,' rather than as a conflict between 'Gothicists' and 'Classicists.' This was certainly the essence of the philosophical position taken by Viollet-le-Duc and Fergusson." *Architectural Judgement,* 171–72.

39. Charles Moore, Foreword, in Sam

Davis, *The Form of Housing* (New York: Van Nostrand Reinhold, 1977), v.

40. Richard Gilman, "Out Goes Absurdism—In Comes the New Naturalism," *New York Times,* March 18, 1978, D1, D6. Gardner, *On Moral Fiction,* 16. Bell, *Cultural Contradiction of Capitalism,* 119.

41. Gardner, *On Moral Fiction,* 9–10.

Chapter 17. Classicism in Context

1. For a discussion of the relationship between the conditions of modernism and Post-Modernism in architecture, world history, and the other arts, see my "Doubles of Post-Modern," *Harvard Architecture Review* (Spring 1980): 74–87. [Chapter 16 in this volume.]

2. For a further elaboration of this, see my "Discontinuity and Continuity in Modern Architecture: Modernism and Post-Modernism," to be published in the catalogue to the exhibition "Forum Design," held at Linz, Austria, June–September 1980. [Chapter 18 in this volume.]

Chapter 18. Discontinuity and Continuity in Modern Architecture

Epigraph: Eugenio Montale, "The Second Life of Art," trans. Jonathan Galassi (1949); reprinted in *New York Review of Books* 26, no. 6 (April 16, 1981): 16–20.

1. This article is an extension of the argument first articulated in my "Doubles of Post-Modern," *Harvard Architectural Review* (Spring 1980): 74–87 [Chapter 16 in this volume], and further developed in my "Notes on American Architecture in the Waning of the Petroleum Era," *GA Documents* I (1980): 6–11.

Chapter 19. Notes on Post-Modernism

1. Robert A. M. Stern, "The Doubles of Post-Modern," *Harvard Architecture Review* I (Spring 1980). [Chapter 16 in this volume.]

2. Charles Jencks, *The Language of Post-Modern Architecture* (London: Academy Editions, 1977).

3. Arnold Toynbee, *A Study of History* (New York: Oxford University Press, 1948–61). Joseph Hudnut, "The Post-Modern House," in *Architecture and the Spirit of Man* (Cambridge, Mass.: Harvard University Press, 1949). Geoffrey Barraclough, *An Introduction to Contemporary History* (New York: Basic Books, 1965).

4. Rackstraw Downes, "Post-Modernist Painting," *Tracks* 2, no. 3 (Fall 1976).

5. Henry-Russell Hitchcock, *Architecture: Nineteenth and Twentieth Centuries* (New York: Penguin, 1971). Reyner Banham, *Theory and Design in the First Machine Age* (New York: Praeger, 1960). Vincent Scully, *The Shingle Style* (New Haven: Yale University Press, 1955).

6. Robert A. M. Stern, "Drawing Towards a More Modern Architecture," *Architectural Design* 47, no. 6 (June 1977): 382–83. Henry-Russell Hitchcock and Philip Johnson, *The International Style* (New York: Norton, 1966).

7. Harold Rosenberg, *The Tradition of the New* (New York: Horizon, 1959).

8. Vincent Scully, "The Death of the Street," *Perspecta: The Yale Architectural Journal* 8 (1963): 91–96.

Chapter 20. On Style, Classicism, and Pedagogy

Author's Note: I wish to thank Gregory Gilmartin for his assistance in the preparation of this text, which is in part based on a transcribed conversation with Daniel Monk and Jeffrey Bucholtz, editors of *Precis* 5.

1. Quoted by Arthur Mizener, "F. Scott Fitzgerald, 1896–1940: The Poet of Borrowed Time," in Alfred Kazin, ed., *F. Scott Fitzgerald: The Man and His Work* (New York: Collier, 1962), 43.

Chapter 21. The Continuity of Post-Modernism

1. Martin Pawley, *Architecture versus Housing* (New York: Praeger, 1971); Robert Goodman, *After the Planners* (New York: Simon and Schuster, 1974).

2. Robert Venturi, *Complexity and Contradiction in Architecture* (New York: Museum of Modern Art, 1966).

3. Robert A. M. Stern, *New Directions in American Architecture,* rev. ed. (New York: George Braziller, 1977), 127, 129, 132.

4. Stern, "The Doubles of Post-Modern," *Harvard Architectural Review* I (Spring 1980): 75–87. [Chapter 16 in this volume.]

5. A notable essay in this vein is Peter Eisenman, "The End of the Classical," *Perspecta: The Yale Architectural Journal* 21 (Summer 1984): 154–72; less compelling, and confusingly argued, but nonetheless important at this moment is Mark Wigley, "Deconstructivist Architecture," in *Deconstructivist Architecture,* exhibition catalogue edited by Philip Johnson and Mark Wigley (New York: Museum of Modern Art, 1988).

Sources

Chapter 1: "Pepsi-Cola Building." Unpublished manuscript, Robert A. M. Stern Papers, Yale University Archives, 1964.

Chapter 2. "Secrets of Paul Rudolph: His First Twenty-Five Years." *Kokusai-Kentiku International Review of Architecture* 32 (April 1965): 55–58 (in Japanese). Written in English as "Paul Rudolph: The First Twenty-Five Years." Manuscript, Robert A. M. Stern Papers, Yale University Archives, 1965.

Chapter 3: "Stompin' at the Savoye." *Architectural Forum* 138, no. 4 (May 1973): 46–48.

Chapter 4: "Current Work/Persistent Preoccupations." Lecture, Institute for Architecture and Urban Studies, New York, April 23, 1974.

Chapter 5: "Post-Modern Architecture." Lecture, Alcan Lecture Series, Montreal, February 18, 1975.

Chapter 6: "Gray Architecture as Post-Modernism, or, Up and Down from Orthodoxy." "Gray Architecture: Quelques Variations Post-Modernistes Autour de L'Orthodoxie," *L'Architecture d'Aujourd'hui* 186 (August–September 1976): 83–98. Reprinted in *Architecture Theory Since 1968*, edited by K. Michael Hays, 240–45. Cambridge, Mass.: MIT Press, 2000.

Chapter 7: "New Directions in American Architecture." *New Directions for American Architects*, Preston Thomas Memorial Lectures, Cornell University College of Art, Architecture, and Planning, Ithaca, New York, October 23, 1976.

Chapter 8: "Over and Under Forty: A Propos the 'Crise à Quarante Ans' Among Second Generation American Modernists." "40 Under 40." Special issue, *A+U: Architecture and Urbanism* 73 (January 1977): 18–28.

Chapter 9: "The Old '40 Under 40': A Retrospective Glance." Curated by Robert A. M. Stern, program director, Architectural League of New York, 1966. All quotations cited in this article are from correspondence in the Robert A. M. Stern Papers, Yale University Archives. "40 Under 40." Special issue, *A+U: Architecture and Urbanism* 73 (January 1977): 29–39.

Chapter 10: "Some Notes on the New '40 Under 40.'" "40 Under 40." Special issue, *A+U: Architecture and Urbanism* 73 (January 1977): 49–69.

Chapter 11: "On the Beaux-Arts Exhibition." In William Ellis, ed., "Forum: The Beaux-Arts Exhibition," *Oppositions* 8 (Spring 1977): 160–75.

Chapter 12: "Drawing Towards a More Modern Architecture." In "America Now: Drawing Towards a More Modern Architecture." Robert A. M. Stern, ed., special issue, *Architectural Design* 47, no. 6 (1977): 382–83.

Chapter 13: "After the Modern Movement." October 4, 1977 (revised March 20, 1978). "After the Modern Movement," *Shinkenchiku* (December 1977): 13–17 (in Japanese). Translated into Italian as "Dopo il Movimento Moderno." *Parametro* 9, no. 72 (December 1978): 36–41.

Chapter 14: "Venturi and Rauch: Learning to Love Them." In *Venturi and Rauch: The Public Buildings,* edited by David Dunster, 93–94. Architectural Monographs 1. London: Academy Editions, 1978.

Chapter 15: "New York, New York: Pluralism and Its Possibilities." *Arquitectura,* no. 218 (May–June 1979): 14–17.

Chapter 16: "The Doubles of Post-Modern." *Harvard Architecture Review* 1 (Spring 1980): 75–87. Excerpted in *Architectural Design* 62 (March–April 1992): xxviii. Reprinted as "The Doubles of Post-Modernism." In *New Classicism: Omnibus Volume,* edited by Andreas Papadakis and Harriet Watson, 167–76. New York: Rizzoli, 1990. Reprinted in *America Builds,* edited by Leland M. Roth, 646–66. New York: Harper & Row, 1983. Translated as "Las Duplicidades del Postmodernismo." *Arquitectura* 63 (September–October 1982): 26–29, 68–75.

Chapter 17: "Classicism in Context." In *Architectural Design Profile: Post-Modern Classicism,* edited by Charles Jencks, 37–38. London: Academy Editions, 1980.

Chapter 18: "Discontinuity and Continuity in Modern Architecture: Modernism and Post-Modernism." "Modernismus und Postmodernismus: Diskontinuität und Kontinuität in der modernen Architektur." In *Design ist Unsichtbar,* edited by Helmuth Gsöllpointner, Angela Hareiter, and Laurids Ortner, 259–72. Vienna: Löcker, 1981. Published for the exhibition "Forum Design" in Linz, Austria. For Yukio Futagawa.

Chapter 19: "Notes on Post-Modernism." In *Yale Seminars in Architecture,* vol. 1, edited by Cesar Pelli, 1–35. New Haven: Yale University School of Architecture, 1981. Translated into Japanese as "Issues in Architecture." *A+U: Architecture and Urbanism* 152 (May 1983): 31–39.

Chapter 20: "On Style, Classicism, and Pedagogy." *Precis* 5 (Fall 1984): 16–23. Reprinted in *Architectural Monographs* 17. New York: St. Martin's, 1991. Excerpted in *Theories and Manifestoes of Contemporary Architecture,* edited by Charles Jencks and Karl Kropf, 183–84. Chichester, England: Academy Editions, 1997.

Chapter 21: "The Continuity of Post-Modernism." Unpublished essay, September 22, 1988, Robert A. M. Stern Papers, Yale University Archives.

Index

Index

Index

Index

Illustration Credits

Chapter 1: Ezra Stoller © Esto. All rights reserved. (figs. 1 & 2)

Chapter 2: Paul Rudolph Archive, Library of Congress Prints & Photographs Division (figs. 1 & 13); Ezra Stoller © Esto (figs. 2–8, 17); Robert A. M. Stern Architects (figs. 9, 11, 14, 15); Richard Johnson, courtesy of Manuscripts and Archives, Yale University Library (fig. 10); Susan Grant Lewin, courtesy of Robert A. M. Stern Architects (fig. 12); © Wayne Andrews/ Esto (fig. 16)

Chapter 3: John Hejduk Fonds, Collection Centre Canadien d'Architecture / Canadian Centre for Architecture, Montréal (figs. 1 & 2); Courtesy of Eisenman Architects (figs. 3 & 4); Courtesy of Michael Graves & Associates (fig. 5); © 2008 Artists Rights Society (ARS), New York / ADAGP, Paris / FLC (fig. 6); Laurin McCracken, Courtesy of Michael Graves & Associates (fig. 7); Leni Iselin, Courtesy of Venturi, Scott Brown and Associates, Inc. (fig. 8); Ezra Stoller © Esto. All rights reserved. (figs. 9, 11, 15); Courtesy Richard Meier & Partners Architects LLP (figs. 10 & 12); Courtesy of Gwathmey Siegel & Associates Architects LLC (fig. 13); Bill Maris (fig. 14)

Chapter 4: Robert A. M. Stern Architects (figs. 1, 3–5); Edmund Stoecklein (fig. 2)

Chapter 7: Norman McGrath (fig. 1); Rob Super, courtesy of Turnbull Griffin Haesloop Architects (fig. 2); Courtesy Centerbrook Architects and Planners Records, Manuscripts and Archives, Yale University Library (fig. 3); Courtesy of Michael Graves & Associates (fig. 4); Robert A. M. Stern Architects (fig. 5); *Building News,* April 28, 1882 (fig. 6); Woody Simes (fig. 7)

Chapter 8: Yale University Art Gallery Archives, Photograph by Lionel Freedman (fig. 1); Ezra Stoller © Esto (figs. 2 & 3); Yale University (fig. 4); Courtesy of Kevin Roche John Dinkeloo and Associates (fig. 5)

Chapter 9: John Hejduk Fonds, Collection Centre Canadien d'Architecture / Canadian Centre for Architecture, Montréal (fig. 1); George Cserna, Avery Architectural and Fine Arts Library, Columbia University (fig. 2); Rollin R. La France (fig. 3); © Office of Lawrence Halprin (fig. 4); Courtesy of Kevin Roche John Dinkeloo and Associates (fig. 5)

Chapter 10: Peter Chermayeff (fig. 1); © Norman McGrath/Esto (fig. 2); Roger Gain, Courtesy of Peter Hoppner (fig. 3); Morley Baer © 2008 by The Morley Baer Photography Trust, Santa Fe. All reproduction rights reserved (fig. 4); Jeremiah O. Bragstad (fig. 5); David Sellers (fig. 6); Photograph by Hans Namuth, © Hans Namuth Ltd. (fig. 7)

Chapter 16: Robert A. M. Stern Architects (fig. 1); Courtesy of Eisenman Architects (fig. 2); Courtesy of Michael Graves & Associates (fig. 3); © Timothy Hursley (fig. 4); Courtesy of Arquitectonica (fig. 5); Tom Bernard, Courtesy of VSBA (fig. 6); Courtesy of VSBA (fig. 7); Courtesy of Stuart Cohen & Julie Hacker (fig. 8); Nick Merrick/Hedrich Blessing. Courtesy of Stuart Cohen & Julie Hacker (fig. 9); Thomas Gordon Smith (figs. 10–13)

Chapter 18: Robert A. M. Stern Architects (figs. 1 & 2); Courtesy of Michael Graves & Associates (fig. 3); Cervin Robinson, Courtesy of VSBA (fig. 4); William Watkins, Courtesy of VSBA (fig. 5); Courtesy of Allan Greenberg (figs. 6 & 13); Edmund Stoecklein (figs. 7 & 8); © Peter Aaron/Esto (fig. 9); Tom Bernard, courtesy of VSBA (fig. 10); Howard N. Kaplan © HNK Architectural Photography (fig. 11); Courtesy of Michael Graves & Associates (fig. 12)

Chapter 19: Richard Caspole, Yale Center for British Art (fig. 1); Tom Bernard, courtesy of VSBA (fig. 2)